INSTRUCTIONAL DESIGN

IMPLICATIONS FROM COGNITIVE SCIENCE

INSTRUCTIONAL DESIGN

IMPLICATIONS FROM COGNITIVE SCIENCE

Charles K. West • **James A. Farmer** • **Phillip M. Wolff**

University of Illinois at Urbana-Champaign

ALLYN AND BACON
Boston London Toronto Sydney Tokyo Singapore

Library of Congress Cataloging-in-Publication Data

West, Charles K.
   Instructional design: implications from cognitive science/
Charles K. West, James A. Farmer, Phillip M. Wolff.
     p. cm.
   Includes bibliographical references and index.
   ISBN 0-13-488578-3
   1. Instructional systems—Design. 2. Cognitive learning.
3. Learning. Psychology of. I. Farmer, James A. II. Wolff,
Phillip M. III. Title.
LB1028.35.W47 1991   90-40589
370.15′23—dc20   CIP

Copyright © 1991 by Allyn and Bacon
A Division of Simon & Schuster, Inc.
160 Gould Street
Needham Heights, MA 02194

Printed in the United States of America

10 9 8 7 6 5 4 3   96 95 94 93

ISBN 0-13-488578-3

Contents

Preface

In this book we present implications of research on cognitive strategies for instructional design. This research has largely been conducted since 1970, a year selected somewhat arbitrarily within our field to mark the onset of what is often called the cognitive revolution. Much understanding about learning and cognition has been achieved during this revolution. As a result, many of us in the field are substantially more sanguine about the practical uses of the psychology of learning than we were in the sixties.

In Chapters 2 through 10 we present cognitive strategies and explain how to use them in instructional design. Included are generally brief discussions of the theory and research from which the strategies flowed. Although some users of this text may wish to know about the theory and research background, others may not. To accommodate different readers' purposes, the chapters have been written and organized so that they can be studied selectively.

In the book we attempt to activate cognitive strategies in systematic ways to help readers learn about the strategies and their design uses. Metaphors, concept maps and frames are used in Chapter 1, for example. We activate the cognitive strategies in ways that we hope will promote their comprehension.

Over the past two decades we have worked with numerous graduate and undergraduate students in applied learning and instructional design courses. As cognitive strategies appeared in the literature, we taught them and used them to improve the courses. Typically these courses included practical exercises in which students used the strategies to plan lessons, units and programs. As a result, many of the strategies are now being successfully used in classrooms and in other ways, including such contexts as computer-aided instruction, computerized instruction for adults and staff development in industry and government.

Because instructional designers make many decisions in addition to those of selecting appropriate cognitive strategies, we include as the two final chapters a process explanation that serves as a template—a guide for these numerous and complicated decisions. Professor James A. Farmer Jr. authored these chapters.

After each chapter a few exercises are included. These exercises are designed to provide students with experiences in the use of strategies, to sensitize students to their current repertory of strategies and to help them learn the content of the book. In our own courses we have often taken class time to have students do these exercises in cooperative learning groups in order to field test the exercises. The exercises can be done individually, however, if the instructor or students prefer.

Appreciation must be extended to former students and colleagues who worked with us as we formulated the ideas for this work, particularly those students who, within the past three years, studied primarily within the framework of this text and suffered through many revisions of the chapters—those who enabled us to field test this work so thoroughly. The students are too numerous to name, but colleagues include Frank Mabry, director of the Professional Computer Systems Laboratory in the College of Education, University of Illinois at Urbana-Champaign, who was instrumental not only in encouraging us to complete this work, but also in providing funds for research assistance and computers, the "machineries of joy." Other colleagues who nourished and/or encouraged us include Thomas H. Anderson, Barak Rosenshine and Rand Spiro—all affiliated with the University of Illinois at Urbana-Champaign. We also wish to express appreciation to the same university for the sabbatical in which the first author wrote most of the first ten chapters of this text and to the 21 reviewers outside this university, most of whom are anonymous, who critiqued parts or all of this manuscript. Two of these reviewers were very hostile, two were "on the fence" and the rest were very favorable; but we learned immensely from all.

CKW
Champaign, Illinois

Acknowledgments

Appreciation is expressed to the Evelyn Singer Literary Agency and Evelyn Singer for permission to reprint an excerpt from *Face of North America* by the late Peter Farb (New York: Harper & Row, 1963). The excerpt is reprinted in Chapter 7, on page 132 as Box 7-1.

The authors also express their appreciation to the American Academy of Orthopaedic Surgeons for permission to adapt two figures from the *Handbook for Orthopaedic Educators* 11th edition, by Frederick G. Lippert III, James A. Farmer Jr. and Michael F. Schafer. The adapted figures appear in Chapter 12 on pages 245 and 247 as Figures 12-3 and 12-5.

INSTRUCTIONAL DESIGN

IMPLICATIONS FROM COGNITIVE SCIENCE

Introduction to Cognitive Science and Instructional Design

Learning is at the center of our ability to adapt to the most trivial and the most profound environmental demands. It makes the difference between purposeful action and directionless activity. Indeed, it is the crucial process necessary for knowing a world rich with experience and opportunity. That we might better aid learning is what this book is about. Specifically, it is about *how we know and how instruction can be better designed.*

Two categories of persons have been charged particularly with aiding learning: teachers and instructional designers. It is to these that we direct this text. Our point of view is that all teachers design instruction (Briggs, 1977, p. 179) in some sense, and all instructional designers "teach," even if designers are often physically remote from a classroom and even if teachers unfortunately have scant opportunity during the work day for instructional planning.

In this book we present cognitive strategies derived from recent research and the historical underpinnings of that research—the developments in the field of cognitive science over the past decades, some might say even the past century. This research into how the mind works is rich with practical implications for instructional design. The practical implications of the research and some of the theoretical concepts underlying specific cognitive strategies—*framing, chunking, concept mapping, the advance organizer, metaphor, rehearsal, imagery* and *mnemonics*—are presented in the first ten chapters of this book.

In focusing the first ten chapters on these nine cognitive strategies we may seem to be neglecting much of the substance of instructional design. This is not our intention. We delay discussion of many of the traditional and important design operations until Chapters 11 and 12. We discuss the cognitive strategies first because, from our perspective, *these strategies are the primary contributions of cognitive science to instructional design.*

Traditionally, instructional designers have organized their work around five steps or stages. There are many versions of these steps [for example, Dick and Reiser (1989)]. Some models contain more steps than five and are more detailed and complex, with subroutines and feedback loops. A very influential example of a more elaborate system with more steps or phases is that of Dick and Carey (1985, pp. 2–3), which has served to sequence design procedures not only for themselves, but also for Gagne, Briggs and Wager (1988, p. 22).

In Figure 1-1 we show a typical model consisting of five steps: (1) setting the *objectives*; (2) *preassessment*, that is, determining whether the target students have the prerequisites to benefit from the instruction; (3) *planning the instruction*; (4) *trial*, that is, presenting the instruction for developmental purposes; and (5) *testing and evaluation*. Examples of feedback loops are revising the objectives after preassessment and revising the instructional plan after evaluation. An example of a subroutine would be the steps in deriving objectives from social conditions and individual needs.

We present these five steps here so that we can illustrate the implications of cognitive psychology in overview form here and in later sections of this chapter.

FIGURE 1-1
Five steps in instructional design with two sample feedback loops.

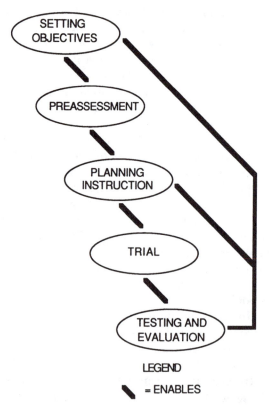

In Chapters 11 and 12 we present a substantially revised version of the simplified system shown in Figure 1-1. For now, however, we wish to restate that in our view the primary, but not exclusive, contributions of the cognitive revolution (or evolution) to the applied science of instructional design are at the phases of planning instruction and the actual instruction itself. At these stages of design our knowledge of the cognitive strategies with which people learn can be put to use as *designer techniques*. Other significant additional contributions to design flow from this emphasis on strategies and are presented later in this chapter.

OVERVIEW OF THE BOOK

In the first chapter we provide an introduction to cognitive psychology with emphasis on schema theory and a brief introduction to the nine strategies, which are themselves schemata of a type. We also discuss an assortment of related ideas that have captured the imaginations and energies of cognitive scientists.

In the introductory chapter we begin with a discussion of the theoretical background, mention some of the "parents" of the cognitive revolution and provide an overview of schema theory. This overview consists of a section on the definitions of schema and the functions of schema. Next, two issues about learning and knowledge are examined: "How is schematic knowledge learned?" and "Toward what kinds of knowledge is this schematized learning directed?" The discussion then turns to some of the practical dimensions of the cognitive revolution with a brief section on how students learn cognitive strategies (metacognition) and monitor their use of these strategies. We provide brief introductions to the nine strategies and then turn to an overview of implications for instructional design.

In the next nine chapters we present the nine strategies. Each chapter begins with an explanation of the strategy, then the research and development are presented and a guide for instructional designers comprises the final major section. In the final two chapters we present a detailed model for instructional design, which we call the *instructional design template*.

THEORETICAL BACKGROUND

Before the strategies and their applications are discussed we examine their history and background. The history of the psychology of learning as an area of inquiry exemplifies the kind of meanderings and transformations characteristic of a well-worn problem domain. Explanations are proposed, only to shift with new evidence and then seemingly to break off in radically new directions. Some of the researchers in the field think of the change occurring primarily over the past two decades as a revolution in psychology—from behavioristic to cognitive (Gardner, 1987). We consider the period of change from behaviorism to cognitive psychology to be longer, with both coexisting over an extended period; thus we speak of evolution.

Some of those who prefer the metaphor of a cognitive revolution apparently enjoy its attendant drama. There are the feelings of newness, of radical departures, of new battles in new territories. Theirs are the glories of marshaling forces, pitched battles and even victory—metaphors all, semantically related to the metaphor "revolution." In many ways designing instruction using the implications of recent cognitive science does seem a radical departure.

By contrast, we prefer the metaphor of evolution to refer to the changes taking place in cognitive science itself and their implications for instructional design. (Readers may draw their own conclusions on this issue.)

Evolution builds on the past: sometimes gradually and sometimes saltatorially; which brings to mind a close cousin metaphor of evolution, "mutation." Whether the developments in cognitive science were gradual or rapid, these two psychological perspectives, behavioristic and cognitive, coexisted side by side, but not peacefully. Evolutionists and mutationists, and even some revolutionaries, honor the past through reference to and discussion of previous research. In this book previous perspectives and research are presented, albeit very briefly and selectively in this chapter. Later, as each strategy is presented, we discuss the appropriate research in greater detail.

David Zeaman (1959) once wrote that the primary difference between the natural sciences and the social sciences is that natural scientists tend to stand on the shoulders of their predecessors, whereas social scientists stand in their faces! For this book, we hope to stand on many shoulders but tread on few faces. Unlike revolutionaries, who tend to tread on faces, we prefer an evolutionary stance on the shoulders.

Presenting a thorough and complete overview of our theoretical background is difficult. Work in the field of cognitive science is rich and complex and anchored in a variety of related perspectives and research strategies. Certain threads in the history of the cognitive strategies and their theoretical underpinnings extend back to the beginnings of empirical psychology—some might even say back into the roots of Western philosophy. The vast majority of research efforts have been undertaken within the past two decades, however, so the perspective can be characterized as essentially new.

The label that best represents this shift in perspective is *cognitive science*. This term subsumes endeavors in numerous fields that are aimed at better understanding the nature of the mind at both physical and highly abstract levels. Although such fields as linguistics, computer science and neurology have made important contributions to cognitive science, the primary parent field is cognitive psychology. The tasks of cognitive psychologists have been to articulate and explore the issues surrounding the ways in which people come to know.

Before we briefly discuss the history of cognitive science, it may be helpful to define the word *cognitive*. It has been used in two ways: first, *cognition* is a word meaning *"coming to know,"* which includes such internal processes as learning, perception, comprehension, thinking, memory and attention. A second use of the term *cognitive* is *to identify a perspective or theory in contrast to one which is an emphasis on observable behavior.* Cognitive theorists emphasize internal processes and knowledge representations which are impossible to observe directly, but which are inferred. In the chapters which follow both definitions are pertinent, and one can infer from context which meaning is intended.

These internal cognitive processes have been emphasized for many decades. The cognitive perspective, or facsimiles of it, existed side by side with behaviorism. A case could even be made that the study of cognitive processes, and the perspective of the centrality of inferred internal intellectual processes, actually predated behaviorism and that behaviorism was itself a revolutionary reaction.

The work of the German structuralist E. B. Titchener (1910) on the structure of consciousness stands as a harbinger of modern schema theory. Much to his chagrin, Titchener observed that subjects often committed what he called *stimulus error*, that is, when observing objects or events, they reported previous knowledge rather than attributes of the objects or events themselves. His angry and nagging efforts to compel subjects to avoid this stimulus error rarely worked. *What to Titchener was error to be avoided and an irritating intrusion of prior knowledge is seen by cognitive scientists today as the basic nature of perception and comprehension.*

The structure of consciousness, or mind, as a problem for psychologists turned even more toward schema theory in modern form with the work of the Swiss psychologist, Jean Piaget (Inhelder & Piaget, 1958). The concepts of "scheme," "schemata," "structures," "strategies" and "operations" used in the context of mental development and cognition occur frequently in the writings of Piaget over many decades extending back to the 1920s. To Piaget, mental growth consisted of the development of increasingly logical, complex and numerous schemata. His essential contribution is the description of how those mature schemata, so numerous and complex, develop or evolve from infantile reflexes (schemata) such as sucking and palmar grasping.

Such is the legacy of Piaget, but even this giant parental figure was not alone. Over many of those same years in which he wrote, the Gestalt psychologists (Koffka, 1935; Kohler, 1925; Wertheimer, 1945) were also investigating ideas which hint of modern schema theory. Such ideas as "wholes," "patterns" of organization, "structures" and "insight" are forerunners of modern views of mental operations and of the modern, unabashed focus on internal mental constructs.

Perhaps, however, the most specific European legacy for the research presented in later chapters is English. The Englishman Bartlett (1932) found that people seemed to be guided in their interpretations of text passages, one of which was entitled "the war of ghosts," by preexisting knowledge or themes. He named these preexisting themes *schemata*.

The European influences from Piaget, the structuralists, Bartlett and the Gestaltists were substantial. But the cognitive focus was not solely European. Here in the United States, Jerome Bruner [see Bruner (1973) for a volume which provides samples of his work across its first three decades] contributed substantially to the acceptance of the validity of internal constructs with his research over four decades, from the 1940s to 1986. Especially influential is his work on categorizing strategies, the role of theme in learning and thinking and the research on representation of knowledge.

While cognitive psychology was being "Americanized," it developed in breadth and complexity along several lines of inquiry. A very critical contribution advanced during the mid-1950s centered on the understanding that the human mind could be compared to the electronic computer. Attempting to invest machines with intelligence forced researchers to explain exactly their thoughts concerning many of the pivotal issues of mind. The products of their thought have had powerful consequences for educational theory and practice. Newell and Simon (1972) were some of the first to construct programs that solve school-like problems using domain-independent strategies. Their success suggested how strategies might be critical to human problem solving and learning. Some of their failures also suggested that learning and problem solving strategies are sometimes domain specific or otherwise tailored to the type of knowledge being manipulated or acquired. Here again, work with computers has advanced cognitive theory through helpful distinctions with regard to the nature of knowledge. With these distinctions, researchers have been able to probe the knowledge structures of experts in a given field as well as those of novices. This focus on mind and the methods used in artificial intelligence have brought freshness and excitement into the awakening field of cognitive science.

Further U.S. developments in cognitive psychology were stimulated by Miller, Galanter and Pribram (1960) on structural or patterned problem solving. Also very significant is Ausubel's (1968) work on subsumption theory and the advance organizer. Equally significant were Bandura's (1969) incorporation of imagery into his social learning theory; Chomsky's (1951, 1965) infusion of structuralism into linguistics; and the popularization of work of the Russian L. S. Vygotsky on cognitive development after the 1962 publication (well after his death in 1934) of the English translation of *Thought and Language*.

These developments in the cognitive revolution or evolution have lead to empirical, usually experimental and quasi-experimental, efforts by large numbers of researchers whose contributions are discussed in later chapters. Research methods have been of several types. First, records, or protocols, have been made of persons who are considered "experts" in a field. These protocols are analyzed for several purposes, including the detection of the "schemata" or strategies the experts use to learn, or solve problems; and the detection of how the expert represents, or organizes, the knowledge. A second and related research method is to take protocols of "novice" learners for similar purposes. Often the records of the expert are compared with the record of the novice. A third method begins with techniques borrowed from books on memory improvement, followed by experimenting in standard ways with the techniques as treatments, and other techniques as controls. Finally, the traditional qualitative and quantitative research strategies are used in the research. Often these efforts have had intriguing and direct practical implications. Often the efforts have been conducted in school and instructional design settings, employing tasks which are very relevant to schooling and the many ways learning takes place in schools. They have revealed a variety of ways experts and novices learn.

While the research tradition is rich, applied and diverse in theoretical ideas and research methods, one concept helps to establish a bond for the diversity. That relatively central bond is the internal representation of knowledge and the acknowledgement of internal structures which have had the greatest effect (Gardner, 1987). An interrelated bond is that learning is a mentalistic activity, an internal structuring of knowledge. Much of the very applied work has been based on schemata as the inferred internal structure. *The genesis of knowledge, its representation and its transformation earmark the agenda of current cognitive science.*

SCHEMATA AND FUNCTIONS OF SCHEMATA

With many traditions converging from previous research, it is to be expected that numerous definitions exist for the concept of schema. As used in modern literature of cognitive science, schema definitions seem to include elements from many of the traditions presented briefly in the previous section. Rumelhart and Ortony (1977) define *schema* by including such ideas as: (a) schemata are mental data structures; (b) schemata represent our knowledge about objects (Anderson, 1985, p. 130), situations, events (Anderson, 1985, p. 130), self, sequences of actions and natural categories (Anderson, 1985); (c) schemata are like plays and scripts of plays (Schank & Abelson, 1977); and (d) schemata are like theories. In other words, schemata are like packets or bundles in which the mind stores knowledge: they are *patterns, structures, scaffolds.*

But the idea that knowledge is stored and retrieved in bundles or packets is only one kind of schema, called *data schemata* or *state schemata*. There are also *process schemata* (Rumelhart & Ortony, 1977; West & Foster, 1976; West, 1981), which are procedures or ways of processing and organizing information.

It is the process schema which reflects and constitutes an example of the profound influence of the computer revolution on cognitive science (Turkle, 1984). A broad analogy is drawn between computers and mind, and a more specific analogy is drawn between programming and the process schema: *state schemata are to data files as process schemata are to programs which are in execution.* Programs are the intelligent strategic actions, as state schemata are the knowledge structures (organized knowledge "about" something). For knowledge "of or about" there exist state schemata, but for knowing "how" (accent progressive tense) there exist process schemata.

This broad analogy with the computer is so ubiquitous that the term *programmed* is beginning to replace *conditioned* in everyday language. We are no longer said to be "conditioned" by our parents to read Hemingway or to brush our teeth or to appreciate Bach; we are now "programmed" for these enthusiasms and habits by parents, by society, by television, by schools. Before the cognitive science revolution we were "conditioned" by parents, schools, television, society.

To reiterate, there are at least two kinds of schemata, the content or data array—state schemata—and the process schemata. Our organized knowledge as well as our organizing patterns, whether that knowledge is in the form of bundles of content (states), or in the form of procedures, are thought to be schemata. In other words there is *schematic* knowledge "of" and *schematic* knowing "how" (Mayer, 1987). The strategies which we discuss in the nine chapters which follow may be thought of as examples of process (knowing how) strategies on which instructional designers capitalize by turning them to techniques.

How do these state and process schemata function? First of all, *schemata direct perception* (Rumelhart & Ortony, 1977). Within the cognitive science revolution, perception is defined as active, constructive, selective and schema driven as opposed to the earlier conceptualization that perception is passive, receptive, nonselective and event driven. In the modern view, typically, many events occur more or less simultaneously; one perceives some portion of these events, or even some part of one complex event. This selectivity is schema driven (West, 1981). What we perceive is partially a function of what we know and an attendant schema. The meaning of the event is constructed in terms of the person's schema.

How different this modern view is from the outdated perspective that perception is like photography (note the analogy)! In an older analogy of perception, the camera lens passively receives the view and records that view as it appears, as it is. To the cognitive scientist the better analogy is once again the computer. During perception a program (schema) is "on," the program actively operates to select from the context of the event and constructs a meaning of that which was selected. The constructed meaning is program (schema) driven rather than event (or phenomenally) driven; that is, it is "top down" rather than "bottom up."

Without the schemata "in mind," perception may not even be possible. Consider the situation of meeting the alien at the edge of the galaxy, a familiar theme from science fiction. Would our human emissary perceive anything if the extraterrestrial were really alien? Probably not. But it is very difficult to conceive of what form a completely alien entity would take. If it took a recognizable form (round) it would mesh with some human experience and some human schemata, and thus would not be totally alien. If it were amoeba-like with extrudable pseudopods covered with hair from which each strand dripped viscous purple liquid, many familiar schemata would likely be activated. Perception would be possible, if not routine—but the extraterrestrial would not be very alien.

Meanwhile, however, back on terra, perception seems to go awry when a poor match exists between the event and the schema "in place" or activated at the time. Suppose that you knew nothing about stretching out before and after exercise. Suppose you see a woman pushing at the trunk of a large tree. It would seem a bizarre scene. You might assume that she was attempting to uproot a very large tree with her bare hands. Suppose you next see, sitting on the grass of a park, a man in shorts and canvas shoes apparently trying to tear off his leg. The world is full of interesting events, whether or not one's schemata are in order and fashionable. These two events were perceived in terms of the schemata available.

It is difficult to predict what schemata will be activated and, thus, what meaning will be derived. Whatever perception is, it is primarily folding or wrapping something relatively new within what we already know. That is, *perception is primarily the construction* of meaning via massaging the new with the old, within the schemata available and activated by an event. Persons have many schemata. Events have many attributes. Knowing *what* schema will be activated, in a *person*, by attributes of *events* is low-probability prediction. That is to say, we cannot always know what schemata will be activated and which parts of the event are together partially determining the meaning derived.

The foregoing description of schema activated in or by a context or event hints of an incomplete or partial truth. During human perception schemata are often already "booted up" or active in our minds as we observe an event. The ideas of "present in immediate memory" or "in consciousness" are tempting. But if a schema is present in mind as we observe, it may determine the perception, the meaning we derive or construct from the event. Up until the cognitive revolution such present-in-mind schema dominations were most often called *perceptual sets* and there is substantial research on that construct (see, for example, West and Foster, 1976; West, 1981; Bower, 1981). Some of the "sets" are emotional and some are intellectual. Such present-in mind schemata may preclude the activation of more pertinent or more predictable or more appropriate schemata.

These perceptual functions of schemata have profound implications for learning, instruction and instructional design because perception is the complex process of attaching meaning to events or constructing meaning from events. Deriving or constructing meaning is essential in learning. It is basic to cognitive processing for recall. There may be little perception without relevant schemata. There is no learning without perception.

Thus schemata serve as guardians against premature intellectual atrophy—without schemata reality is "without form and void"—but they are also the sentinels of our illusions and delusions. Our best features, our ethics, our theories are comprised of schemata; but so also are our worst features, our biases, our stereotypes.

One very important implication for instructional design is at the pre-assessment stage listed in Figure 1-1. Historically, designers have pretested for knowledge; but, for the most part, not pretested for schema, or for how that prior knowledge may be organized. The schemata, or how any prior knowledge is organized, is as important as any prior knowledge, particularly since the schemata will exert strong influences on perception during instruction or learning. Any schema present during instruction will also serve as the constructive core around which detail will be added.

The idea that perception is constructive rather than receptive is beginning to redirect designers away from another historic design preoccupation with "How shall we best present so students will receive the information in the best manner possible?" The constructive function of perception should result in a redirection of focusing on what the learner is doing mentally during instruction (Andre & Phye, 1986, p. 2) in this constructive process and planning for ample opportunity to actively, mentally process.

A second function of schemata in addition to directing perception is *making learning and comprehension possible* (Anderson, 1984). The mind seems to fit new information into the existing structures. The schemata make learning possible. It is generally assumed that a person cannot or does not learn if pertinent schemata are not available. Consider the statement, "The seams were split so the notes were sour" (Bransford & McCarrell, 1974). It is impossible to learn this in any meaningful way, to decode the statement, to make sense of it, without the concept "bagpipe." Once the concept (some say schema) "bagpipe" is presented or activated in a person, the statement makes sense. One can then understand and learn the statement.

Not only do schemata allow perception, comprehension and learning, they also *aid recall* (Anderson, 1984). That is, we tend to remember material we learn in terms of a relevant schema. Schemata can influence what is learned and remembered. In one study, for example, two groups of students were asked to study a passage about houses; one group was instructed to take the perspective of a homeowner and the other was asked to take the perspective of a burglar (Anderson & Pichert, 1978). Those students who were asked to study the passage about a house from the perspective of a homeowner remembered items in the house which were quite different from those items recalled by students who were asked to study the same passage from the perspective of a burglar. The perspective, or schema, also influenced what was remembered when students were asked to take the other perspective but not restudy the passage.

Figure 1-2 is a summary of functions of schemata. These functions, including those of perception, learning, comprehension and recall, extend to everyday experiences as well as experiences in formal instruction. In both of these contexts *schemata of learners exert powerful influences on input of information*

FIGURE 1-2
A summary of the functions of schemata.

1. SCHEMATA AID PERCEPTION.
   A. Facilitate selective allocation of attention.
   B. Perception is schematically constructed.
2. SCHEMATA AID LEARNING, COMPREHENSION AND RECALL.
   A. Provide ideational scaffolding for the assimilation of events, text information.
   B. Allow inferential elaboration.
   C. Allow orderly and consistent search of memory.
   D. Aid editing, abstracting and summarizing.
   E. Permit inferential reconstruction.

Based on Rumelhart and Ortony (1977) and Anderson (1984).

(*perception*), *the processing of that input* (*comprehension*) *and recall of abstractions of that input.* It is probable that the more complex the event or experience, the greater the influence of the schema.

The nature and functions of schema in cognition discussed in this section reveal a complex picture of the cognitive revolution or mutation. It is very apparent that the perspectival change from behavioristic to cognitive consists of more than merely a shift from the emphasis on the study of observable behavior to the emphasis on organized internal representations such as schemata. A second shift of emphasis is from cognition (which includes perception, comprehension, learning and recall) as a part-to-part, then part-to-whole mechanism, to a *holistic* mechanism. That is, earlier perspectives were based on the idea that cognition is "bottom up," from pieces of the world determining cognition, to "top down," or patterns of internal representations (wholes) primarily determining cognition. The cognitive perspective is that these wholes allow cognition, and that the direction of cognition is generally whole-to-part, then part-to-whole, as opposed to part-to-part or part-to-whole. A third shift of emphasis in the cognitive revolution is the change from a direction of concrete to abstract to the obverse. Wholes, patterns, schemata are abstractions. Knowledge is abstract. Cognition is an abstractive process. Cognition does not necessarily begin with concreteness.

A fourth shift of emphasis is that cognition is a *constructive/reconstructive* process rather than a discovery/retrieval process. That is, cognition is the creation and recreation of knowledge rather than the discovery or retrieval of knowledge. Humans construct knowledge through mental interaction with the physical and social world, as opposed to merely retrieving knowledge from that world (diSibio, 1982; Spiro, 1977). By discovery in this context we are not speaking of "discovery learning." A fifth change of emphasis, which may be as important in the cognitive revolution as the others, is a *metaphorical shift* from such static and sequential metaphors as "mind as an assembly line," an entity which assembles parts, or the "mind as a print medium," to "the mind as a fluid medium, a computer" (Andre & Phye, 1986, p. 1). A sixth change is that of emphasis on outcomes in the earlier period to the cognitive emphasis on process [in a way that is quite similar to cognitive therapy as presented by Beck and Weishaar (1989)]. These six changes or "fronts" of the cognitive revolution, summarized in Figure 1-3, are hints that not only have there been changes in the psychology of cognition, but also changes in the philosophy of the science—its metaphysics, its metaphors and its assumptions.

The idea that a metaphorical shift such as that described in Figure 1-3 is a profound piece in the cognitive revolution or mutation is based on the important role which Pepper (1961) assigns to metaphor in changes in thought patterns and theory. These changes manifest themselves in the culture at large and among scholars in the disciplines. According to this line of thought, metaphors play a vital role in changes in thought and revolutions in science and other fields of knowledge. Change entails shifts in metaphor.

For some, if not all, of these six "fronts" mentioned in Figure 1-3, we can see parallel changes in instructional design. That is to say, instructional designers traditionally focused on overt behavior, breaking instruction into

FIGURE 1-3

Six fronts of the cognitive revolution.

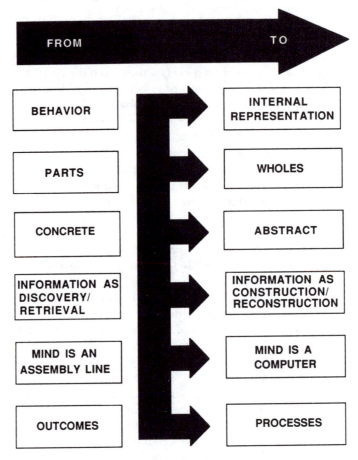

parts, concreteness, and so on. As a result of the cognitive revolution, instructional designers emphasize the internal representations concomitant with instruction and the active intellectual processing which must occur if learning is to take place. It is also more acceptable today to begin with the whole (van Dijk & Kintsch, 1983; Mandl & Schnotz, 1987) or with a general overview, as with the elaboration model of Reigeluth and Stein (1983, pp. 335–381) rather than always break the instruction into component parts. An example of a holistic approach is the emphasis on text structure in comprehension, as opposed to an emphasis on words and sentences. Many of the features of the cognitive strategies to be discussed in later chapters are related to one or more of these "fronts."

In this section we have examined issues about kinds of schemata, the features of schemata and their functions. We have also discussed the cognitive revolution as more than merely a rejection of the overt behavior focus of behaviorism. Now we turn to the question, "Is schema *the* internal representation?"

A QUINTESSENTIAL SCHEMA?

A major misdirection is to assume that the schema or any one of the cognitive strategies discussed in this book or found elsewhere is the quintessential one. There is the possibility that advocates, not the scholars themselves, may have represented a particular strategy as the generic or quintessential one. Some candidates for this misrepresentation are the advance organizer (Ausubel, 1968); schema (Bartlett, 1932); strategies of categorization (Bruner, 1973); frames (Minski, 1975); metaphor (Ortony, 1979); imagery (Pavio, 1971); scripts (Schank & Abelson, 1977); and TOTE units of Miller, Galanter and Pribram (1960) (while solving problems, the mind *Tests ideas, Organizes results, Tests again until Exiting from the problem*). A more useful direction of thought is to be skeptical of the idea that there is any one transcendent, basic, generic or supraordinate intellectual strategy. Rather, given the state of the knowledge, the *strategies presented in this book are an assortment of intellectual strategies which are items in a repertoire available to persons as learners and/or a "tool kit" for instructional designers.*

There is probably no schema or strategy which renders all unknowns known, as a mental elixir or mental "philosopher's stone," although there may be schemata which we hold about the nature of knowledge which influence learning in very broad and powerful ways (Schommer, 1989). When the first author was ten or so, he fantasized that there was some secret strategy which could serve this purpose. He even suspected that some adults knew but would not tell.

Childhood imagination aside, the strategies presented in this book are an assortment of true strategies or schemata, true in the sense of Rorty's (1979) truth: truth is a compliment we pay to beliefs which help us do what we want to do. These strategies are "true" schemata which help us do what we must do—learn and comprehend and help others learn and comprehend.

All of these strategies should be understood as actually in use by some of the people, some of the time, on some content rather than by all of the people, all of the time, on all content. The transcendent, elixir-like schema may not exist. After all, the human brain has marvelous, multifunctional, multipurpose, self-programming capabilities; it is fairly portable; and it is often, but not always, relatively easily programmed—if not always user friendly. Perhaps it requires no quintessential program. Perhaps it does.

For the present volume, however, the cognitive strategies may be considered relatively independent of each other, even though some can be used together. They also may be considered as known schemata, known strategies of learning. Yet none should be seen as *the* way to learn. Further, all may be thought of as intellectual programs, process schemata, which may be learned and used. The instructional designer deploys these as *techniques of design.*

In the following section we discuss some of the issues which determine the appropriateness of the use of strategies. These issues, generally speaking, grew out of developments in schema theory and research.

KINDS OR MODES OF LEARNING AND TYPES OF KNOWLEDGE

Cognitive psychologists are not only intrigued by these nine useful, rich, varied and complex strategies; they are also interested in the diverse ways in which new knowledge is incorporated into existing knowledge, the diverse kinds of knowledge, the issues about well-structured and ill-structured knowledge, and the possibilities of matching strategies with the various kinds of knowledge.

Kinds or Modes of Learning

Piaget (1952) claimed that there are two kinds of cognitive processing: *assimilation* and *accommodation*. *Accommodation*, according to Piaget, is the cognitive operation of mind by which it conforms to the demands of the environment. In recent schema theory this is analogous to learning a new schema. *Assimilative* learning is fitting the environment to the demands of mind. In recent schema theory this is analogous to adding facts, concepts or detail to a schema. Accommodative learning generally occurs less often and is considered more complex and difficult than assimilative.

It does seem that most formal and informal learning is assimilative rather than accommodative. For most learning we are, it seems, adding detail to schemata. For this, Rumelhart and Norman (1978) use the concepts of accretion and tuning.

Accretion is like putting new wine in old bottles or adding moss to sedentary rocks. Detail is added to schema, to the knowledge structure. Suppose, for example, a child had the schema of "dog" as a creature with four legs. If someone points to a dog and refers to it as a brown dog, the child may add the detail that a dog may be brown. The schema of "dog" accrues more detail as the child learns about ranges of size, color and shapes of dogs. Accretion is routine fact learning.

Tuning is typically more complex than accretion, for it involves minor modification of the schema (the old bottle, the stone). Suppose, for example (and this is an actual parental experience), a two-year-old son's schema for dog did not include very large four-legged animals. A Saint Bernard might be identified as a bear, assuming the child had the schema "bear." To the child, a very large four-legged animal had to be a bear. Should the schema "dog" be modified to include Saint Bernards, tuning would have occurred.

There is a point in the modification (tuning) of a schema in which a prior schema must be so reorganized that it is quite different from the old one.

Piaget termed this *accommodation*, whereas Rumelhart and Norman (1978) write of *restructuring* the schema. This difficult and significant kind of learning usually takes a substantial amount of time and effort, perhaps even a number of years.

It may help to think of these kinds of learning as a continuum from adding detail to a schema (accretion), through tuning, to restructuring. Most learning is the gradual addition of facts, details and concepts to existing schemata which are adequate to those additions. When existing schemata become less adequate to encompass the additions, one fine tunes the schema. As new information becomes increasingly discrepant with an existing schema, mere accretion or tuning may be inadequate, so restructuring is required.

As one learns a new field and, more broadly, adapts to social changes, one may be required to adopt new schemata (Farmer, 1983, 1985). This generally proceeds, however, from the attempt to use known schemata with efforts made to tune gradually those known and thus make them work for the new field. But knowledge of new fields does typically require the formulation of new schemata (LeGrand, 1987). It is very probable that quick formulation of new schemata does not occur, but, rather, it is a gradual progression from attempts to accrete, to tuning, to restructuring.

One reason that restructuring or accommodation is difficult is that learning is often not free of affect or belief. Humans often have attitudes, beliefs and values attached to their knowledge. These affective or motivational variables sometimes create resistance to change and to learning new structures. Learning is not merely a rational (cold cognition) process; it often entails emotion (hot cognition) (Bower, 1981; Paris, 1988; West, 1981, West & Foster, 1976).

Types of Knowledge

Not only are cognitive psychologists interested in the variation in learning, they are also interested in the complex, varied nature of the knowledge toward which the strategies are directed. What are some patterns of knowledge? kinds of knowledge? Are there patterns that indicate which strategies work best for specific kinds of knowledge?

Several kinds of knowledge have been identified (Anderson, 1985; Gagne, 1985; Tulving, 1972). The first, *declarative* (*factual or propositional*) knowledge, is thought of as "knowledge that" or "knowledge about." Some cognitive scientists think that all declarative knowledge is stored, or represented, in memory in the form of propositions (Anderson, 1985) and networks of propositions. This idea is appealing because concepts and facts, for example, often seem to make sense only within more complex principles or connected concepts. They seem interactive and webbed in seemingly endless networks.

This networking in declarative knowledge can itself take several forms (Tulving, 1972; Anderson, 1987). The networks may be *semantic*, composed of lists and elements (disjointed bits of information, and some facts connected in space) or may be *episodic* (connected chains such as some historical and story narratives, merely connected by time). In all cases, however, declarative knowledge is "knowledge that." Declarative knowledge which is patterned may be seen as state schemata, one of the two kinds of schemata discussed in a previous section.

A second type of knowledge is *procedural*—knowing how, that is, statements of instruction such as "perform A then B then C." A substantial portion of knowledge is of this type. Figure 1-1 contains procedural knowledge. The "As," "Bs" and "Cs" vary in kind also. The steps may be members of classes, items in a list or even subprocedures. In all cases, however, what distinguishes procedures as a type of learning is that there is an *order-specific and time-dependent requirement*. The knowledge demand is that one must perform the subtasks in the stated and required order.

There is a third kind of knowledge recently defined by Paris, Lipson and Wixson (1983): *conditional*. Conditional knowledge is knowing when and why to use a procedure. It is a description of contexts (Prawat, 1989) and circumstances under which an application or procedure is appropriate. Paris, Lipson and Wixson (1983) discuss this within the context of metacomprehension, that is, learning *when and why* a particular cognitive strategy is appropriate. In the same sense, we could think about conditional knowledge as the specifications of use of strategies as design techniques. When and why does a designer use an advance organizer, for example, as opposed to a metaphor? These specifications have preoccupied us throughout the development of this text.

More broadly, whenever procedures are taught, if there is to be proper use of those procedures, learners must also learn the specifications—when and why this procedure is applicable. It is an essential component of proper application and transfer of procedures. The format of conditional knowledge is typically hypothetical: *If* these conditions obtain *then* do thus and so.

Reflecting on kinds of knowledge can be quite helpful to instructional design. Often the strategy *qua* technique chosen by a designer will be partially determined by the kind of knowledge to be taught.

Structure of Knowledge

There is another way of characterizing knowledge, that of its logical structure. Some knowledge domains, such as mathematics and natural science, are very logical and are called *well-structured knowledge domains*. Others, such as psychology, are not very logical and have been termed *ill structured* (Spiro, et al., 1987). The relative structure, however, should not be expected to run throughout all the knowledge in a discipline. Some parts of even the most structured of disciplines could be ill structured. On the other hand, some parts of ill-structured domains can be well structured.

The structure of knowledge may be viewed as a property of the physical world which is manifested in the knowledge available to us, or it may be seen as a property of mind manifested in that knowledge. In the latter case the human mind constructs the logic or organization of the knowledge domain. We have already seen that cognitive theorists generally favor the constructivistic view. Still, this is a contentious issue which is both metaphysical (involving questions about the nature of reality) and epistemological (involving questions about the nature of knowing), but the significance for this text and for instructional design lies in the extent to which structure is thought to be contained in the specific material to be taught which is provided by the expert.

Well-structured knowledge may be characterized in several ways: it has considerable logical order; it may have the kind of theory which allows powerful predictions, not just the kind of theory which is a label for a perspective or point of view; and it may contain families of theories or other general principles which allow inferences about facts, and which allow general principles to be developed from facts or observations—which ultimately allow predictions. Structure appears to accrue either through being rule governed, as in mathematics, or some combination of being very empirical and rule governed, as in the physical sciences. This, however, does not mean that in the highly structured domains there is no room for creativity, spontaneity and intuition in its development or learning.

There is often the expectation that some fields such as history and the social sciences, which may now be characterized as ill-structured domains, may ultimately become well structured. This supposedly would depend on further development, advances and constructions/discoveries in the field. Domains such as the physical sciences and mathematics, domains of high structure, are sometimes referred to as *mature* with the unflattering label *immature* reserved for ill-structured domains. Whether the social sciences will ever become mature in this sense is still open. Judgments about the worth of a discipline should not be made on the basis of structure. Relative structure, however, is an important basis for designer decisions about strategy use.

The questions for the instructional designer, in the meantime, are "To what extent is this material which is to be taught structured?" and "If it is structured, how?" It is probable that well-structured knowledge can be more readily learned with some strategies, while ill-structured knowledge must be learned with other strategies. These are important questions which will be addressed in later chapters, when we provide implications for choice of strategy and implementation of strategies.

From this discussion of kinds of learning and types of knowledge it should be obvious that the issues about the types of knowledge, kinds of knowledge and knowledge representation are complex. It is clear that *procedural knowledge contains declarative knowledge so that these categories are not mutually exclusive.* In some of the literature, imaginal knowledge is added as a third category of knowledge representation. All do not agree that all declarative knowledge is propositional. To complicate the situation further, some question the usefulness of the distinctions.

In this text we will test the usefulness of the distinctions among declarative knowledge, procedural knowledge and conditional knowledge, and the concept of the structure of knowledge, by alerting the reader in each of the chapters on the nine strategies as to whether the usefulness of a particular strategy is constrained by these distinctions. The distinctions will be highlighted in the specification charts in later chapters. There are some patterns of constraints, some of which are summarized in Figure 1-5.

In the section just completed we have discussed how cognitive psychologists view several types of learning and how structures or schemata interplay with that learning. As we observe the preoccupation of cognitive scientists with these characteristics of knowledge, we see parallel concerns among instructional designers. We have also discussed the kinds of knowledge, or the ways knowledge is represented. We focus in the next section on cognitive strategies in formal learning through research on metacognition and reciprocal teaching. In this section we further establish the applied design value of research attendant with the cognitive revolution.

METACOGNITION AND RECIPROCAL TEACHING

Ann Brown and her colleagues (Brown, 1975, 1978, 1980; Brown & Campione, 1981), Flavell (1985) and (Duell, 1986) have investigated students using cognitive strategies, students learning more strategies, students becoming aware of their learning strategies, their self-monitoring of use of the strategies and their employment of particular strategies both consciously and deliberately. These operations are called *metacognition*. Research on these operations has been systematic and well designed. Much of this research has been conducted in classroom settings as opposed to laboratories.

From this research it is clear that there is a developmental progression in metacognitive sophistication. Even young children use strategies of learning. *As development progresses students learn more about their own cognitive strategies and begin to monitor those strategies.* Later, an ability to reflect on the strategies while learning develops. Even later, students become able to plan their learning, check progress toward goals, monitor the effectiveness of any strategy used and try another if necessary.

While such a progression may emerge in students without intervention during the years of growth and schooling, it is possible to intervene. This intervention is termed *reciprocal teaching* (Palincsar & Brown, 1984; Brown & Campione, 1977; Brown, Campione, & Day, 1981; Brown, Palincsar, & Armbruster, 1984). This reciprocal teaching involves teaching the strategies while students are learning instructional content. Furthermore, reciprocal teaching involves the emphasis that the strategies work, which probably acts as motivation for later use. The idea is that strategy learning improves content learning and vice versa. There is a reciprocal relationship, in other words.

In a series of studies Palincsar and Brown (1984) selected four activities for intervention. Students were trained to engage in summarizing, questioning, clarifying and predicting. These activities were taught by first having an adult, usually a parent or teacher, demonstrate the activities—developing summaries and asking questions about the material under study; clarifying its meaning; and predicting questions, meaning and ideas to follow in the material. The child initially merely observed. The adult gradually turned the activities over to the child. In the final stages of training the child performed these activities and was able to be self-critical in the use of the activities.

The effects of reciprocal teaching are very positive even when peers are the models for learning the strategies. Students can learn to use the strategies and can become convinced that they aid learning and comprehension of material. The improvements in strategy use and content learning seem to persist, and the strategies transfer to other classroom material.

In these studies the strategies taught, while very useful in themselves, are basic and occur concomitantly with some of the more advanced strategies presented in this text. These four basic strategies and several others are discussed in depth in Chapter 9 on rehearsal.

The emphasis on the ideas of metacognition and reciprocal teaching is yet another relatively new emphasis for instructional design. We saw in Figure 1-1 that objectives (for the present and until Chapter 11), very generally defined to include goals and outcomes, have traditionally been considered the initial stage of design. Within this emphasis on objectives, and because of the potential of reciprocal teaching, *we advocate that designers include an objective to teach or improve a cognitive strategy (an emphasis on process) along with whatever else the objective might be.* Content objectives should be supplemented by strategic objectives. Landa (1983, pp. 55–69) also makes a case for this.

FROM SCHEMATA AND METACOGNITION TO COGNITIVE STRATEGIES

While schema theory is not the exclusive tradition of the strategies (Anderson, 1987), the emphases on schemata and metacognition have engendered considerable attention and research about the strategies which can be used by persons as they study. This book is about specific sets of these learning strategies and how they can be used to improve the design of instruction. It is important to emphasize that these are mental strategies which occur in the minds of persons, but learning these strategies is aided by their incorporation into instruction.

These cognitive strategies are intellectual "waldoes." The *waldoe* is a machine which magnifies strength and increases dexterity, so named by Robert Heinlein in *The Roads Must Roll* after the fictional character who invented them. The name has been carried over from science fiction to robotics. Heinlein thought of the waldoe as an extension of the hand and arm. The intellectual waldoe extends mind. In our complex and varied environment we need all the help we can get. Much of that help can be provided systematically through instructional design.

OVERVIEW OF STRATEGIES

Since, in each later chapter, from 2 through 10, we suggest hybridization, or the combination of cognitive strategies, it should help to have a brief introduction to the strategies. This overview follows the order presented in the chapters to follow.

The cognitive strategies may be grouped roughly into four "families," as in Figure 1-4. In family A are the *chunking, or organizing, strategies.* In family B are the *spatial learning strategies.* These are frames, type one, frames, type two, and concept mapping. These strategies generally consist of patterns which may be visually displayed and consist of a "big picture" displaying and organizing substantial amounts of information. Family C may be termed the *bridging strategies*: they help students apply their prior knowledge to new information in relatively systematic ways. Members of this family are the advance organizer, metaphor and frames, type two (which is also a member of the second family). Family D is composed of *general purpose strategies*: rehearsal, imagery and mnemonics. These are called general purpose because they may be used to process many kinds of material for many purposes.

Naming the strategies has posed problems for us. A strategy is a *process* and we would prefer that all the names were progressive tense verbs. On the other hand, we refuse to create clumsy new words. (Framing exists, so that we do not need to transform from frame to framing; but we cannot bring ourselves to transform metaphor, for example.) On the other hand, *neither a frame nor a concept map is a strategy. They are the results, or products, of framing and concept mapping.* In the coming chapters we rely on you to make this distinction, even though we may persist in the use of the noun form as we discuss the strategies and show examples of products.

Chunking

Chunking comprises a large assortment of organizing strategies. These strategies enable the rational ordering, classifying, or arranging of complex arrays. They aid persons in intellectual management of large amounts of data or very complex processes or events. These organizational strategies are preparatory, and deeper processing through other cognitive strategies is re-

FIGURE 1-4
Four families of cognitive strategies.

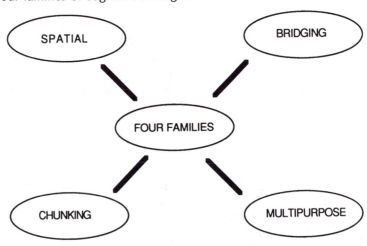

quired for better comprehension and learning, although when one rechunks or reorganizes, one's comprehension is likely to be aided.

Frames, Type One

This type of frame is a matrix or grid (see Figure 1-5 which is an example). Names of concepts, categories or relationships are headings for columns and rows of the grid. Students, teachers or instructional designers supply information in the slots.

Frames, Type Two

Type two frames are grids or matrices which look very similar to type one frames. The main difference is that type two frames are governed by some general principle which allows students to use logic to fill information into slots. Students can infer information from slot to slot and from general principle to slot.

Concept Maps

Concept mapping is the arrangement of major concepts from a text or lecture into a visual arrangement. Lines are drawn between associated concepts, and relationships between the connected concepts are named. These concept maps reveal the structural pattern in the material and provide a "big picture."

Advance Organizer

Presented prior to the new material, the advance organizer is a brief, abstract passage of prose. It is a bridge, a transition statement, which is not only a summary of prior learning prerequisite to new material but is also a brief outline of the new material. *The advance organizer is unique among the strategies in that generally students cannot be expected to create advance organizers. This is the task of the designer or teacher.*

Metaphor, Analogy, Simile

These strategies are used to transpose meaning from one idea, concept, procedure or event to another. They help to sensitize students to similarities across knowledge arrays. Like the advance organizer, the metaphor is a bridge from something known to new knowledge. A metaphor, in contrast to the advance organizer, is often more connotative, less definitive and less detailed.

Rehearsal

Rehearsal is a category name for another set of miscellaneous ways of study or comprehension. Examples are reviewing material, asking questions, answering those questions, predicting possible questions, predicting material to follow and summarizing. Rehearsal is a bit different from the others in that most of these are strategies that only students can use, and the designers' task is to provide time for use, instruction in their use, and opportunities for use.

Imagery

Imagery is the mental visualization of objects, events and arrays. The typical technique is to ask students to form a mental picture. This can be a very powerful learning aid. It is considered to be the second encoding process, with verbal being the other. Imagery is a major way of storing knowledge in mind.

Mnemonics

Mnemonics are called artificial aids to memory. There are numerous types, one of which is first letter coding. First letter coding is the formation of some word or sentence or some other verbal string to aid recall. For example, a reader might note the first letter of the name of each of these cognitive strategies, then create a memorable sentence of words beginning with the letters.

INSTRUCTIONAL DESIGN AND COGNITIVE STRATEGIES

The cognitive strategies are mental activities performed by persons. In instructional design, the designers' task is to plan the instruction so that the student can use one or more of the cognitive strategies to learn the material, to actively, *mentally* process the content. As the designer plans the instruction, decisions must be made about what strategy or strategies are most appropriate for the content and for the particular students. To design instruction without the aid of cognitive science and these strategies is like playing soccer without using the head.

In addition to the goal of using strategies to learn the content is a complementary goal of strategy learning. The designer ideally should try to incorporate the cognitive strategies explicitly as an additional outcome while teaching content. The goals are to learn to learn, or to learn cognitive strategies—to become metacognitively sophisticated—and to master specific material, tasks or skills.

If learning to learn does occur, the student becomes more effective as a learner. A repertoire of cognitive strategies is accumulated, each of which increases the efficiency and effectiveness of learning and instruction. Students become increasingly able, that is, they become *metacognitively sophisticated*.

An exceedingly crucial design task is to decide *which* cognitive strategy to use for *what* content for *which* students, and at *what* point during the instruction. Knowledge of this sort is an example of *conditional knowledge. Such matching is often a matter of trial and error or "tinkering."* We have already mentioned that not all strategies are appropriate for all content for all persons at all points during instruction. In later chapters conditions of use are discussed as each strategy is presented. At this time, however, we present a matrix (frames, type one) and a brief overview of some of these considerations.

Figure 1-5 is a frame, type one, a summary of some of the major ideas and issues discussed in this book. Column one is a list of the cognitive strategies, and the chapters follow the order of the listing. Column two is a listing of chapter numbers in which the strategies are discussed.

There are many features of content or disciplines which largely determine the appropriateness of a strategy. Among these features of content are the abstractness or concreteness (column three) of the lesson content and the relative structure of the content (column four). The feature abstractness/concreteness is the extent to which the material approximates everyday experience and to which it can be visualized, or more or less directly sensed. The feature required structure is an allusion to the extent of the structure of the discipline necessary for the strategy use.

For examples, we mentioned earlier that math and the natural sciences are well structured. In math much can be deduced from general principles. This is true of much knowledge in the natural sciences. By contrast, psychology is not a highly logical discipline. One generally cannot predict human behavior very specifically or accurately through logic or theory. This may not be the fault of the scholars in the discipline, for human behavior is not necessarily based on logic or reason, or, when it is reason based, it is only partially so.

Column five is a list of the utility of the strategy for declarative, procedural, or conditional knowledge. Column six is an estimation of the extent to which the cognitive strategy, properly used, with appropriate content and persons may be expected to aid long-term recall of the content. For example, creating a mnemonic almost always aids learning and recall for a short while, but the fading from memory is typically rapid.

The ratings are not to be taken literally, but are to be taken as a way of estimating recall potential among the strategies. The rating scale is like the hardness scale used with rocks, gems and minerals.

Column seven in Figure 1-5 is the result of a metaphor of mind as a freight hauler. Data is to mind as tonnage is to a freighter. Just as some freighters carry more materials, some minds carry more data than others. So also can some of the strategies aid the recall of more data, or information. This rating is again merely used as a way to represent conveniently the comparison among the strategies.

Column eight is an average of columns six and seven. It is an estimation of the instructional/learning power or effectiveness and possible efficiency (Smith, 1987) of each strategy—assuming, of course, appropriateness of the strategy with the content and audience.

In column nine are listed other strategies which may act in combination with the particular strategy. Long-term recall or data tonnage could be increased when, for example, a metaphor contains an image, or when images are produced by the metaphor. Many metaphors are rich in imagery.

FIGURE 1-5

A decision matrix for selecting strategies for use.

	Chapter #	Abstract/ Concrete	Required Structure	Declarative/ Procedural/ Conditional	Long-Term Recall Potential (10 = high, 0 = low)	Data Tonnage (10 = high, 0 = low)	Power (10 = high, 0 = low)	Hybrid With
Chunking	2	either	varies	type dependent	2	varies	3	all
Frames, type one	3	either	medium	any	7	10	8	any below
Frames, type two	4	either	high	any	10	10	10	any below
Concept mapping	5	either	medium	map dependent	6	8	7	any
Advance organizer	6	abstract	medium	any	9	4	7	imagery
Metaphor—analogy	7	either	medium	any	8	2	5	any
Rehearsal	8	either	low	any	4	4	4	all
Imagery	9	concrete	low	any	7	7	7	metaphor most all
Mnemonics	10	either	low	any	2	7	3	most all

The ideas summarized in Figure 1-5 are discussed in some detail in the later chapters. In the next section we present some common functions of the nine strategies.

GENERAL COMMENTS ABOUT THE COGNITIVE STRATEGIES

Before the reader moves on to the chapters on the cognitive strategies, we present a few general ideas about these strategies. This will aid the reader by providing an overview of what to expect and some of the pitfalls in using the strategies in designing instruction.

Who Is the Content Expert?

An important perspective is that neither the applied cognitive psychologist nor the instructional designer is an expert in all academic, or content, fields. The instructional designer, however, is much more likely to be more expert than the cognitive psychologist in at least one content field—that field in which the designer plans instruction. The designer, therefore, must make the decision about what cognitive strategy is best to use with the content, when to use it and where in the sequencing of parts of lessons, units and courses it is to be used. There will be occasions, however, when this decision should be shared with an expert in the knowledge domain. Proper use, even then, may be a matter of trial and error, or tinkering.

The idea that the designer is likely to be expert in the knowledge domain may be problematic. From time to time the *designer will need to consult with experts or learn a substantial amount of new content.* Ideally designers would have access both to experts for content and to cognitive scientists for learning strategies. This book provides some of that access to cognitive science.

From time to time the instructional designer may be aided by experts by following one of the favored research strategies in cognitive psychology, that of observing how experts in a field solve problems or represent knowledge in their field. As was discussed in an earlier section, cognitive psychologists have used records of these observations to study the structures of knowledge and to reconstruct how the experts represent their knowledge. The hope is that these records yield insight into how to aid the novice, the person for whom instruction is often designed. Some of the more difficult design problems may be resolved in this way.

Our own design experience with getting the help of experts in the knowledge domain has been invaluable, particularly for the design of instruction for advanced students and continuing education learners; and also particularly when it is expected that extremely large amounts of information are to be covered. This latter case is fairly common when one attempts to design entire courses and programs. These experts have often been excited by the aid strategies can provide. Also, often the experts have reported familiarity of these strategies but have called them by other names or have no name for them. The main idea, however, is that *involving experts can be very fruitful.*

The designer seems often a surfer in a strong crosscurrent. The designer is caught in the currents of the needs of the novice, the characteristics of the knowledge, the nature of knowing and the demands of the expert; and these are only a few. The task of designing instruction is demanding and complex.

Cognitive Strategies Are a Repertoire of Ways to Learn

The cognitive strategies are a collection of known ways that people learn. These strategies become techniques in the hands of teachers and designers. Much of the research on which the strategies are based has been conducted with people in school-like or actual school situations and other contexts in which people want or are expected to learn. Therefore, some of these strategies will be familiar even though the names are not. By learning about the others not used, one becomes familiar with more tools of learning and design. These research efforts have shown that most of these are *true strategies used by real people,* by either novices or experts and sometimes by both.

Indeed, observations support the fact that good students are likely to use some of these strategies, sometimes unconsciously, but poor students rarely or never use any of the strategies. This is probably why good students are effective learners and poor students are ineffective. The strategies may be why some are considered bright and some dull. Many good students are aware of their strategic use and monitor the appropriateness of the particular strategy for the particular task.

These findings are based on research in the areas of metacognition and reciprocal teaching. Brown, Palincsar and Armbruster (1984) and others are currently conducting further research on how students can learn the use of cognitive strategies; how, in other words, poor students can become good students, and how good students can become better through learning the cognitive strategies and their appropriate uses. Better students are also conscious of their strategic use, monitor which strategies they are using at the time and have the capability of changing to another strategy when one is not helping.

The concepts of metacognition and reciprocal teaching are similar to their predecessors' "mathemagenic behaviors" (Rothkopf, 1970); "learning to learn" and "generative" learning (Wittrock, 1974); cognitive style, learning style and transfer of learning. Some readers may wish to examine the research in these areas conducted before 1976.

Match the Cognitive Strategy to the Task or Content

Not all strategies are appropriate for all content. Imagine the difficulty of forming a mental picture of the meaning of *hypothesis.* By contrast, it would be very easy to form a mental picture of an isosceles triangle or a doric column.

Figure 1-4 can provide some help in matching strategy to content. Additionally, as each strategy is presented in later chapters further explanations and help will be provided for this matching through the issues about the structures and kinds of knowledge and other specifications. Once again, this is *conditional knowledge*. It is the conditional knowledge as it develops in reading this text which will ultimately determine personal use of these strategies. As one teaches or designs instruction, one is likely to be the expert on one's target learners and the knowledge domain of the instruction.

Change of Pace

It would be very confusing and perhaps boring to use the same strategy lesson after lesson, day after day. The instructional designer must know which strategies are appropriate and use them judiciously. It is likely that *using one strategy constantly would reduce its effectiveness*; for example, in the case of imagery, mental images would blur in the mind and interfere with each other during learning and during recall.

USES OF COGNITIVE STRATEGIES AND MIND-TO-MIND CONTACT

Much of instructional design in the past has been preoccupied with objectives and how to state them, presentation of stimuli, overt responding (drill and practice), sequencing parts of lessons and media selection. More simply, the focus has been on what stimuli to present, how they should be presented, and what overt response should be forthcoming. While these are important considerations, designers have had students primarily occupied with either overt activity or media exposure including observing movies, slide shows, videotapes, and so on—with very little active intellectual processing or involvement. With both print and electronic media, students can be intellectually inactive, merely exposed. With many of the cognitive strategies turned to techniques and designed into instruction, however, students become intellectually active and are much more likely to construct those mental representations which we think of as knowledge. Minds engage each other and minds engage material. If the designer gives instructions to image, or uses an appropriate metaphor, the probability is increased that active intellectual involvement has occurred and that one mind has contacted another mind, in a social situation or even through media such as texts and computers.

For decades in pedagogy there has been talk of the necessity of involving students in learning. *An important new element in the cognitive revolution is intellectual involvement, active cognitive processing*, as contrasted to merely physically responding. This is the most important single idea in cognitive science and its applications to instruction. The use in design of cognitive strategies increases the probability of this kind of involvement.

Motivation and Cognitive Strategies

Just because students can use cognitive strategies does not guarantee that they will. This difference between skill and will (Paris, 1988) attests to the power of motivation in learning. Substantial research exists on the cognitive components of motivation and the interrelationships between motivation and cognition (Ames & Ames, 1984; Dweck, 1986; Weiner, 1980). One view in the motivation literature is that first one becomes motivated; then one learns. Another view, by contrast, is that first one learns; then one becomes motivated. It is very likely, however, that there are reciprocal relationships between the two, and that either could occur seemingly initially, with each influencing the other, perhaps in a cyclical pattern. Keller (1983) developed a model which incorporates several possibilities of cyclical patterns and which includes several variables other than abilities, performance and motivation.

Within this cycle one might also posit important "schemata" [Prawat (1989) terms these *dispositions*] which are significant in the will to learn. Dweck (1986) and Dweck and Leggett (1988) have explored two such dispositional schemata which are *performance* and the *mastery*. Those who are disposed toward mastery are concerned with competence while those who are concerned with performance are preoccupied with gaining positive evaluations from others. Those with the mastery orientation view errors as giving helpful information and are likely to attribute success and failure to their own effort. They also tend to view teachers as resources or guides rather than dispensers of punishment.

It is very likely that the use of cognitive strategies will increase learning, which often will motivate students for further effort and study. Their use may also help to inculcate the schema of mastery with its accompanying effort attributions. That is to say, academic success appears to lead to the cognitive components of motivation such as internal attributions that "I can learn this when I study hard" (an effort attribution). On the other hand, academic failure appears to lead to external cognitions such as "The teacher does not like me" or "I had bad luck, so there is no use in trying hard" (Ames & Ames, 1984; Weiner, 1980). Using the cognitive strategies should increase learning, should help to create internal attributions (which lead to more effort rather than less) and should promote the viewing of teachers as resources for further learning.

Model Their Use

In general, learning by imitation can be very effective (Bandura, 1969). Not only can students learn content by imitation, they can learn the use of cognitive strategies by observing the instructor use them and by observing other students use the strategies (Madden, Slavin, & Stevens, 1986). Both serve to familiarize students with the strategies and their many uses in study and learning.

Some of the strategies can be used in group activities. Students can use the strategies during cooperative learning (Slavin, 1983). This too can serve the objective of metacognitive sophistication, for students can learn strategies from each other.

Reinforce Their Use

Reinforcement is a powerful force in human affairs and human learning (Skinner, 1953). During instruction rewards should be provided to students when the students use cognitive strategies. The strategies should be recognized, emphasized or somehow highlighted so the student can be aware of exactly what is being reinforced. Reinforcement increases the probability of such responses occurring again. Therefore, if a student uses imagery or a particular metaphor *that use should be reinforced.*

Cognitive Strategies Are to Be Designed into Instruction: Strategy Training

Cognitive strategies are not only ways real people learn, *they can be activated in systematic ways.* The instructional designer can carefully design a metaphor, for example, one which is developed particularly for the lesson or idea to be conveyed.

It is true that some of the better students might use a strategy on their own to learn the material. Many will not. Some students will partially use a strategy which might be less helpful than the particular one the designer plans.

There is again the objective beyond helping the student to learn the specific lesson. That is the additional objective of "learning to learn" or becoming metacognitively sophisticated. That is to say that, as a student learns the material, the student is hopefully learning how to use imagery or frames or rehearsal strategies—the cognitive strategy used as a technique by the instructional designer.

Designers can use these strategies in at least three ways (Reigeluth & Stein, 1983). *First is the use of a strategy to convey the content, or to activate the internal processing necessary for learning.* For example, an appropriate analogy is presented by the designer. *Second, the designer may in a variety of ways activate a strategy known by the learner.* For example, the learners are asked to create or think of an appropriate analogy. *Third, the strategy is taught along with content, as in reciprocal teaching.* Generally speaking, the more advanced the learner, the more typical is the second use.

Our knowledge based on cognitive science, reciprocal teaching, modeling and reinforcement may be incorporated into a very simple model for strategy training. This model is shown in Figure 1-6. This model reflects considerable research and development in strategy training [see Dubois and Kiewra (1989) and Pressley and Levin (1983) for examples]; and, obviously, it also reflects applications from behaviorism, social learning theory and cognitive science. Thus it is eclectic or multimodal, drawing, as is most good technology or practice, from several theoretical sources [see Lazarus (1989), for

FIGURE 1-6

A model for strategy training.

MODEL STRATEGY

MAY REQUIRE MANY
DEMONSTRATIONS
WITH VARIED
CONTENT; LET PEERS
DEMONSTRATE ALSO

THEN

STUDENT PERFORMS (GUIDANCE)

GRADUALLY "FADE",
REINFORCE, EXPLAIN;
PROVIDE KNOWLEDGE
OF RESULTS
(FEEDBACK);
RETURN TO DEMOS IF
NECESSARY

THEN

STUDENT PERFORMS WITHOUT GUIDANCE

STUDENT
PRACTICES IN
A VARIETY
OF CONTENT
AREAS

example, for an eclectic psychotherapy based on both behaviorism and cognitive theory]. *Despite our emphasis on cognitive theory we are advocating an instructional design approach which is eclectic.*

Briefly, learning to use a strategy cannot be divorced from its use in content learning. Learning a strategy may require many demonstrations with a variety of content. As progress is made, peers who master the strategy first may demonstrate or tutor, as is incorporated into reciprocal teaching. When students use a strategy, knowledge of results should be provided and effort should be reinforced (Kulhavy, 1977). Another important feature of this model is *fading, the reduction of the support provided by modeling and reinforcement.* Considerable explanation and further demonstration by the teacher or peers may be necessary. The goal is that the student will be able to use the strategy without guidance in a variety of content settings. This simple model, or parts of it, is used in many strategy training efforts.

SUMMARY

In this first chapter we have provided a complex background from the literature on the cognitive mutation/revolution, and we have drawn several broad implications for instructional design. This background has included a short history of the emphasis on "internal representation" and its centrality in the cognitive mutation. We have emphasized that schema is the favored, but not the sole, "internal representation." We have also provided an overview of nine cognitive strategies, themselves "internal representations."

In each of the following chapters to which we now turn, we have presented relatively brief research backgrounds so that readers will have some familiarity with the basis for our claims of the usefulness of the strategies. Most chapters are organized with introductory material and general explanations of the strategy presented initially; then the research is discussed; then a designers' guide to the use of the strategy is presented. Our primary emphasis is the provision of a guide for the use of the strategies by the instructional designer and teacher. The final two chapters are a general guide to instructional design, a procedural explanation named the instructional design template for the many decisions instructional designers must make. These decisions include, but are not restricted to, choices about the cognitive strategy. In this next chapter we turn to the first family of cognitive strategies: chunking or organizing strategies.

EXERCISES

1. Examine Figure 1-5 carefully. Feel free to examine the relevant text. Paraphrase what is meant by the column and row headings. Inspect the slots (the intersections of rows and columns) and think about the information in those slots. Learn and then test yourself for the names of the nine strategies and their definitions.

2. What is your name for any strategies you used to learn the names of the nine strategies in exercise number one?

3. What is the name of the strategy of which Figure 1-5 is an example?

REFERENCES

Ames, C., & Ames, R. (1984). Systems of student and teacher motivation: Toward a qualitative definition. *Journal of Educational Psychology, 76*, 535–556.

Anderson, J. R. (1985). *Cognitive psychology and its implications.* New York: Freeman.

Anderson, J. R. (1987). Skill acquisition: Compilational weak-method problem solutions. *Psychological Review, 94*, 192–210.

Anderson, R. C. (1984). Role of reader's schema in comprehension, learning, and memory. In R. C. Anderson, J. Osborn, & R. J. Tierney (Eds.), *Learning to read in American schools: Basal readers and content texts.* Hillsdale, NJ: Lawrence Erlbaum Associates.

Anderson, R. C., & Pichert, J. W. (1978). Recall of previously unrecallable information following a shift in perspective. *Journal of Verbal Learning and Verbal Behavior, 17,* 1–12.

Andre, T., & Phye, G. D. (1986). Cognition, learning, and education. In G. D. Phye & T. Andre (Eds.), *Cognitive classroom learning.* New York: Academic Press.

Ausubel, D. P. (1968). *Educational psychology: A cognitive view*. New York: Holt, Rinehart & Winston.

Bandura, A. (1969). *Principles of behavior modification*. New York: Holt, Rinehart and Winston.

Bartlett, F. C. (1932). *Remembering*. Cambridge, England: Cambridge University Press.

Beck, A. T., & Weishaar, M. E. (1989). Cognitive therapy. In R. J. Corsini & D. Wedding (Eds.), *Current psychotherapies* (4th ed.). Itasca, IL: F. E. Peacock.

Bower, G. H. (1981). Mood and memory. *American Psychologist, 36,* 129–148.

Bransford, J. C., & McCarrell, N. S. (1974). A sketch of a cognitive approach to comprehension. In W. B. Weimer & D. S. Palermo (Eds.), *Cognition and the symbolic processes*. Hillsdale, NJ: Lawrence Erlbaum Associates.

Briggs, L. J. (1977). Designing the strategy of instruction. In L. J. Briggs (Ed.), *Instructional design*. Englewood Cliffs, NJ: Educational Technology Publications.

Brown, A. L. (1975). The development of memory: Knowing, knowing about knowing, and knowing how to know. In H. W. Reese (Ed.), *Advances in child development and behavior* (Vol. 10). New York: Academic Press.

Brown, A. L. (1978). Knowing when, where, and how to remember: A problem in metacognition. In R. Glaser (Ed.), *Advances in instructional psychology*. Hillsdale, NJ: Lawrence Erlbaum Associates.

Brown, A. L. (1980). Metacognitive development and reading. In R. J. Spiro, B. C. Spruce, & W. F. Brewer (Eds.), *Theoretical issues in reading comprehension*. Hillsdale, NJ: Lawrence Erlbaum Associates.

Brown, A. L., & Campione, J. C. (1977). Training strategic study time apportionment in educable retarded children. *Intelligence, 1,* 94–107.

Brown, A. L., & Campione, J. C. (1981). Inducing flexible thinking: A problem of access. In M. Friedman, J. P. Das, & N. O'Conner (Eds.), *Intelligence and learning*. New York: Plenum Press.

Brown, A. L., Campione, J. C., & Day, J. D. (1981). Learning to learn: On training students to learn from texts. *Educational Researcher, 10,* 14–21.

Brown, A. L., Palincsar, A. S., & Armbruster, B. B. (1984). Inducing comprehension-fostering activities in interactive learning situations. In H. Mandl, N. Stein, & T. Trabasso (Eds.), *Learning and comprehension of texts*. Hillsdale, NJ: Lawrence Erlbaum Associates.

Bruner, J. (1973). *Beyond the information given*. New York: Norton.

Bruner, J. (1986). *Actual minds, possible worlds*. Cambridge, MA: Harvard University Press.

Chomski, N. (1951). *Syntactic structures*. The Hague: Mouton.

Chomsky, N. (1965). *Aspects of a theory of syntax*. Cambridge, MA: M.I.T. Press.

Dick, W., & Carey, L. (1985). *The systematic design of instruction* (2nd ed.). Glenview, IL: Scott, Foresman.

Dick, W., & Reiser, R. A. (1989). *Planning effective instruction*. Englewood Cliffs, NJ: Prentice-Hall.

diSibio, M. (1982). Memory for connected discourse: A constructivist view. *Review of Educational Research, 52,* 149–174.

DuBois, N. F., & Kiewra, K. A. (1989). The development of a multi-level research program to evaluate the effects of strategy training on study behaviors. Paper read at the annual meeting of the American Educational Research Association, San Francisco.

Duell, O. K. (1986). Metacognitive skills. In G. D. Phye & T. Andre (Eds.), *Cognitive classroom learning*. New York: Academic Press.

Dweck, C. S. (1986). Mental processes affecting learning. *American Psychologist, 41,* 1040–1048.

Dweck, C. S., & Legett, E. L. (1988). A social-cognitive approach to motivation and personality. *Psychological Review, 95,* 256–273.

Farmer, J. A., Jr. (1983). The three foci model. *Proceedings of the 23rd Annual Conference on Research in Medical Education* (pp. 272–277). Washington, DC: Association of American Medical Colleges, Group on Medical Education.

Farmer, J. A., Jr. (1985). Adult education: counseling. *International encyclopedia of education: Research and studies* (3rd ed., pp. 1072–1074). Oxford: Pergamon Press.

Flavell, J. H. (1985). *Cognitive development* (2nd ed.). Englewood Cliffs, NJ: Prentice-Hall.

Gagne, E. D. (1985). *The cognitive psychology of school learning.* Boston: Little, Brown.

Gagne, R. M., Briggs, L. J., & Wager, W. W. (1988). *Principles of instructional design* (3rd ed.). New York: Holt, Rinehart & Winston.

Gardner, H. (1987). *The mind's new science: A history of the cognitive revolution.* New York: Basic Books.

Inhelder, B., & Piaget, J. (1958). *The growth of logical thinking from childhood to adolescence.* New York: Basic Books.

Keller, J. M. (1983). Motivational design of instruction. In C. M. Reigeluth (Ed.), *Instructional design theories and models.* Hillsdale, NJ: Lawrence Erlbaum Associates.

Koffka, K. (1935). *Principles of Gestalt psychology.* New York: Harcourt Brace Jovanovich.

Kohler, W. (1925). *The mentality of apes.* New York: Harcourt Brace Jovanovich.

Kulhavy, R. W. (1977). Feedback in written instruction. *Review of Educational Psychology, 47,* 211–232.

Landa, L. N. (1983). Descriptive and prescriptive theories of learning and instruction: An analysis of their relationships and interactions. In C. M. Reigeluth (Ed.), *Instructional-design theories and models: An overview of their current status.* Hillsdale, NJ: Lawrence Erlbaum Associates.

Lazarus, A. A. (1989). Multimodal therapy. In R. J. Corsini & D. Wedding (Eds.), *Current psychotherapies* (4th ed.). Itasca, IL: F. E. Peacock.

LeGrand, B. (1987). *A study of graduates of off-campus graduate programs of the University of Illinois at Urbana-Champaign: Change and related learning.* Ph.D. dissertation.

Madden, N. A., Slavin, R. E., & Stevens, R. J. (1986). *Cooperative integrated reading and composition: Teacher's manual.* Baltimore, MD: Johns Hopkins University, Center for Research on Elementary and Middle Schools.

Mandl, H., & Schnotz, W. (1987). New directions in text comprehension. In E. De Corte, H. Lodewijks, R. Parmentier, P. Span (Eds.), *Learning and instruction: European research in an international context* (Vol. I). Oxford: Pergamon Press.

Mayer, R. E. (1987). *Educational psychology: A cognitive approach.* Boston: Little, Brown.

Miller, G. A., Galanter, E., & Pribram, K. H. (1960). *Plans and the structure of behavior.* New York: Holt, Rinehart and Winston.

Minski, M. (1975). A framework for representing knowledge. In P. H. Winston (Ed.), *The psychology of computer vision.* New York: McGraw-Hill.

Newell, A., & Simon, H. (1972). *Human problem solving.* Englewood Cliffs, NJ: Prentice-Hall.

Ortony, A. (Ed.). (1979). *Metaphor and thought.* New York: Cambridge University Press.

Paivio, A. (1971). *Imagery and verbal processes.* New York: Holt, Rinehart & Winston.

Palincsar, A. S., & Brown, A. L. (1984). Reciprocal teaching of comprehension-fostering and comprehension-monitoring activities. *Cognition and Instruction, 1,* 117–175.

Paris, S. (1988). Fusing skill and will: The integration of cognitive and motivational psychology. Address given at the annual meeting of the American Educational Research Association, New Orleans, LA.

Paris, S., Lipson, M. Y., & Wixson, K. K. (1983). Becoming a strategic reader. *Contemporary Educational Psychology, 8,* 293–316.

Pepper, S. C. (1961). *World hypotheses.* Berkeley: University of California Press.

Piaget, J. (1952). *Origins of intelligence in children.* New York: International Universities Press.

Pressley, M., & Levin, J. R. (Eds.). (1983). *Cognitive strategy research.* New York: Springer-Verlag.

Prawat, R. S. (1989). Promoting access to knowledge, strategy, and disposition in students: A research synthesis. *Review of Educational Research, 59,* 1–41.

Rorty, R. (1979). *Philosophy and the mirror of nature.* Princeton, NJ: Princeton University Press.

Reigeluth, C. M., & Stein, F. S. (1983). The elaboration theory of instruction. In C. M. Reigeluth (Ed.), *Instructional-design theories and models: An overview of their current status.* Hillsdale, NJ: Lawrence Erlbaum Associates.

Rothkopf, E. Z. (1970). The concept of mathemagenic activities. *Review of Educational Research, 40,* 325–336.

Rumelhart, D. E., & Ortony, A. (1977). The representation of knowledge in memory. In R. C. Anderson, R. J. Spiro, & W. E. Montague (Eds.), *Schooling and the acquisition of knowledge.* Hillsdale, NJ: Lawrence Erlbaum Associates.

Rumelhart, D. E., & Norman, D. A. (1978). Accretion, tuning, and restructuring: Three modes of learning. In J. W. Cotton & R. Klatzky (Eds.), *Semantic factors in cognition.* Hillsdale, NJ: Lawrence Erlbaum Associates.

Schommer, M. (1989). The effects of beliefs about the nature of knowledge on comprehension. Unpublished doctoral dissertation. University of Illinois at Urbana-Champaign.

Schank, R. C., & Abelson, R. (1977). *Scripts, plans, goals, and understanding.* Hillsdale, NJ: Lawrence Erlbaum Associates.

Skinner, B. F. (1953). *Science and human behavior.* New York: Macmillan.

Slavin, R. E. (1983). *Cooperative learning.* New York: Longman.

Smith, K. A. (1987). Heuristics for improving learning effectiveness and efficiency. *Engineering Education, 77,* 274–279.

Spiro, R. J., Vispoel, W. L., Schmitz, J. G., Samarapungavan, A., & Boeger, A. E. (1987). Knowledge acquisition for application: Cognitive flexibility and transfer in complex content domains. In B. C. Britton & S. Glyun (Eds.), *Executive control processes.* Hillsdale, NJ: Lawrence Erlbaum Associates.

Spiro, R. J. (1977). Remembering information from text: Theoretical and empirical issues concerning the "state of schema" reconstruction hypothesis. In R. C. Anderson, R. J. Spiro, & W. E. Montague (Eds.), *Schooling and the acquisition of knowledge.* Hillsdale, NJ: Lawrence Erlbaum Associates.

Titchener, E. B. (1910). *Text-book of psychology.* New York: Macmillan.

Tulving, E. (1972). Episodic and semantic memory. In E. Tulving & W. Donaldson (Eds.), *Organization of memory.* New York: Academic Press.

Turkle, S. (1984). *The second self: Computers and the human spirit.* New York: Simon & Schuster.

van Dijk, T. A., & Kintsch, W. (1983). *Strategies of discourse comprehension.* New York: Academic Press.

Vygotski, L. S. (1962). *Thought and language.* Cambridge, MA: M.I.T. Press.

Weiner, B. (1980). *Human motivation.* New York: Holt, Rinehart & Winston.

Wertheimier, M. (1945). *Productive thinking.* New York: Harper & Row.

West, C. K., & Foster, S. F. (1976). *The psychology of human learning and instruction in education.* Belmont, CA: Wadsworth.

West, C. K. (1981). *The social and psychological distortion of information.* Chicago, IL: Nelson-Hall.

Wittrock, M. C. (1974). Learning as a generative activity. *Educational Psychologist, 11,* 87–95.

Zeaman, D. (1959). Skinner's theory of teaching machines. In E. Galanter (Ed.), *Automatic teaching: The state of the art.* New York: Wiley.

CHAPTER 2

Chunking: Organizing Strategies

In this chapter we turn to the first family of cognitive strategies: chunking, or organizing, strategies. This chapter is a discussion of a relatively few general organizing strategies (Mannes & Kintsch, 1987), or text structures (Meyer & Rice, 1984) which recur in prose. These chunking strategies are often "preparatory" to other strategic processing. Even more, they are intrinsic to knowledge, for we often (perhaps always) require some organization before we render a judgment that something has the status of knowledge.

As we introduce this first family we must emphasize as we did in Chapter 1 that the *strategies are processes*. This may seem strange to repeat, yet it is very essential that you recognize that examples of text or a figure are not strategies themselves but results of strategies. The strategy in this chapter labeled with its most general name is *sorting*.

Mother Nature and her consort Father Probability, while splashing in the gene pool, perhaps in the Olduvai Gorge a few million years ago, must have taken a moment to implant in humans a command or program, "Think categories!" Those ancient humans or human prototypes in the Gorge must have obeyed enthusiastically, for so many of our modern mental operations are sorting activities. The command, or genes, took well and spread far.

The booming success of the commands may be attributable to their functionality, their aiding of adaptation. For example, imagine the necessity of sorting objects into classes such as edible and inedible, or persons into categories such as friendly versus hostile, for examples. Having classes of things which we recognize and the knowledge that we can respond to events and things as classes rather than having to respond to each event or thing as unique reduces the complexity of living (Bruner, Goodnow, & Austin, 1967).

It is difficult to imagine human life without adroitness in categorization. Seemingly, such cognitive skills are very basic to human functioning (Bruner,

Goodnow, & Austin, 1967). Perhaps those who were adroit in these skills survived in greater numbers and were thus, collectively, more proficient in passing on the command to offspring.

Perhaps Plato, not Mother Nature and Father Probability, is responsible for our proclivities toward chunking for he, a master sorter, divided people into three types: philosopher kings, soldiers, and workers. Not satisfied with classification of persons, he continued with a three-part sorting of soul and five-part sorting of types of government. Only the names and numbers of types have changed. All this classification was part of a search for the ideal, the true form.

Social scientists, following in the footprints of Plato, may have gotten more than their fair share of chunking genes or commands: we make up stages or steps for anything! When stages do not fit, types or classes are used in apparently endless contexts on an infinite variety of objects and phenomena.

Jesting aside, the endless use of chunking is testimony to its vitality as a set of ways of functioning intellectually. These chunking strategies are real examples of schemata which people use to describe, comprehend, represent and remember events and objects. These schemata function in ways that are equivalent to those functions presented in Chapter 1 (pages 7–11) of enabling perception, comprehension and recall.

In the literature on writing [see Lane (1983) for example], many of the chunking strategies presented in this chapter are recommended as organizing strategies. Novice writers are urged to be aware of the organizing strategies; and, as one of the earlier of several steps in writing, select the organizer that is particularly suitable for the topic and use it to organize their writing.

In contrast to selecting an organizer from someone's list, expert and prolific writers may have a large repertory of chunking strategies. Or, if the person is a master of one genre, the writer may use a few very elaborate appropriate strategies, each with many interesting variations.

Even for the novice, including the young, chunking does seem to be a very natural activity. Children, early in their development, seem to be able to easily sort by obvious characteristics of an array such as size, color or shape. Initially, they sort by one obvious feature and are unable to sort by another characteristic. As they develop, however, they become able to sort by one feature, then another. For example, a child might sort a group of blocks by size, then by color, then by shape.

Piaget and Inhelder (1969) and Inhelder and Piaget (1964) have interesting discussions of their research on the development of chunking, or classification, skills. Sorting skills develop in a general pattern from being based initially on single, concrete, observable features to being based on more abstract and multiple qualities.

Without the development of these chunking strategies intellectual management of the very complex environment would probably be impossible. The amount of information available today is massive and complex and stresses human capacities in perception, discrimination, comprehension, recall and judgment. Miller (1956) has placed the human capacity for adequate processing before overload at between five and nine bits of information.

This capacity is also reflected in the work of Meehl (1954) on personal judgments. We often must make decisions from information arrays that are so dense and complex that our judgments cannot incorporate enough of the information. When the amount of information reaches a certain point, between five and nine for most people, our judgments about the information do not improve with further data. Beyond that finite number we cannot resolve conflicts and properly weigh implications. For example, a medical doctor's diagnosis of an illness would not necessarily be more accurate with a total of seven symptoms and indicators, than it would be with five.

Computers can be used as intellectual "waldoes" to stretch this capacity (Warfield, 1976). So many decisions and judgments, to be accurate, must incorporate very dense and complex data arrays. Computers do provide fantastic aid.

Miller has further shown that people, however, can substantially stretch this capacity for perception, discrimination, recall and judgment by forming categories, and that each category can contain between five and nine bits. If the produced bits are also categories, these too can contain more bits of information.

The increased capacity enabled by chunking has been a focus of research for several years by many researchers. The label for what is called chunking is varied: Bousfield reports *clustering* (1953); Miller (1956) terms it *chunking*, as do we; Jenkins and Russell (1952) write of *structuring*; Mandler (1966) names it *organizing*; and Katona (1940) calls it *grouping*. The varied labels are perhaps excessive and mildly confusing, but the aiding of cognition is clear.

Bousfield's (1953) study is a concrete illustration of how chunking helps recall. Subjects were presented 60 words in four categories: names, animals, vegetables and professions. The words were given in random order. They were asked to list all the words they could remember. The subjects did recall more words that they could from lists of unorganized words. Furthermore, many subjects often grouped the recalled words into the categories.

Bousfield's study and similar research clearly demonstrate the intellectual aid provided by one form of chunking. In the following sections a variety of chunking strategies is presented, with examples and with applications for instructional design.

CHUNKING STRATEGIES

In the following sections several typical chunking strategies are organized (chunked) into two broad categories: linear/spatial; and, second, classification. The list of strategies should not be thought of as complete; but rather as partial, yet still including most of the major typical chunking strategies used when we organize and try to comprehend ordinary events and which we find in many formal educational materials.

The array of typical chunking strategies in Figure 2-1 attests to the complexity of the human environment, the complexity of human intellect, and the various multifaceted twists which the structure of knowledge about that environment can take. They are, again, real intellectual patterns used by experts and novices alike. The more expert one becomes, the more obvious and elaborate become the chunking strategies used.

At this point we need to share with you that we have used the word *structure* (as in text structure) in what seem to be two ways so far in this book. In this we are consistent with the literature. In chapter 1 we wrote of the structure of knowledge and referred to it as though it were a *quantitative* variable as in high structure, medium structure and low structure (or well-structured and ill-structured). In this chapter, on the other hand, we are discussing several types of structures, so that we are recognizing *qualitative* differences in structure in this chapter. We can blend these by showing that the different types of text structure (the qualitative) vary in structure—quantitatively. That is to say, some of the types of text structure are more (quantitatively) structured than others. We note this in Figure 2-1 by using the words high, medium and low in parentheses to communicate the extent of relative *quantitative structure*.

A large part of becoming an expert is, of course, being very aware of the structure of knowledge in the content domain, both its qualitative or quantitative structural characteristics. This awareness includes knowing the typical and appropriate chunking strategies. For some knowledge domains the chunking scheme is the sole structure. For other domains, other structures exist which can be made apparent in well-designed instruction. The "chunking of chunking" done here and listed in Figure 2-1 is so ubiquitous that it is difficult to think of knowledge and the communication of that knowledge without these chunkings.

FIGURE 2-1

Types of chunking strategies with ratings of relative quantitative structure.

I. LINEAR/SPATIAL STRATEGIES
  A. Spatial (low)
  B. Narrative (low)
  C. Procedure (medium)
  D. Exposition (high)
II. CLASSIFICATION
  A. Taxonomies (high)
  B. Typologies (medium, low)
  C. Multipurpose sorting
    1. Causes and effects (medium)
    2. Similarities and differences (medium to low)
    3. Forms and functions (medium)
    4. Advantages and disadvantages (low)

In design, the appropriate chunking strategy, suitable to the knowledge domain and perhaps combined with any other cognitive strategy, should be selected and made obvious during the instruction. Since the chunking strategies are not among the more memorially powerful cognitive strategies presented in this text, combining appropriate chunking schemes with another cognitive strategy is frequently helpful. Most of the time, however, the chunking will have been done by those who prepare instructional material.

This hybridization is often helpful or necessary because so much of our knowledge and so many explanations consist of chunkings—typologies, classification, procedures, and so forth. That is to say, knowledge is so replete with classes, class names and concepts that they often are unnoticed. They are "invisible" in the sense that fish may be unaware of water. Therefore, in instructional design the primary chunkings must be emphasized in more memorable ways.

We now turn to a discussion of the first set of chunking strategies. We call these "tales of space, time, procedures and logic." In other documents (Meyer & Rice, 1984) these are called *text structure*.

Spatial/Linear Strategies: Tales of Space, Time, Procedure and Logic

There are four common classes of linear and spatial strategies reflected in text and other forms of written and spoken communications (sometimes called connected discourse) (Goetz & Armbruster, 1980). We call these space, time, procedures and logic (exposition). (Please see Figure 2-1.) This classification of text structure is similar to Brewer (1980). In the following subsections we describe these. It is important to remember that all four classes have the potential to organize an infinite amount of information. Often that information is rich and dense, and often structures are not easy to detect.

Space

Some arrays of information can only be made orderly by *spatial* chunking (Anderson, 1985; Santa, 1977). For everyday examples, one could, and likely would, use a spatial strategy to answer a question about what a new apartment was like. One would begin the description at a place of choice, perhaps the kitchen, and "map" or describe the kitchen, then the living room, then the bedroom, then the bath, and so on.

Such a strategy is also commonly used as one observes and describes a painting. It is mentally divided into components or parts, or subspaces; then examined carefully. Foreground might be examined, then background.

Another example of this type of chunking is from the geography of the contiguous United States. Starting in the east on a topographic map is the tidewater region, then the Appalachian mountain chain, intermittent tall grass prairie with the Great Lakes region to the north, the Great Plains, the desert region, the western mountains and the western seacoast.

In a more formal educational context, the first author's son, Kenyon, while in the seventh grade, was assigned the task of memorizing the countries of Europe. His efforts were observed as follows:

"I think I can divide this (the European) map into parts. There are northern countries and southern, and central, western, and eastern. Then there are island countries."

He then continued by examining the parts, or sections, making a list for each section; then, seemingly easily memorizing the countries in each section. The next day he remembered more than required for an A on the exam.

Santa (1977) has conducted research which provides some guidelines for the kinds of knowledge appropriate for choosing between linear/spatial strategies. For the purposes of instructional design, spatial strategies are most appropriate for helping recall of geometric figures, and probably other relatively concrete arrays.

Time (Narrative or Sequencing)

By contrast, when time is the basic organizer, sequencing or narration (Bruner, 1986) is the appropriate strategy. Time or narration is the basic, simple format of "storytelling"—no flashback permitted (in the simple story)! If a friend asks what you did on your vacation, it's your choice, of course, exactly what you tell and how you tell it; but often our replies to such questions are organized by time. It's simple. It is a communal format, not likely to confuse, but, for detailed and lengthy stories, very likely to overload the cognitive system.

Narration, or time, is also a "natural," but not the sole chunking strategy for history. This is not meant to be an oversimplification. It is true that "History has many cunning passages; contrived corridors. . . ." (Eliot, 1962). It seems appropriate to organize the stories of the exploration of the western hemisphere by Europeans according to the order in which Europeans are thought to have visited. So it happens that Leif Ericson's exploration might be told first, then Christopher Columbus's and so on.

Another narrative example often presented is the way in which ancient people occupied North America. The periods are characteristically presented as first Paleo, from at least 15,000 until approximately 9,000 years before present; then Archaic, circa 9,000 BP to circa 3,000 BP; then Woodland, circa 3,000 BP until circa 1,000 BP; then Mississippian; then Historic. Moundbuilders, who continued from Woodland through Mississippian times, could be presented as: first Adena, then Hopewell, then Mississippian. The interesting detail of lifeways and the regional complications and variations in the story, could, and often have, been presented with these time boundaries as the organizer.

While time is the glue that holds together the narrative as an identifiable chunking category, there are many substructures used in stories and histories (Brewer & Lichtenstein, 1982; Meyer, 1975; Mandler, 1987). Frequently researched recently are such narrational substructures as problem, action and result (Armbruster, Anderson, & Ostertag, 1987) which are particularly suited to history; the similar problem-solution of Meyer, Brandt and Bluth (1980); and the story grammar of Mandler and Johnson (1977) and Mandler (1978, 1987). The latter found that episodes were divided and subdivided into such sequences as beginning, development and ending with development subdivided into complex reaction and goal path. Goal path was also subdivided into simple reaction and goal; and, finally, goal was subdivided into attempt and outcome. Some have seen cause-effect as a narrative substructure (Richgels, McGee, Lomax, & Sheard, 1987; Trabasso & Sperry, 1985; Trabasso & van den Broek, 1985; van den Broek & Trabasso, 1986).

Some narrative chunkings may be familiar as flow charts. Flow charts are often used in texts and other media to represent very complex, or rich, information sets. For design purposes it is helpful to be aware that there are at least two types of these flow chart patterns in the organization of knowledge. The *first type is based on time only, while the second type includes procedure.*

Procedures

Dividing certain appropriate information into steps and stages seems an intellectual residual of the comprehension and representation of such life events as seasons; variable climates; phases of the moon; food gathering and preparation; and birth, growth and death. There are many very significant and redundant exemplars in nature, sometimes easily observable, but sometimes not so readily comprehended and represented.

In a more modern industrial context an analogue is the assembly line. On the assembly line complex and lengthy processes are ordered in a necessary sequence. This presumably allows efficient functioning of workers and machinery and maximum production of goods.

Knowledge about some events must be described in the order of a required series of steps or stages. The knowledge is a sequenced set of activities. Should the steps not be followed in the proper order, the procedure does not work. This type of knowledge is about steps or subroutines which must be performed in a particular sequence. *Time is one organizer, but also the necessary sequence must be added.* Procedural organization may be remembered as discourse about the second mode or type of knowledge: *procedural.*

Everyday knowledge, basic book learning and advanced performance all contains many examples of procedural knowledge or procedural chunking. At home we use recipes and try to decode obtuse instructions for IRS filing; at work complex office procedures must be mastered. Consider this procedural chunking, one rutted in the daily routine of writing:

1. Place DOS in drive A.
2. Place working disk in Drive B. (Hard disk will be installed next week! Praise be!)
3. Turn on computer.

4. Wait.
5. Strike RETURN for date.
6. Strike RETURN for time.
7. Wait yet again.
8. In Drive A, replace DOS disk with Word Star disk.
9. Type WS and strike RETURN.
10. Wait some more.
11. Strike L to change logged disk drive.
12. Strike D.
13. Wait some more.
14. Type file name.
15. Strike RETURN. (Chapter draft magically appears!)

This is a necessary sequence for the most part, and if the steps were not followed in the required order the draft would not appear on the screen. When this routine fails, however, it is as though the disorderly familiar, a sprite of convoluted mind, whispers, "Don't you dare consult the manual. Call a friend! Disturb a colleague!"

Ordinary living provides many other examples of such procedures: starting a car, tuning a piano, loading a camera, cooking an egg or beef burgundy and so forth. The logical or other features of the task require performance in a specific order, otherwise failure is guaranteed.

Much to be learned in more formal contexts consists of procedural chunkings. Here is a familiar example (presented also in Chapter 1) from instructional design, one which extends back in time to the turn of this century to early time and motion studies (when slightly modified for other tasks), an "assembly line," and one which is considered basic in more detailed form in instructional design literature:

1. State objectives for lesson (or unit).
2. Pretest.
3. Plan and sequence instructional activities.
4. Teach.
5. Evaluate and/or test.

In another knowledge domain, supposedly *the* scientific method or *the* problem-solving process, proper steps are said to be:

1. Becoming aware of a problem
2. Defining the problem

3. Stating the hypotheses

4. Selecting the most probable hypothesis

5. Testing or observation

6. Formulating the conclusion.

This is similar to Dewey's list of how thought progresses (Dewey, 1910). It is offered as the scientific method in many texts.

An example of a procedural strategy in science is contained on page 149 of a junior high school text (Brandwein, Yasso, & Brovey, 1980). It is in prose form in the original. Preceded by the common how question, the topic is the formation of radioactive fallout. Here is the procedure, or process, in abbreviated format: explosion, fireball formed, fireball touches or comes close to ground, fireball sweeps earth into air, earth becomes fine dust, dust spreads widely, radioactive products contaminate dust, dust settles to ground.

By way of review, notice that there are two organizers in these examples from everyday life, from the problem-solving literature and from physical science. *The first organizer is the necessary sequence* imposed by the nature of the knowledge; a specific sequence must be followed. One step follows another and one step is a necessary condition for the next and, in some cases, can even be simplistically thought to be a causal chain. The second organizer is merely time.

Logic

Expository or logical organizations are those which are structured around induction and deduction. Such "stories" unfold from statements, assumptions, theories, postulates or hypotheses; then other statements follow in a chain, each of which is logically induced or deduced from the prior statement.

Summary of Linear/Spatial

Three of the four chunking strategies (space, time and procedure) of this first type discussed in this section are relatively weak in the sense that they tend not to be very memorable and yet often contain so much information that the mind of the student, or listener, becomes overloaded with information. That is why hybridization with other strategies is needed. In the fourth, expository or logical, inference reduces the necessity for recall.

While these three are relatively weak compared with other strategies presented in this book. they are much better than no strategy at all. Imagine attempting to design instruction or even to attempt to master the kinds of rich arrays in some of the examples discussed with no organizing pattern at all. Actually, it may be impossible to have no chunking strategy. It would be almost impossible for most of us. In the absence of organizing patterns the material would be so inchoate and chaotic that we would not consider it to be knowledge; thus it would not be considered worth teaching.

FIGURE 2-2

Type of "story," basis and exemplification.

	Basis	Exemplified or Found in
Spatial	Description of scene, parts, maps	Geography. Structural features of living beings in botany and zoology.
Narrative	Time	Fiction, history, newspaper story, biography, audiobiography
Procedure	Time and one step are necessary for next step.	Recipes, instructions for starting auto. Functional descriptions.
Exposition	Induction and deduction, (following rules of formal logic).	Philosophy (logic) Math

In Figure 2-2 we present the four linear/spatial strategies in a frame, type one. This figure includes the class name of the strategy (which some scholars including Brewer have called the underlying text structure), its basis and some typical disciplines in which it occurs. This figure is very similar to that of Brewer (1980). From space to logic as types of "stories" or text structure which might be found in a knowledge domain, there is a general progression from low structure to high structure.

CLASSIFICATION

In the following sections some standard ways of classifying, or sorting, are discussed. These standard ways are sorted into taxonomies, typologies and multipurpose sortings. This specific three-part sorting should be considered as merely convenient, not a definitive categorization scheme. It is a typology of classification.

Throughout this book the idea of structure of knowledge has been mentioned. In this section it should be clear to the reader that there are types of classification strategies which are appropriate for some knowledge and inappropriate for other knowledge, and that these strategies are related to the structure of the knowledge being classified.

Taxonomies

When knowledge is characterized by logical, law-like—and usually observationally based—interrelationships, taxonomies are appropriate. Perhaps the most widely known example of a taxonomy is the system originated by

Linnaeus, the eighteenth century Swedish naturalist. Today living beings are subdivided according to similarities into three groups: protist, plant and animal. The three groups are further subdivided into phyla and phyla are further subdivided into subphyla. Other subgroupings are species, classes and families.

Given the extremely large number of living organisms, description, comprehension and representation of them would be very difficult without some intellectual strategy. With the taxonomy, however, description, comprehension and representation are made easier. Relationships within the array promote learning.

Another example of a taxonomy, although less orderly than the biological and zoological system, is in the discipline of the psychology of learning—specifically, instructional objectives. Human learning is very complex, and there are many kinds of learning, including both cognitive and affective. Bloom and his colleagues (Bloom, 1956; Krathwohl, Bloom, & Masia, 1964; Bloom, Hastings, & Madaus, 1971) have developed a taxonomy of educational objectives for learning and instruction. The two most widely known domains within this taxonomy are the cognitive and affective domains. (Please see Figure 2-3.)

Within each domain there are several levels of objectives; each level is a prerequisite to the learning and performance of the next higher one. Divided into six levels, the cognitive domain begins with level one, knowledge (mere recall of specifics and universals), continues to level three (application of specifics, concepts and generalizations) to the highest level (evaluation, judging value, appraising worth). Each main level is subdivided into orderly sublevels by Bloom (1956), but we do not do so in this discussion. Please see Figure 2-3 for further information with examples. Notice that the explanations and examples are developed for the use of the cognitive strategies for student learning or in instructional design. We have not included all the sublevels of each of the six levels.

The affective domain (Krathwohl, Bloom, & Masia, 1964) consists of five levels with each level again subdivided into sublevels. The basic level is receiving (allowing an attitude or value to be spoken or advocated in one's presence). The second level is responding, in which the person complies with the attitude, belief or value. The third level is called *valuing*: at this level the person becomes committed and tries to convince others of the worth of the belief. The fourth and fifth levels involve organization and characterization; that is, the belief is made consistent with other beliefs and becomes typical of the person's consistent set of values. It is important to know that affect often involves cognition and vice versa.

Perhaps examples would help to make the affective domain more concrete. Not only do we want students to learn about the cognitive strategies and how to apply them, we want students to value or appreciate their use. We desire this because, unless students develop positive affect about them, these strategies will not be used to design instruction after the course or text is finished. Figure 2-4 is a sketch of objectives about the cognitive strategies within the affective domain. Notice that there is an orderly progres-

FIGURE 2-3

Taxonomy of educational objectives: Cognitive domain.*

1.00 **KNOWLEDGE:** Knowledge is recalled in the form presented or learned. This *knowledge* could be *about* terminology (1.11); facts (1.12); sequences, methods of inquiry and standards of judgments (1.20); conventions and rules in a field (1.21); and classifications (1.23). Despite the sublevel, the emphasis is always on remembering.

Examples: Students can define each of the cognitive strategies. Students will list the nine cognitive strategies from memory.

2.00 **COMPREHENSION:** This involves understanding, or showing that one understands, by paraphrasing or being able to explain or summarize. This can be accomplished by stating in one's own words (2.10, translation), by understanding each part of a communication and being able to understand relationships among the parts (2.20, interpretation), or by going beyond that which was exactly stated in the communication (2.30, extrapolation).

Examples: Students will list and define *in their own words* the nine cognitive strategies. This will be accomplished from memory without the aid of notes or references. Students will give examples of the use of each of the nine strategies.

3.00 **APPLICATION:** Students correctly apply the knowledge remembered in concrete situations. This entails chiefly procedural knowledge.

Examples: Students use each cognitive strategy appropriately to design instruction. Given an article of which the structure is sequential, the student will select an appropriate cognitive strategy to learn it.

4.00 **ANALYSIS:** Students can identify characteristics or elements or interrelationships in the knowledge. This typically involves breaking down material into its important components.

Example: Students can break down the nine cognitive strategies into four classes or categories and understand the parts and interrelationships as to why it is valid to organize in this way.

5.00 **SYNTHESIS:** Students can develop a plan or a proposed set of operations which the student has not seen before.

Example: Given content to teach, student will consider its critical attributes and select a strategy which is appropriate. Student will be able to explain the rationale for the choice in terms of attributes of the content or task and the characteristics or functions of the strategy chosen.

6.00 **EVALUATION:** Judging effectiveness of the value, effectiveness or worth.

Example: Students of instructional design, when provided with knowledge of target students and while considering the relevant characteristics of strategies and attributes of content, can predict the effectiveness of a chosen strategy and provide a rationale for that prediction.

---

* Bloom (1956, pp. 201–207).

sion through the five levels, with one level a seeming prerequisite to the next.

Developmental work for taxonomies is typically lengthy and is usually a cooperative effort. The Linnaeus system took many years to develop and has been revised as discoveries have been made over the past two centuries. The taxonomies of educational objectives were several decades in the making, even though many contributed to them during bag-lunch seminars at the University of Chicago.

In the following section less extensive and less orderly classification schemes are briefly discussed. While their "data tonnage" is often less, they do aid description, comprehension and representation.

FIGURE 2-4
Taxonomy of educational objectives: Affective domain.*

1.0 RECEIVING
  1.1 AWARENESS: Learners are conscious that something exists.
     Example: The learners demonstrate that they are conscious of the cognitive strategies.
  1.2 WILLINGNESS TO RECEIVE: Learners take notice, do not seek to avoid the presentation of the cognitive strategies when there is little else to compete for attention.
     Example: The learners listen to a lecture on the cognitive strategies when there is nothing else to do.
  1.3 CONTROLLED OR SELECTED ATTENTION: The learners direct attention to the desired stimuli even when they could be distracted.
     Example: The students are alert toward the use of the strategies and notice their use, even though there is much to distract them.
2.0 RESPONDING
  2.1 ACQUIESCENCE IN RESPONDING
     Example: The students comply when asked to use a cognitive strategy.
  2.2 WILLINGNESS TO RESPOND: At this level there is voluntary acceptance or use.
     Example: The students cooperate or voluntarily use a cognitive strategy.
  2.3 SATISFACTION IN RESPONSE: At this level the learner shows zest or enthusiasm for the target skill.
     Example: The students display satisfaction in being asked to discuss which cognitive strategy would be most appropriate for specific content.
3.0 VALUING
  3.1 ACCEPTANCE OF A VALUE: Belief in the value or worth of the target skill is displayed.
     Example: Students believe that the use of a cognitive strategy is an important activity.

FIGURE 2-4 (cont'd)

    3.2 PREFERENCE FOR A VALUE: Belief is so strong that students choose the target skill, the new belief, over the previously held one. Time may be spent reflecting on the new belief or skill.

    Example: Students choose concept mapping over an earlier preference for relying on rereading as a study strategy and frequently consider how mapping might be used.

    3.3 COMMITMENT: Belief is strong. Students are certain that "this is the way."

    Example: Students energetically argue in favor of the use of cognitive strategies.

4.0 ORGANIZATION

    4.1 CONCEPTUALIZATION OF A VALUE: Students attempt to identify the characteristics of the favored skill or target stimulus.

    Example: In order to value more deeply, the students try to identify the characteristics which distinguish exemplars of the value or characteristics of the target skill.

    4.2 ORGANIZATION OF A VALUE SYSTEM: The learners bring together elements, characteristics or attributes into a coherent valued whole.

    Example: The learners voluntarily develop a plan for using cognitive strategies in all courses now that they have demonstrated preference for doing so in a course in which they were taught those strategies.

5.0 CHARACTERIZATION

    5.1 GENERALIZED SET: The system of values is internally consistent and has become habitual.

    Example: Students use the strategies in courses, individual learning and personal communications.

    5.2 CHARACTERIZATION: Learners incorporate the value into their philosophy of education and learning in a systematic manner.

    Example: Students demonstrate that they have placed considerable value on the use of the strategies in personal learning, teaching and instructional design. Furthermore, the strategies have implications for such teaching/design operations as the articulation of objectives and the evaluation of learning. In other words, the strategies are believed to deserve special consideration in the curriculum beginning early in the school years.

* Krathwohl, Bloom and Masia (1964, pp. 176–185).

Typologies

For most detailed and complex arrays there are few, if any, nonarbitrary, logical, law-like interrelationships. The typology scheme is less logically based than the taxonomy, and certainly more pervasive across knowledge domains. Usually these are based on obvious features, easily observed. Common examples are by size, color, shape and texture. Most typologies are based on structural features and each type is based on similarities across exemplars of the type. Of course, functional similarities can be bases for types.

A complete list of typologies would be infinite. Bodies of water are divided into streams, rivers (large streams), lakes, seas and oceans. Land is typed by deltas, deserts, plains and so on. Types of soils are classified as loam, sand, clay and so forth. Humans are divided by cognitive style types, personality types, stress types, social class membership and body types. These are but a few.

The task for designing instruction is to examine the material for critical information and highlight any typological scheme which could help students organize and learn that material. The types may not be obvious to the student, who may then not learn as efficiently as is possible when the types are made obvious.

Multipurpose Sorting

In the immediately preceding section it was seen that most types were based on relatively concrete, and often easily observable, features. In this section are briefly discussed multipurpose sortings, which, while commonly used, are more abstract in origin. These types do, however, help to simplify and order complex arrays.

Causes-Effects. One of the multipurpose, abstract sorting or classification schemes, used frequently is cause-effect (Richgels, McGee, Lomax, & Sheard, 1987; Trabasso & van den Broek, 1985; Trabasso & Sperry, 1985; van den Broek & Trabasso, 1986). This scheme is so useful, so "usefully true" in the Rorty (1979) sense, that it dominated Western science for many centuries until the advent of relativity theory early in the twentieth century. Continuing to our day, cause-and-effect sorting and its accompanying reasoning pervades everyday interactions with environment. It even helps children remember stories when embedded as a narrative substructure (Trabasso & Sperry, 1985; Trabasso & van den Broek, 1985).

It works to the extent that Wartofsky (1968) conceptualized numerous types. He does, however, emphasize that, while cause-and-effect reasoning is helpful, it is harmful as a core principle for a philosophy of science: ". . . causality suffices for the rough and ready uses of everyday life, but is too inexact, too ambiguous, or worse, explicitly pernicious when carried over into science" (Wartofsky, 1968, p. 291). Travers (1981) agrees with Wartofsky. Others, however, are more sanguine about the role of cause and effect, including Ennis (1973, 1982a, 1982b) and Mackie (1974).

In design one might, for example, organize a lesson on photosynthesis around its causes and effects. Examples of causes might be considered (1) presence of light, (2) presence of carbon dioxide, (3) presence of water and (4) increased temperature. Production of carbohydrates and oxygen could be considered effects.

Experts in this field might not think that cause-and-effect sorting is the proper way to organize such a unit or lesson. The expert might think that a procedural explanation would be better. It could be that there are better options or that a procedural explanation combined with cause-and-effect sorting would be more acceptable. Such decisions are best left to the experts.

Similarities and Differences. A second multipurpose sorting device is similarities and differences or comparison/contrast (Richgels, McGee, Lomax, & Sheard, 1987). Good students often seemingly automatically think about similarities and differences on their own. It is a typical organizing strategy for essays. It is, incidentally, also intrinsic to metaphor.

For example, in Armbruster, Mitsakos and Rogers (1986), students are asked about the similarities between Rotterdam and a U.S. city. Such a request is a prompt for students to think about something they know and transfer or compare that with some new information. Getting students to remember and apply what they know is often difficult and will happen infrequently unless there is at least prompting. Students might think they know nothing about Rotterdam, but looking for similarities can convince them otherwise.

Other examples are similarities and differences in governments, occupations and the treatment accorded native populations in Africa, Australia and the western hemisphere by Europeans. The list is practically endless.

Forms and Functions. For some content it is meaningful and instructionally sound to organize material by structure and function. In a unit on cells in plants or animals, many concepts could be organized by the dichotomy, structure and function. What are the structures and functions of cell walls, the nucleus, the protoplasm? What is the structure of the cell itself, its parts? What are the functions of the cell parts? Form questions are: "What is x like?" and "What is its structure?" A function question is: "How does x work?"

Another example of the use of structural and functional analysis and sorting is in the area of ecosystems or communities. Structural concepts are such notions as the plant and animal species present, and the patterned relationships among these species. Boundary characteristics are another.

Such considerations as energy and material consumption and transfer could be treated as functional. So also could the details of the process of transformation from one ecosystem to another—from a grass meadow to a forest, for example.

Advantages and Disadvantages. A fourth multipurpose chunking strategy, and last to be discussed, is sorting by advantages and disadvantages. It is helpful for numerous information arrays, but is especially suitable for material around which argument is based. Thus pros and cons could help organize material about different sources of energy: coal, oil, municipal waste, nuclear, solar, winds and tides. Other examples are product comparisons and government comparisons.

Bases for Categorization. There is some work on the bases of categorization which is very interesting (Murphy & Medin, 1985; Medin, Wattenmaker, & Hampson, 1987). The question, put most simply, is, "Why are certain objects 'lumped' together?" Of course, it is not just a lumping exercise because we must often split an array before lumping. Murphy and Medin (1985) argue that there are at least two bases for the formation of categories. First, there is the fact of similarity. They argue that categorical coherence is often simply assembly based on similarity of characteristics or relations. In the case, for example, of stone artifacts found at a complex archaeological site, representing many cultures over thousands of years, we could categorize (lump and split) the stone objects by such common features as size, edge wear pattern, type of stone, sharp and pointed versus dull and not pointed and so forth. But Murphy and Medin add a second basis, that of assembly (and splitting, we add!) or categorization being based on persons' theories of the world. Thus, in the case of the artifact assembly already mentioned, we could categorize depending on our theory of culture. Should our theory of culture be focused around economic factors or subsistence pattern we would group in certain ways. Should our theory be one of the centrality of symbolism in cultures, other groupings emerge. Of course, categorization based on similarity is often theory based. Theory provides the basis for what features are critical for the selection of *which* characteristics or relations are to be the basis for the grouping.

To these two bases of categorization we add convention or societal origin. Cultural attitudes, values, often determine categories. For example, in Jewish tradition certain animals are considered clean or unclean for dietary purposes. Further discussion of the significance of convention can be found in the literature on the sociology of knowledge (for example, Curtis and Petras, 1970).

Summary of Categorization. In the preceding sections we presented a variety of classification strategies, from those which are logical, those which are based on rather concrete attributes, to those which are very abstract—but multipurpose. The classification strategies, including multipurpose, can be observed as substructures of, and thus supplemental to, the four types of stories (or the four types of text structures). We now turn to suggestions for instructional design.

DESIGNERS' GUIDE

We have written of the ubiquity of chunking strategies reflected in knowledge. We have also stressed that chunking strategies are not as powerful in terms of aiding recall as many of the other strategies discussed briefly prior to this chapter. Their omnipresence and relatively modest memorial power require supplementary strategies for powerful instruction. They must be supplemented whenever possible by other strategies; yet, at the same time, they are preparatory for other, more powerful, strategies.

Thus, chunking stands in an unusual relationship with other strategies. Chunking is required for preparing knowledge for strategies such as framing and mapping, *and* in some cases a chunking strategy determines the type of map which can be used. Chunking is required for many of the rehearsal strategies, but rehearsal must be used for deeper active cognitive processing.

In order to create some order about this unusual and complex relationship, some of the implications for the design use of chunking are presented in Figure 2-5. The first step in designing instruction consists of analyzing the chunking strategies used in the content, particularly if the instructional content is already developed for use. One must be very conscious of how that content has been organized. The second step is to determine whether there is a more appropriate strategy which could be developed and used during the instruction. The next step is to rechunk if doing so is desirable.

Clearly, when text contains many steps as in procedurally structured text, or numerous items of information or numerous categories, it is essential that the designer or teacher rechunk or develop more general typologies. Whether that classification is a taxonomy or a typology depends on the nature of the content as previously discussed. Remember that Miller (1956), Mandler (1966) and Bousfield (1953), among others, have demonstrated the cognitive benefits of categorization and the recall benefits of categorizing and recategorization. Often the teacher or designer can use the multipurpose sorting strategies in this manner and for this purpose.

Fourth, the specific chunking and recategorization should be emphasized during the instruction. Some have gone so far as to alert the reader to the text structure early in the lesson or in the introduction to the text and have found this to benefit learning (Dixon, 1987; Fitzgerald, 1984; Mannes & Kintsch, 1987). Much of the instructional design effort should go into the full

FIGURE 2-5

Steps in designers' guide to chunking.

1. ANALYZE CHUNKING STRATEGIES USED IN CONTENT.

2. DECIDE IF THERE IS A MORE APPROPRIATE STRATEGY.

3. RECHUNK IF DESIRABLE.

4. EMPHASIZE CHUNKING STRATEGY IN THE DESIGN.

5. COMBINE CHUNKING USED WITH OTHER STRATEGIES.

FIGURE 2-6

A frame showing hybridization of chunking with other strategies.

	Preparatory for	Combine for Recall Aid	Structure of Knowledge
Exposition	chain map	chain map, others	high
Procedure	chain map	chain map, rehearsal, imagery	medium
Time	chain map	chain map, rehearsal, imagery, mnemonics	low
Space		rehearsal, imagery, mnemonics	low
Taxonomies	spider map, hierarchy map	spider and hierarchy maps, rehearsal, imagery	medium to high
Typologies	spider map, hierarchy map	spider and hierarchy maps, rehearsal, imagery, plus mnemonics	low
Cause/ Effect	chain map frames	chain map plus frames	high to medium
Similarities/ Differences	frames, type one	frames, type one, plus most others	medium to low
Form/ Function	frames, type one	frames, type one, plus most others	medium
Advantages/ Disadvantages	same as above	frames, type one, plus most others	low

comprehension of the organizing strategy. The last step is to combine the chunking used in the lesson with other cognitive strategies. Some of the more explicit combinations are listed in Figure 2-6.

Notice that in Figure 2-6 rows follow the order of that in Figure 2-1 and that specific recommendations about hybridization are presented in the columns. Notice that there are very specific implications for mapping. By way of interest, the last column is a crude indication of the required structure of knowledge within each chunking strategy. It is obvious that many of the uses of the chunking strategies in instructional design involve hybridization. Nonetheless, one of the most important decisions in materials preparation and lesson design is the choice of the organizing strategy.

SUMMARY

In this chapter we explored the numerous and more common types of chunking. We saw that chunking of large and/or complex arrays aid recall when used by themselves and that they extend recall beyond the magical number "seven plus or minus two." *The more important function of chunking, however, is one of preparation.* The effects of chunking on recall are greatly enhanced because of the implications for hybridization. We presented the research on the types of chunking and, finally, discussed some of the implications for instructional design. We now turn to other strategies, the family called spatial learning strategies.

EXERCISES

1. Think of the nine cognitive strategies as a chunking exercise. Most are really chunks or sets. What type of chunking is that (from Figure 2-1)?
2. Examine another text. Open it randomly several times and note the types of chunkings which are present. Do the same ones occur over and over again? In your opinion, are these typical of the structures (qualitatively) in the knowledge domain of that text?

REFERENCES

Anderson, J. R. (1985). *Cognitive psychology and its implications.* New York: Freeman.

Armbruster, B. B., Mitsakos, C. L., & Rogers, V. R. (1986). *America's regions and regions of the world.* Lexington, MA: Ginn.

Armbruster, B. B., Anderson, T. H., & Ostertag, J. (1987). Does text structure/summarization instruction facilitate learning from expository text? *Reading Research Quarterly, 22,* 331–346.

Bloom, B. S. (1956) *Taxonomy of educational objective: The classification of educational goals—Handbook 1: Cognitive domain.* New York: McKay.

Bloom, B. S., Hastings, J. T., & Madaus, G. F. (1971). *Handbook on formative and summative evaluation of student learning.* New York: McGraw-Hill.

Bousfield, W. A. (1953). The occurrence of clustering in the recall of randomly arranged associates. *Journal of General Psychology. 49,* 229–240.

Brandwein, P. F., Yasso, W. E. & Brovey, D. J. (1980) *Energy: A physical science.* New York: Harcourt Brace Jovanovich.

Brewer, W. F. (1980). Literary theory, rhetoric, and stylistics: Implications for psychology. In R. C. Spiro, B. C. Bruce, & W. F. Brewer (Eds.), *Theoretical issues in reading comprehension: Perspectives from cognitive psychology, linguistics, artificial intelligence, and education.* Hillsdale, N.J.: Lawrence Erlbaum Associates.

Brewer, W. F., & Lichtenstein, E. H. (1982). Stories are to entertain: A structural-affect theory of stories. *Journal of Pragmatics, 6,* 473–486.

Bruner, J. S., Goodnow, J. J., & Austin, G. A. (1967). *A study of thinking.* New York: Science Editions.

Bruner, J. (1986). *Actual minds, possible worlds.* Cambridge, MA: Harvard University Press.

Curtis, J. E., & Petras, J. W. (Eds.) (1970). *The sociology of knowledge.* New York: Praeger.

Dewey, J. (1910). *How we think.* New York: Heath.

Dixon, P. (1987). The processing of organizational and component step information in written discourse. *Journal of Memory and Language, 26,* 24–35.

Eliot, T. S. (1962). Gerontion. *The Complete Poems and Plays, 1909–1950* (pp. 21–23). New York: Harcourt, Brace & World, Inc.

Ennis, R. H. (1973). On causality. *Educational Researcher, 2,* 4–11.

Ennis, R. H. (1982a). Abandon causality? *Educational Researcher, 11,* 25–27.

Ennis, R. H. (1982b). Mackie's singular causality and linked overdetermination. *PSA (Philsosophy of Science Association) Newsletter, 1,* 55–64.

Fitzgerald, J. (1984). The relationship between reading ability and expectations for story structures. *Discourse Processes, 7,* 21–41.

Goetz, E. T., & Armbruster, B. B. (1980). Psychological correlates of text structure. In R. J. Spiro, B. C. Bruce, & W. F. Brewer (Eds.), *Theoretical issues in reading comprehension: Perspectives from cognitive psychology, linguistics, artificial intelligence, and education.* Hillsdale, N. J.: Lawrence Erlbaum Associates.

Inhelder, B., & Piaget, J. (1964). *The early growth of logic in the child: Classification and seriation.* London: Routledge and Kegan Paul.

Jenkins, J. J., & Russell, W. A. (1952). Associative clustering during recall. *Journal of Abnormal and Social Psychology, 47,* 818–821.

Katona, G. (1940). *Organizing and memorizing.* New York: Columbia University Press.

Krathwohl, D. R., Bloom, B. S., & Masia, B. B. (1964). *Taxonomy of educational objectives. The classification of educational goals: Handbook II: Affective domain.* New York: McKay.

Lane, L. (1983). *Steps to better writing: A guide to the process.* New York: St. Martin's Press.

Mackie, J. L. (1974). *The cement of the universe: A study of causation.* Oxford University Press (Clarendon Press)

Mandler, G. (1966). Organization and memory. In K. W. Spence & J. T. Spence (Eds.), *The psychology of learning and motivation.* New York: Academic Press.

Mandler, J. M. (1978). A code in the node: The use of a story schema in retrieval. *Discourse Processes, 1,* 14–35.

Mandler, J. M. (1987). On the psychological reality of story structure. *Discourse Processes, 10,* 1–29.

Mandler, J. M., & Johnson, N. S. (1977). Remembrance of things parsed: Story structure and recall. *Cognitive Psychology, 9,* 111–151.

Mannes, S. M. & Kintsch, W. (1987). Knowledge organization and text organization. *Cognition and Instruction, 4,* 91–115.

Medin, D. L., Wattenmaker, W. D., & Hampson, S. E. (1987). Family resemblance, conceptual cohesiveness, and category construction. *Cognitive Psychology, 19,* 242–279.

Meehl, P. E. (1954). *Clinical versus statistical prediction. A theoretical analysis and a review of the evidence.* University of Minnesota Press.

Meyer, B. J. F. (1975). *The organization of prose and its effect on memory.* Amsterdam: North-Holland.

Meyer, B. J. F., Brandt, D. M., & Bluth, G. J. (1980). Use of top-level structure in text: Key for reading comprehension of ninth-grade students. *Reading Research Quarterly, 16,* 72–103.

Meyer, B. J. F., & Rice, G. E. (1984). The structure of text. In D. Pearson (Ed.), *Handbook of reading research.* New York: Longman.

Miller, G. A. (1956). The magical number seven plus or minus two: Some limits on our capacity for processing information. *Psychological Review, 63,* 81–96.

Murphy, G. L. & Medin, D. L. (1985). The role of theories in conceptual coherence. *Psychological Review, 92,* 289–316.

Piaget, P., & Inhelder, J. (1969). *The psychology of the child.* New York: Basic Books.

Rorty, R. (1979). *Philosophy and the mirror of nature.* Princeton University Press.

Richgels, D. J., McGee, L. M., Lomax, R. G., & Sheard, C. (1987). Awareness of four text structures. *Reading Research Quarterly, 12,* 177–196.

Santa, J. L. (1977). Spatial transformations of words and pictures. *Journal of Experimental Psychology: Human Learning and Memory, 3,* 418–427.

Trabasso, T., & van den Broek, P. (1985). Causal thinking and the representation of narrative events. *Journal of Memory and Language, 24,* 612–630.

Trabasso, T., & Sperry, L. L. (1985). Causal relatedness and importance of story events. *Journal of Memory and Language, 24,* 595–611.

Travers, R. M. W. (1981). (Letter to the editor). *Educational Researcher, 10,* 32.

van den Broek, P., & Trabasso, T. (1986). Causal networks versus goal hierarchies in summarizing text. *Discourse Processes, 9,* 1–15.

Warfield, J. N. (1976). *Social systems: Planning, policy, and complexity.* New York: Wiley.

Wartofsky, M. W. (1968). *Conceptual foundations of scientific thought.* New York: Macmillan.

CHAPTER 3

Frames, Type One

In this chapter we present the first member of the spatial learning family of cognitive strategies, *frames, type one*. These spatial strategies share the characteristic of *providing a visual display of substantial amounts of information*. They differ, however, in how the information is displayed, the kinds of information which are displayed and the intellectual operations which are involved in constructing them.

We have organized this chapter into five sections. First, we provide some introductory and background material on frames, type one, which includes definitions and examples. Second, we discuss specific research and development efforts. Next, a designers' guide is presented, which is followed by a section on hybridization and a chapter summary.

INTRODUCTION TO FRAMES, TYPE ONE

While reasonably well-designed or written text, or other instructional material, has an intrinsic structure around which the main ideas, concepts or facts are organized, students often become so embedded in the material that they never become aware of the structure, if it is present (Goetz & Armbruster, 1980), or the main ideas. This becoming embedded is problematic for, as most cognitive scientists believe, learning best begins with a big picture, a schema, a holistic cognitive structure, which should be included in the lesson material—often in the text. If a big picture resides in the text, the designers' task becomes one of emphasizing it. If this big picture does not exist, the designers' task is to develop a big picture and emphasize it, assuming the material is amenable. Without awareness of the text structure and/or a big picture in the form of main ideas, learning is rote and piecemeal at best; and, if there is piecemeal learning, it will probably be forgotten quickly.

Using a big picture such as a frame may provide help in a variety of ways. First, it may supply a coherent structure within which detail may be organized. Second, it may display a large number of meaningful connections (van den Broek & Trabasso, 1986) among details and concepts which are integrated into the whole. Third, it may provide hints to students about what is important in the instruction. For some of these functions, particularly the display of a few connections rather than many, Reigeluth and Stein (1983) employ the metaphors of wide-angle and telescopic lenses. The spatial strategies allow looking at the big picture and telescoping, or zooming, to the detail and back and forth.

Cognitive psychologists offer several strategies which are particularly suited to providing a big picture so that students can relatively easily grasp this big picture and fit the detail from the text or other materials into that structure, or mold (Davies & Greene, 1984). Students, in other words, must either have a big picture or learn one, then assimilate the facts, concepts, ideas into the structure, the schema, the big picture.

There is a large and complex body of research literature on spatial learning strategies (Holley & Dansereau, 1984; Stewart, Van Kirk, & Rowell, 1979; Stewart, 1982). Within this literature two promising but intertwined strategies have emerged: framing and concept mapping. For the purposes of clarity and communication of applications for instructional design, in this and the next two chapters of this text we attempt a convenient and rational separation. We delay the discussion of concept mapping until Chapter 4.

In this chapter we discuss research and applications of interesting research on frames. In discussing frames we employ several perspectives. An early introduction of the concept "frames" into cognitive science was made by Minsky (1975), and Winograd (1976) developed it further. Minsky (1975, 1986), in his classic papers, offered frames as the general intellectual mechanism for knowledge and knowing: to him frames had the generic or all-encompassing status of scripts (Schank & Abelson, 1977), schemata (Bartlett, 1932), or the image (Boulding, 1956) in writings by others.

Even earlier than its use in cognitive science by Minsky, the word *frames* was used in the context of programmed instruction by psychologists such as Skinner (1968), Markle (1969), and Glaser (1965). In programmed instruction, a *frame* is a unit of instruction which usually consists of a presentation of a short and simple item of information, a question and a place for an answer to the question. Students supply the answer, usually in short-answer or multiple-choice format.

In the area of story grammars (see Stein and Trabasso, 1981, for example) the word *frame* is also used by some. Some story frames are organized around characters, setting, plots, conclusions and so on. In Fowler (1982), for example, the frame consists of blanks left in a passage for students to complete. The blanks are to be filled with character names, intentions of characters, actions of characters and narrative conclusions.

In computer-based instruction the frame has been considered to be like the frame in a movie. In this context, the frame is the appropriate set of information which should and can be presented on the computer screen at one time (McAleese, 1985, 1986).

Specifically in this text, however, the concept *"frames, type one," is reserved to mean a grid, a matrix or a framework for representing knowledge*; one of a number of cognitive strategies which can be used to design instruction for individuals and groups, for ordinary classroom instruction, for sequencing and synthesizing information for the purposes of design (Van Patten, Chao, & Reigeluth, 1986), for making text friendlier (more easily comprehended) and for other types of instruction including computer-based instruction. Usually frames are two-dimensional matrices, but three dimensions may be used and recorded on paper or on a computer screen. The two-dimensional frames are most typical and appropriate for most instructional uses.

Notice that the illustrative frames of Figures 3-1, 3-2 and 3-3 are visual or graphic displays (spatial learning strategies) which show how information on a topic is organized. We have decided not to provide the information in some of these. The intent is to show the organization. *The frames include labels of main ideas in rows and columns.* Frames allow information about relationships among the main ideas to be entered in "slots" (Minsky, 1975). This information can consist of facts, ideas, examples, concepts, descriptions, explanations, processes and procedures.

Text authors, teachers, individual students and cooperative groups of students can insert information into the slots. Practically any source of information can be searched, or these slots can, of course, be filled from memory.

A frame, type one, developed by a former student and actually used in a unit on earth science in a middle school is shown in skeleton form as Figure 3-1. Along the rows are types of rocks. Columns consist of how the rocks were formed, their composition, specific common subtypes and uses of subtypes. Notice that a great deal of information can be recorded in the slots.

In Chapter 1 a type one frame is included as Figure 1-5. It is a visual display of the organization of this text and many main ideas from the text.

FIGURE 3-1

A frame for a unit in earth science on rocks.

	Formation	Composition	Specific Types	Uses of Types
Igneous Rocks				
Sedimentary Rocks				
Metamorphic Rocks				

FIGURE 3-2

A three-dimensional frame on forms and functions of memory.

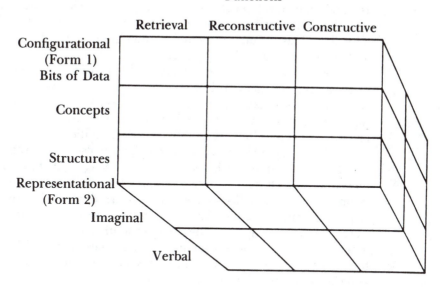

FIGURE 3-3

A frame of the human digestive system.

	Function	Subparts	Function of Subparts
Mouth			
Swallowing Tubes			
Stomach			
Small Intestine			
Large Intestine			
Rectum			

Source: See Vaughan (1984) for further details.

RESEARCH AND DEVELOPMENT BACKGROUND

As is the case with much of the research on other cognitive strategies, the research and development on framing has occurred in educational settings including elementary schools, middle schools, high schools and universities. The disciplines include elementary reading, middle and high school history, and secondary and university science.

Armbruster and Anderson (1982, 1984) used a frame which has broad applications, especially in history. They term it the *goal frame*. This type of frame appears to have been derived from research on story (narrative) grammars. An entire junior high school colonial history course was organized around this frame (see Figure 3-4 for an adaptation).

The *story frame* is a variant of the plans-goals-actions frame. In an example of research on this variation, Dreher and Singer (1980) worked with intermediate grade students in reading. This type of frame includes characters, setting, plot and conclusion labels for row headings and different stories for column headings. Students learned the structure and parts of a story and then were able to correctly fill in the slots for another story. Good readers recalled more than poor readers after using the frames, as would be expected; but there was no observed difference between good and poor readers in their knowledge of the story frame.

This kind of work has had substantial influence in schools particularly in story writing. Teachers report that, given a frame similar to that of Dreher and Singer (1980), training in reading stories with the frame as a guide, and further training in writing with the frame as a guide, elementary students are able to write their own stories.

With older students in college physiology and neuroanatomy, and high school biology and history, Vaughan (1984) investigated effects of framing on learning and recall. Figure 3-3 is a frame adapted from their work. The medical school classes received a four-week program, the high school tenth-grade biology classes received 12 weeks of instruction, and the eighth-grade history classes were taught for 19 sessions (time not specified).

FIGURE 3-4
A goal frame for colonial U.S. history, seventeenth century.

Goal → Plan → Action → Outcome

English				
Dutch				
Blacks				
Native Americans				

Source: See Armbruster and Anderson (1982) for further details.

Vaughan tested for both immediate and delayed recall. The tests consisted of open-ended questions, with cues taken from the students' textbooks. Three levels of questions were designed and administered: superordinate, questions about the gist of long text passages; subordinate, questions about major subtopics including enough detail to understand the subtopics; and specific, questions about nonessential detail.

These three studies resulted in substantial support for the use of framing. For the medical students, *framing aided recall* of specific-level information. For the tenth-grade students, framing aided superordinate and subordinate recall, but not specific-level recall. *Framing, type one, also had significant effects on both immediate and delayed recall* for the eighth-grade students.

For the eighth-grade students, no differences were found between controls and experimentals on the superordinate questions, in the immediate test. On the delayed test, however, the framing group recalled significantly more of what they had learned. It seems that the frame aided better long-term memory.

In a series of experiments Broadbent, Cooper and Broadbent (1978) compared recall of material presented in three ways: (1) the matrix subtype of frames, type one, (2) lists of unorganized words and (3) a hierarchy. The hierarchic organization looked similar to that presented in Figure 3-5 and is very similar to concept maps which will be presented in Chapter 5. Both the hierarchy and the matrix produced recall superior to the unorganized listing. The authors note that there is no consistent superiority of either of the two organizations over the other. Their reasoning for this is that in the hierarchy there is one strong retrieval path from the superordinate categories to the subordinate. In the matrix, however, there are several retrieval paths, none of

FIGURE 3-5

Spatial learning strategies.

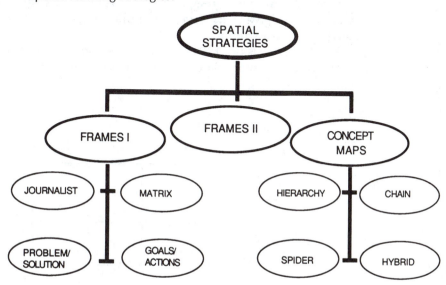

which is very strong; but the many make up for the strength of the one in the hierarchy. In the matrix, for example, there are cues (retrieval paths) from the column headings and the row headings.

Armbruster, Anderson and Ostertag (1987) used a problem/solution frame (see Figure 3-6 for an example) in four fifth-grade social studies classes. The experimental group students were trained to develop the frames and actually used these frames to study passages from their textbooks. Students were tested for two kinds of knowledge: knowledge about the relationships (problems/solutions) and more specific knowledge about passages read, a portion of which was specific to problems/solutions and a portion of which was not. Experimenters gave both an essay test and a short-answer test. Most of the short-answer test items were independent of the problem/solution frame.

After 11 days of instruction the group which was trained to use the frame recalled more than controls on the essay test. On the short answer test, however, there were no training effects.

An interesting twist in this study is that information recalled on the essays written was scored for five levels of importance from the most important (level 1) to the least important (level 4) and extraneous (level 5). The training group remembered more ideas from levels 1 and 5, but fewer from level 4, the least important.

Another interesting effect of the training is that the training group wrote essays with greater focus, better organization, better integration of ideas and more support for the ideas presented. Two raters judged the essays independently. Judges were classroom teachers trained in the procedures but not otherwise involved in the study.

In a long-term science education effort reported in Davies and Greene (1984), frames became the favored strategy to aid reading comprehension. These researchers think that frames are derived from the structures of knowledge in the minds of the authors of science texts, and that frames give coherence to text. Furthermore, they recommend frames as a major way of communicating knowledge and its structure so that students can better understand material and learn from it.

Davies and Greene (1984) identify three categories of frames in science texts: those that contain descriptions of observations and classifications de-

FIGURE 3-6
Problem/solution frame.

	Problem of	Action	Results
#1			
#2			
#3			

Source: See Armbruster, Anderson and Ostertag (1987) for further details.

rived from observations (see Figure 3-1 for an example), those that are used to describe interpretations of those observations and those that involve setting up observations (see Figure 3-7 for an example of a combination of the two latter categories).

This third type of frame is particularly useful in science because of the centrality of systematic observation to science, the role of the laboratory exercise in science education, and the difficulty many science students have with laboratory exercises. Often students seem to go through the motions of the exercise seemingly without awareness of the event being observed and what they are supposed to be observing. Nor do they have the big picture of how the observation fits with relevant knowledge either from a text being used or already known and brought to the exercise in the minds of the students.

From these research and development efforts conducted with students of a variety of age levels and in several knowledge domains, it is clear that *frames, type one, can be a very powerful strategy for learning.* Framing works. It aids learning and comprehension. As verbal ability develops during early years, the usefulness of frames will, of course, improve.

FIGURE 3-7

A skeleton frame as a guide to measure heat produced by a Bunsen burner flame.

Step/Procedure/ Action	Materials Required	Apparatus Required	Condition	Result	Interpre- tation
Measure Mass					
Add to the Beaker					
Measure Mass of Beaker & Water					
etc. etc. (steps continued)					
Record Temp. of Water					
Calculate					
Calculate					
Calculate					

Source: See Davies and Greene (1984) for further details.

One issue related to the research is whether framing aids the recall of relationships, concepts or detail—or all of them. The mixed findings are a bit of a puzzle and are likely to lead to more research. There are at least *two plausible hypotheses*, a design explanation and an intention explanation, with perhaps a third hypothesis, an interaction between design and student intention.

Consistent with the *design explanation*, it seems that if the designer had the objective of increasing recall for relationships, concepts, facts or all three, then the frame should be specifically developed so that its slots would be consistent with the objective. Designers could "tinker" with various formats for frames. Not every frame will suit every objective.

The second hypothesis is about the *intentions of the student*. Students may be accustomed to study for detail because they expect to be tested for detail; thus, they intend to learn detail. Vaughan (1984) suggests that his high school subjects were caught in this intention, studied for detail, and thus recalled detail. He suggests that the medical students, by contrast, typically intend to recall relationships, concepts and ideas. So their use of frames and the benefits derived followed their intentions.

The idea of student intentions recalls a large group of learner attributes which generally cannot be controlled completely, if at all, by the instructional designer: age, intentions, ability and motivation, to name a few. For ability, researchers observe that, while framing can help in all ability groups represented in classrooms (Fitzgerald, 1984), interactions between ability and framing treatments do occur in other studies (Dreher & Singer, 1980). In some studies low-ability students benefit more than high-ability students, probably because high-ability students have more effective strategies prior to the experiment or, more specifically, are more familiar with story frames during study of narratives. As for motivation, it seems that highly motivated students are more likely to use framing assiduously than poorly motivated students (McKeachie, 1984).

Despite the complexity of these issues, for the present frames, type one, exist as an important cognitive strategy. *Improved learning* may be expected to occur when frames, type one are designed into instruction. In the following section the important design considerations are presented.

PRACTICAL ISSUES AND USES: A DESIGNERS' GUIDE

We have shown that the frame is a useful technique for instructional design. There are many very practical questions which are significant for designers. As is true of all the strategies, whether the strategies are to be taught, activated or simply used to present content will influence responses to issues and questions. In this section some of these most important questions or issues will be discussed:

What conditions determine the use of frames, type one?

How is a frame constructed?

When, during the lesson or unit, should the frame be used?

Can students learn to build frames?

Can frames be used for accommodative learning or are they only assimilative aids?

Are frames useful for factual and procedural knowledge?

How often should frames be used?

Should students be given completed frames or complete the frames themselves?

Can frames aid discussion, writing, thinking, creativity and cooperative learning?

How are large information sets managed?

What Conditions Determine the Use of Frames, Type One?

While there are numerous uses of frames, type one (Armbruster, 1985, 1987) and we do not wish to overprescribe, there are important specifications for the use of frames. Many of these are included in Figure 3-8. Briefly, the specifications are included in Figure 3-8 as three types of variables: content variables, task variables and outcomes (from Gagne & Driscoll, 1988). We have already discussed all the content variables in the two previous chapters, so that you should be familiar with these. In the rows of the task variables we include integrative (synthesis, or wholes) and disintegrative (parts). By *integrative*, we mean instructional tasks which are largely holistic or helping to intellectually manage relatively large amounts of information. By disintegrative (parts) we mean those tasks which involve learning of parts, or breaking into parts without being preoccupied with assembly into wholes. *Bridging* is the task of transfer of learning. That is, of trying to teach something new with students using prior learning as a major prerequisite to that new knowledge.

The last four rows contain four types of outcomes identified by Gagne and Driscoll (1988). There are other ways of categorizing outcomes such as the taxonomies of educational objectives we discussed in the last chapter. We adopt these four outcomes because of their relative simplicity. Gagne and Driscoll describe information as declarative knowledge which includes facts, generalizations and principles (1988, pp. 44–46). They describe intellectual skills as procedural knowledge and include such processes as discriminations (least complex) to concepts, rules and higher-order rules (most complex) (pp. 47–55). In cognitive strategies (pp. 55–57) as an outcome, they include some of those presented in our nine chapters. By attitude outcomes they mean essentially the same things as those in the affective taxonomy discussed in the last chapter—feelings, values and ethics. The last outcome listed in Figure 3-8 is motor learning. These would be included in such outcomes as typing, driving an automobile and putting in golf.

We should mention that the major use of frames in the latter two categories would be in the conveyance of information about the attitudes and motor skills. Rarely would one try to teach attitudes or motor skills without present-

FIGURE 3-8
Specifications chart for frames type one.

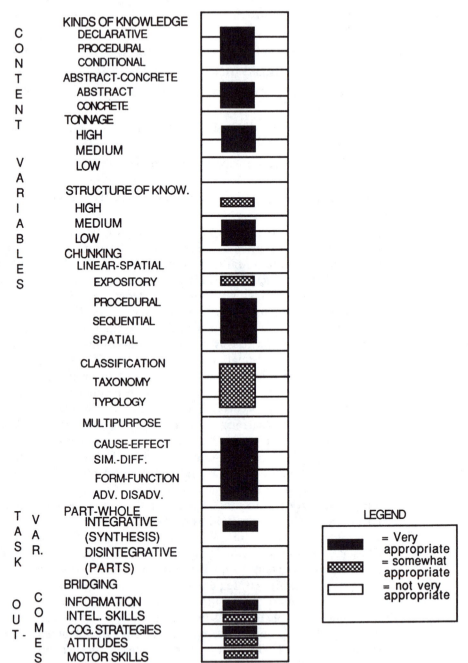

ing some essential information. *When information is presented, even during instruction driven by these outcomes, frames may be used, of course depending on the other specifications or conditions presented in Figure 3-8.*

By inspecting the slots in Figure 3-8 one should be able to determine those best uses of frames, type one. Notice that we recommend frames, type one, particularly for integrative tasks, for content of medium structure and in content chunked by the multipurpose strategies, for examples. In the next chapters, we use for all strategies a specifications chart with these same row headings to help you understand the conditions of use of each strategy.

How Is a Frame Constructed?

The initial step in frame construction is to inspect the material in the lesson or unit to discover the major ideas, concepts and principles. Help will be provided by the apparent organizational efforts of the author, if the material is prepared for the designer—which is usually the case. Examine topics, transition statements, introductions and summaries. Highlight main ideas. It may be necessary to list these. Then it is essential to examine the relationships among the ideas.

Should the designer author the instructional materials, those materials should be written and organized following the frame and its structure. If the authored material does follow the frame in this manner the horizontal (row) and vertical (column) labels or phrases can become sectional headings. The prose sections may be sequenced by the vertical or horizontal labels or phrases. In this manner the frame replaces the traditional outline.

For computer-based authoring it is possible to use the frame slots as windows or files. Students could use the frame slots to access information from the frame. The author may even wish to organize material in some slots as supplemental frames for instruction. If it is possible to retain a basic organizing frame for a course or unit in a window on the screen, the big picture would be constantly present and would be very helpful. Such a technique of accessing the files and subfiles from the frame while retaining the frame in a window retains the big picture for inspection.

The next step in framing is to decide whether the material lends itself to a matrix such as Figures 3-1 or 3-2 or to some other organizing strategy such as plans (intentions), actions and outcomes (see Figure 3-6). The matrix frame easily lends itself to organizing strategies such as comparison/contrast, simple causes/effects, forms/functions or advantages/disadvantages—the multipurpose sorting strategies discussed in the chapter on chunking. The final step is to draw the frame and name or label the rows and columns.

During the construction of the frame the idea of the structure of knowledge, or the structure of the textual material, should become apparent to the designer. The same or similar structures will usually recur in a discipline, so that frame construction becomes more efficient, and frame use becomes habitual. If so, awareness of the forest may be assured while trees are studied.

Recently written texts and other material on which instruction is based may actually provide substantial help in the detection of the organizing strategy, the forest. This is because cognitive scientists have had some success in convincing some publishers and authors to provide well-organized material. Some texts may even provide frames which are usable as printed.

When Should the Frame Be Used?

This is the choice of the designer. Frames aid learning so substantially that a lesson or unit is likely to benefit from frames presented and used as an introduction, during the lesson, and at the end (or during review). Assuming that the designer constructs the frame, maximum benefit is likely to occur when the frame is used throughout, from the introduction through review. If, on the other hand, students construct the frame, they would have to inspect the material from which the frame is constructed. In this case the frame is developed during the lesson and could be used for study and review.

Can Students Learn to Build Frames?

Researchers have demonstrated that students can learn to frame (Armbruster, Anderson, & Ostertag, 1987; Vaughan, 1984). This finding extends across a substantial age span from fifth grade through junior high and senior high to medical school. The effect has also been found with a variety of subject matter—history, social studies and biology.

Tuning or Restructuring?

Whether the learning is tuning or restructuring largely depends on whether the frame, this particular structure, is a big picture new to the student. If it is new to the student, and then learned by the student, it may be restructuring. If the frame, in contrast, is either already known by the student or merely used as a device into which information of various types is recorded, the learning is tuning. It should be remembered, however, that most learning is assimilative (Piaget, 1952) or accretion and tuning (Rumelhart & Norman, 1978). Should the frame-based learning involve accommodation (Piaget, 1952) or restructuring (Rumelhart & Norman, 1978), the designer should be aware that substantial instructional time must be available.

Declarative, Procedural and Conditional Knowledge?

We have seen that frames may provide the big picture and substantial supporting knowledge for *both declarative and procedural knowledge*. While there is no research and development which we have located which uses framing for conditional knowledge, we think that framing could be used on that knowledge also. Should the instruction be on procedural knowledge, however, special care should be taken in the design of the frame. This is because in a frame, sequential order is not always obvious. Ordinary prose, in English, is read left to right and top to bottom. Frames may be inspected in the same way, but inspection and study involve inspection of columns and rows, and often either may be read first. Furthermore, in many frames any row or any column may be examined and comprehended initially. Students can move about the frame with impunity and not have their learning impaired. By contrast, *for procedural frames, the proper sequence of the steps in the procedure must be followed,* either in the rows or in the columns, left to right or top to bottom.

How Often Should Frames Be Used?

Overuse of any one cognitive strategy, including frames, can become boring and can result in poor recall. Too many frames can begin to interfere with each other and produce negative transfer. Varying the cognitive strategies is very crucial, not only because not all strategies are appropriate for all content, but also because students need to learn all the strategies to become metacognitively sophisticated. Proper attention to the characteristics of the material, including its structure, may preclude overuse because other strategies may be more appropriate as new material is introduced.

Should Students Construct Frames or Should Frames Be Provided?

Answers to this question must be left to the designer. Frames do aid learning. Designers can supply frames. Students can learn to construct frames. Answers depend greatly on the objectives of the lesson or unit and whether students have learned to frame. Since, however, it has not been established firmly that a frame "discovered" or created by a student is better for learning than one provided by the text or designer, the designer should develop framing skills while conducting instruction so that students *can* frame on their own without supervision. There will be times, on the other hand, even after students have developed framing skills, that the designer or teacher will want to develop the frames. Designer-developed frames may be better representations of the knowledge than student-developed frames. This is another question which can be resolved by teachers and designers through trial and error with their own students and their own content.

If the objective is to teach framing, it seems essential to provide instruction which includes practice. As with all the cognitive strategies, goals should consist not only of teaching content but also of teaching strategies of learning, as we emphasized in Chapter 1. *The important goal is metacognitive sophistication, learning to learn.*

Can Frames Aid Discussion, Writing, Thinking, Creativity and Cooperative Learning?

Some educators have raised substantial issues about formal instruction including, for example, the idea that well-planned instruction stifles problem solving, thinking and creativity. Such an idea has little basis in the context of frames particularly.

Frames can be an aid to group discussion. During both construction of the frame and the completion of slots, frames can provide a lively basis for idea generation and evaluation. A frame can provide prompts for those who are often reluctant to contribute. Both groups and individuals can build and complete frames. Frames can also be used in brainstorming to generate divergent ideas and, later, to evaluate those ideas.

For writing, frames provide just the help some novice writers need. Teachers are currently using story frames as an aid to teach writing—as early as the first grade. It is likely also that experts, prolific writers in their own genre, often use frames unconsciously. Remember that Armbruster, Anderson and Ostertag (1987) found that the use of frames improves essay writing. These uses imply that frames, type one, can be properly used to promote thinking, decision making and creativity—some of those higher-order outcomes contained in the taxonomy of educational objectives, cognitive domain.

How Are Large Information Sets Managed?

The larger the information set toward which the instruction is directed, the greater is the need for spatial strategies: providing a big picture becomes almost mandatory at some point. In framing there are at least three responses to the challenges of large/dense information arrays. These are: (1) having many columns and/or rows; (2) creating frames within frames (in slots); and (3) developing three dimensional frames such as that shown in skeleton form as Figure 3-2.

Having many columns and rows is a reasonable adjustment to more information, but the upper limits of amounts which can be represented visually in a medium such as a book (one page, a double page with facing pages or a foldout) or a computer will be reached relatively quickly. In books, however, it is possible to disassemble a frame with many rows and columns and place each piece on a page, but the more the parts of the frame are separated, the less it serves the function of providing the big picture. Thus having many columns and rows can also be done in the computer medium but, as with the size of book page, screen size constrains the amount of information represented. Computers, however, are much more "fluid" than books so that it should be possible to rapidly and systematically scan pieces of larger frames and retain the intellectual augmentation which the frame provides.

Somewhat akin to rapid scanning of pieces of frames is the "frame within a frame." Suppose, for example, we were to modify Figure 3-4 by creating a frame within a frame of the slot "Native American—Goal." Row headings might be the names of five, for illustrative purposes, of the most powerful Northeastern tribes in the seventeenth century (perhaps the Iroquois Confederacy). Column headings might be the subgoals of religious, economic and territorial natures (again for illustrative purposes and not that they are completely separate). Many if not all of the slots in Figure 3-4 could serve as locations for comparable frames within frames. In the design of courses, each frame within a frame could provide the big picture of a unit. Or, in the case of designing a program, each frame within a frame could represent a course.

The third option for the management or representation of husky bodies of information via framing is the three-dimensional frame, type one. (Please see Figure 3-2 for an example.) A three-dimensional goal frame for U.S. history with a third dimension added to Figure 3-4 could be constructed. This third dimension could be time, with the first series of slots as the 17th century. The second series of slots (or cross-sectional slice) would follow these threads for the 18th century, and a third series could be entitled "19th century." Of course, modifications would be made in the row entitled "Dutch" for historical authenticity so that other peoples could be included in the frame within appropriate time slots.

Such a frame might be most worthwhile if it were presented with the computer medium using HyperCard, hypertext or hypermedia. These allow rapid movement within the content or frame. Placing the entire frame in a corner of the screen while detail on slots is presented (with perhaps the slot highlighted) retains the big picture with its helpful effects.

These three tactics may, of course, be combined for the representation and management of larger collections of information. Computers with increased memory capabilities, portability, the potential of networks, HyperCard and hypermedia provide exciting opportunities in design.

Yet another design opportunity exists for performance augmentation rather than instruction; that is, substantial reliance on external memory and analysis rather than unassisted human recall and analysis. Given the upper limits of human capability for recall and analysis of implications (Meehl, 1954; Miller, 1956) when data sets are large, and given the fact that so many professional situations require for best performance the recall and analysis of robust data sets, performance could be augmented. Such augmentation systems may be called external intellectual waldoes. Print has served this function relatively well, and still can, but computers could become even more powerful augmentation devices (Warfield, 1976).

Need for the external intellectual waldoe increases, not only as a function of the amount of pertinent information available, but also as a function of such person variables as anxiety and stress. Consider the medical doctor, the lawyer and the tank commander. Each of these persons finds him- or herself in stressful situations in which an already overloaded intellectual system becomes increasingly overloaded as a function of that stress. The waldoe could provide enough aid for proper performance.

Overload is likely to become cyclical, as shown in Figure 3-9. One enters an anxiety ridden situation which requires large amounts of information, or scanning large amounts of information. Analytic capabilities diminish. Anxiety increases. The cycle of stress or anxiety and reduction of intellectual functioning could continue to the point at which performance is extremely impaired. Machine augmentation could reduce this impairment. It is likely that instructional design could contribute to the development of these augmention systems.

HYBRIDIZATION

Frames, type one, may be combined with most of the other strategies. Some students can use *imagery* with frames, especially if the material included in the frame is sufficiently concrete. While studying frames or building frames, students will engage in many of the miscellaneous strategic activities which we have classified as *rehearsal*. In addition, especially when the material cannot be imaged, students may use *mnemonics*.

Because learning the material in a frame, or in any of the spatial learning strategies, may be difficult for some students, and because other cognitive strategies are almost always involved when humans learn, we propose a modest model of learning when the spatial strategies are used as design techniques. Figure 3-10 is a three-phase model. First, someone—a student, a text writer, an instructional designer or a teacher—will have engaged in one or more of the organizing strategies discussed in Chapter 2. Such chunking is inherent in knowing and knowledge communication, and it is preparatory to the creation of some product—any one example of a spatial learning strategy. Second, the product, a frame or concept map, is developed. Finally, the product is intellectually processed (studied) with one or more of the general purpose strategies such as imagery, rehearsal or mnemonics. This three-phase model is consistent with the idea of the desirability of multiple processing.

When the instructional material is complex or when students are expected to struggle, it is usually desirable for the designer to supplement framing with several other appropriate strategies. As students become metacognitively sophisticated, combining strategies and multiple processing becomes easier.

FIGURE 3-9
The cyclical nature of overload.

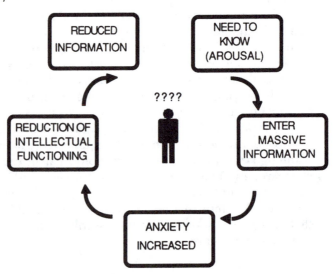

FIGURE 3-10

A simple model for incorporating spatial learning strategies into learning and instruction.

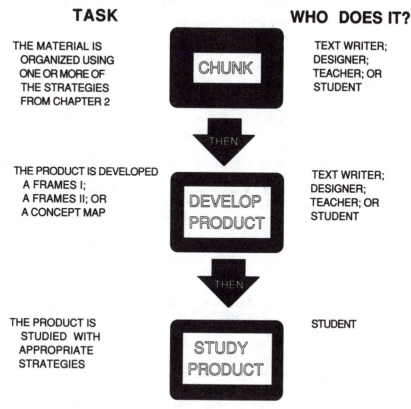

TASK

THE MATERIAL IS
  ORGANIZED USING
  ONE OR MORE OF
  THE STRATEGIES
  FROM CHAPTER 2

THE PRODUCT IS DEVELOPED
  A FRAMES I;
  A FRAMES II; OR
  A CONCEPT MAP

THE PRODUCT IS
  STUDIED WITH
  APPROPRIATE
  STRATEGIES

WHO DOES IT?

TEXT WRITER;
  DESIGNER;
  TEACHER; OR
  STUDENT

TEXT WRITER;
  DESIGNER;
  TEACHER; OR
  STUDENT

STUDENT

CHUNK

THEN

DEVELOP PRODUCT

THEN

STUDY PRODUCT

SUMMARY

In this chapter we presented the first of three spatial learning strategies. The background of research was presented along with a guide for designer development of this type of frame. Several examples of frames were presented. In the next chapter we discuss a frame with unique features and considerable cognitive power.

EXERCISES

1. Select material from the first three chapters and create and complete a frame, type one, (matrix) incorporating the material selected.

2. Study that frame carefully. Name in your own words the strategy or strategies you used during that study. Did having the frame help you learn this material? Why or why not?

3. Is the material in this frame declarative or procedural or conditional? (See Chapter 1, pp. 15–16 if you need a review.)

4. Can you form a mental picture of this frame?

5. Assuming frames help you comprehend and recall, why do you think they help?

REFERENCES

Armbruster, B. B. (1985). A technique to promote meaningful learning in the content areas. University of Illinois at Urbana-Champaign, Center for the Study of Reading.

Armbruster, B. B. (1987). Does text structure/summarization instruction facilitate learning from expository text? *Reading Research Quarterly, 12*, 331–346.

Armbruster, B. B., & Anderson, T. H. (1982). *Structures for explanation in history textbooks: Or, So what if Governor Stanford missed the spike and hit the rail?* (Technical Report No. 252). University of Illinois at Urbana-Champaign, Center for the Study of Reading.

Armbruster, B. B., & Anderson, T. H. (1984). Mapping: Representing informative text diagrammatically. In C. D. Holley & D. F. Dansereau (Eds.), *Spatial learning strategies: Techniques, applications, and related issues.* New York: Academic Press Inc.

Armbruster, B. B., Anderson, T. H. & Ostertag, J. (1987). Does text structure/summarization instruction facilitate learning from expository text? *Reading Research Quarterly, 22*, 331–346.

Bartlett, F. C. (1932). *Remembering.* The Cambridge University Press.

Boulding, K. (1956). *The image.* University of Michigan Press.

Broadbent, D. E., Cooper, P. J., & Broadbent, M. H. P. (1978). A comparison of hierarchical and matrix retrieval schemes in recall. *Journal of Experimental Psychology: Human Learning and Memory, 4*, 486–497.

Davies, F., & Greene, T. (1984). *Reading for learning in science.* Edinburg: Oliver & Boyd.

Dreher, M. J., & Singer, H. (1980). Story grammar instruction unnecessary for intermediate grade students. *The Reading Teacher, 33*, 261–268.

Fitzgerald, J. (1984). The relationship between reading ability and expectations for story structures. *Discourse Processes, 7*, 21–41.

Fowler, G. L. (1982). Developing comprehension skills in primary students through the use of story frames. *The Reading Teacher, 35*, 176–179.

Gagne, R. M., & Driscoll, M. P. (1988). *Essentials of learning for instruction* (2nd ed.). Englewood Cliffs, NJ: Prentice-Hall.

Glaser, R. (1965). *Teaching machines and programmed learning, II: Data and directions.* Washington, DC: National Education Association.

Goetz, E. T., & Armbruster, B. B. (1980). Psychological correlates of text structure. In R. J. Spiro, B. C. Bruce, & W. F. Brewer (Eds.), *Theoretical issues in reading comprehension: Perspectives from cognitive psychology, linguistics, artificial intelligence, and education*, Hillsdale, NJ: Lawrence Erlbaum Associates.

Holley, C. D., & Dansereau, D. F. (Eds.). (1984). *Spatial learning strategies: Techniques, applications, and related issues.* Orlando, FL: Academic Press.

Markle, S. (1969). *Good frames and bad* (2nd ed.). New York: Wiley.

Markle, S. (1978). *Designs for instructional designers.* Champaign, IL: Stipes Publishing Co.

McAleese, R. (1985). Some problems of knowledge representation in an authoring environment: Exteriorization, anomalous state metacognition and self confrontation. *Programmed Learning and Educational Technology, 22,* 299–306.

McAleese, R. (1986). Computer-based authoring and intelligent interactive video. In C. W. Osborne & A. J. Trott (Eds.), *International yearbook of educational and instructional technology.* New York: Kogan Page.

McKeachie, W. J. (1984). Spatial strategies: Critique and educational implications. In C. D. Holley & D. F. Dansereau (Eds.), *Spatial learning strategies: Techniques, applications, and related issues.* Orlando, FL: Academic Press.

Meehl, P. E. (1954). *Clinical versus statistical prediction. A theoretical analysis and review of the evidence.* University of Minnesota Press.

Miller, G. A. (1956). The magical number seven plus or minus two: Some limits on our capacity for processing information. *Psychological Review, 63,* 81–96.

Minsky, M. (1975). A framework for representing knowledge. In P. H. Winston (Ed.), *The psychology of computer vision.* New York: McGraw-Hill.

Minsky, M. (1986). *The society of mind.* New York: Simon and Schuster.

Piaget, J. (1952). *Origins of intelligence in children.* New York: International Universities Press.

Reigeluth, C. E., & Stein, F. S. (1983). The elaboration theory of instruction. In C. E. Reigeluth (Ed.), *Instructional-design theories and models: An overview of their current status.* Hillsdale, NJ: Lawrence Erlbaum Associates.

Rumelhart, D. E., & Norman, D. A. (1978). Accretion, tuning, and restructuring: Three modes of learning. In J. W. Cotton & R. Klatzky (Eds.), *Semantic factors in cognition.* Hillsdale, NJ: Lawrence Erlbaum Associates.

Schank, R. C., & Abelson, R. (1977). *Scripts, plans, goals, and understanding.* Hillsdale, NJ: Lawrence Erlbaum Associates.

Skinner, B. F. (1968). *The technology of teaching.* New York: Appleton-Century-Crofts.

Stein, N. L., & Trabasso, T. (1981). *What's in a story: An approach to comprehension and instruction.* (Technical Report No. 200). University of Illinois at Urbana-Champaign, Center for the Study of Reading.

Stewart, J., Van Kirk, J., & Rowell, R. (1979). Concept maps: A tool for use in biology teaching. *The American Biology Teacher, 41,* 171–175.

Stewart, J. (1982). Two aspects of meaningful problem solving in science. *Science Education, 66,* 731–749.

Van Patten, J., Chao, C., & Reigeluth, C. M. (1986). A review of strategies for sequencing and synthesizing instruction. *Review of Educational Research, 56,* 437–471.

Vaughan, J. L. (1984). *Concept structuring: The technique and empirical evidence.* In C. D. Holley & D. F. Dansereau (Eds.), *Spatial learning strategies: Techniques, applications, and related issues* (pp. 127–147). Orlando, FL: Academic Press.

ven den Broek, P., & Trabasso, T. (1986). Causal networks versus goal hierarchies in summarizing text. *Discourse Processes, 9,* 1–15.

Warfield, J. N. (1976). *Social systems: Planning, policy, and complexity.* New York: Wiley.

West, C. K., & Foster, S. F. (1976). *The psychology of human learning and instruction in education.* Belmont, CA: Wadsworth.

Winograd, T. A. (1976). Framework for understanding discourse. In P. Carpenter & M. Just (Eds.), *Narrative processes in cognition.* Hillsdale, NJ: Lawrence Erlbaum Associates.

Frames, Type Two

In this chapter we discuss a second spatial learning strategy, frames, type two. These frames are matrices or grids which allow organizing relatively large numbers of facts, concepts or ideas. *The distinguishing feature of frames, type two, is that some law-like principle or statement allows, through inference, the completion of slots.* The principle is used to construct facts logically, to elicit personal knowledge from memory and to place that knowledge into the visual array, the grid or frame. In frames, type one, you may recall, the information to be placed in the slots is provided by recall or searched from reference material.

The frame, type two, as presented in this text, is somewhat similar to Papert's (1980) "microworld," and is somewhat reminiscent of the work of Minsky (1975, 1986). Its conception and development are based, however, on extensions of frames, type one, as the first author gave talks on American Indians to elementary students in public schools. Over a 15-year period, elementary teachers invited him to "show and tell" sessions about the art, tools and weapons of American Indians. Specifically he was asked to display his collection and talk a bit.

But artifacts lose their meaning when separated from lifeways and seasonal patterns of those lifeways. The artifacts have less informing value when isolated in this way. The talks evolved into being guided by a frame which served in a modest, and surely partial but intelligent way, to reintegrate the artifacts through helping students make reasonable guesses about lifeways of the people who made the artifacts.

Frames, type two, also evolved out of disenchantment with the ways most authors and teachers approach the writing and instruction about American Indians, at least at the levels of education from elementary through secondary schooling. Depending on the level, teachers assign material on one "tribe" or another for reading or small group study. Then perhaps material on another "tribe" is assigned and studied. Students (or their parents) do posters, dioramas, reports. Every culture, if several are studied, is approached like a new world: few or no attempts are made to understand patterns across the cultures and little is done to connect art or tools or weapons to lifeways and life conditions. What is learned is typically learned poorly. When appreciations emerge, they are ephemeral.

This spatial learning strategy is best discussed by the examination of the following example. Characteristics of this type of frame and how it functions can then be more easily understood and presented.

AMERICAN INDIAN FRAME

When Figure 4-1 is examined it looks exactly like the matrix subtype of frames, type one. There are concepts heading rows and columns in a grid arrangement. There are slots to be completed. The difference is that the grid is "driven" by a general principle which helps the completion of the slots, which helps students supply the information to be placed in the slots. For this frame the general principle is, "Where they lived and the climate tell you much about how they lived." Please note that we did not write that these tell you everything about how they lived.

Note that several habitats are listed as headings of rows and that categories of how they lived are listed as column headings. The instructional use of this frame is illustrated by the narrative which follows. The site is a third-grade mainstreamed classroom in a medium-sized Illinois city. The narrator is the first author.

FIGURE 4-1

American Indian frame, type two.

	Tools	Food	Clothing	Shelter	Art
Coast North South					
Desert					
Plain					
Forest North South					
Mountain East West					

A NARRATIVE

The general principle was presented with a vocabulary which was suited to the level of most students. I promised students the opportunity to examine the artifacts after they participated in discussion about how some American Indians might have lived. They were told that they would be required to think and to remember some information. Students were initially asked to mention some ideas about what is meant when we ask "How did they live?" Several "hows" were mentioned by students—including tools, food, clothing, and shelter. These were placed on the chalkboard as column headings. Then the habitat Coast (Southwest) was placed on the board initially as the sole row heading. A topographic map, present in the classroom, was examined for other habitats. Students did mention that they thought Indians could live in deserts, mountains, forests and so forth. Some students were able to point to these habitats on the map and name them as "places Indians could have lived."

The map examination served as a lead-in to the southern California seacoast. When asked about what that habitat might have been like several thousand years ago, students offered such ideas as "It was warm." "It didn't change much during the seasons!" Several students shared information about the area.

In a shift of discussion students were asked, "What do we call those who study ancient people?" The first enthusiastic response was "Scientists!" Prompting helped elicit "Archaeologists!" Then a brief discussion was held about tools of archaeologists. After some discussion they were told that the primary tool of the archaeologist was the mind. This seemed to be a surprising idea. Students were also informed that archaeologists make guesses both about what they find and what is suggested about how the Indian might have lived from the objects found. The class agreed to pretend to be archaeologists, and to make guesses—to think.

From this discussion the class returned to trying to imagine this habitat, the warm climate on the seacoast. I asked them to "form a picture in your mind of this warm seacoast and what it might have been like to live there." Most students claimed that they could "see it in their minds." First question: "What food items would probably be available?" Reasonable guesses were placed in the appropriate slot, under food. (Students were not bothered by beginning in the middle of the frame. Some adults in other groups have been offended by starting in the second column!) Guesses such as fish, several types of shellfish, birds, seaweed and others were offered and listed.

I then asked the class to think about these food items and what tools would seem to be required to obtain and prepare these food items. Nets, spears, traps, prying instruments and, oddly enough, finally hooks and lines, were suggested. These third graders were very able to think in a very abstract way—to formulate hypothetical syllogisms: "If fish, then nets or spears or hooks." One interesting series of interactions took place when volunteers were asked to go one by one to the board and design spears for large and then small fish.

Notice that two types of inferences were being generated. Initially the general principle provided inference about food items available. This inference was general to specific (deductive). Once specific detail was provided, other specifics could be generated (see Figure 4-2). These are slot-to-slot inferences. In these logical, inferential operations, students were somewhat like the paleontologist who finds a bone in a stream bed. If the bone is tentatively identified as a toe bone, for example, inferences follow. What must be some functions attributable to a toe bone with this structure? Toe bones are connected to foot bones. What must be the structure of such a foot bone? What does that imply about function? What about connective tissue? What kind of leg supports such a foot? What does this imply about speed and strength? The particular chunking of structure/function seems to aid inference.

From guesses about tools the discussion developed to listing materials from which tools could be made which would likely have been available. Possibilities included bone, shell and rocks. There was then talk of shell containers and spades and spears made of bone. These were listed in the slot near tools.

From materials available and more elicitation of ideas about climate, clothing and shelter were described in some detail by the students. I asked such questions as "What materials would likely have been available for clothing? Shelter?" I also asked about the implications of the climate for the clothing. That detail was placed in the appropriate slots. Reasonable guesses were listed about materials available and characteristics of clothing and shelter. No discussion was held with this group about art, which is included in Figure 4-1.

This discussion was followed by some discussion of an Illinois habitat. It began with a discussion of differences between the Southwest coastal climate and the more variable or seasonal climate of Illinois. More slots were filled on food, tools, clothing and shelter, with some detail about climate effects and seasonal rounds. Prompting questions included "What were the people likely to have been doing in winter? Why? Spring? Why? What tools do these activities require? What materials might have been available?"

FIGURE 4-2

Slot-to-slot inferences.

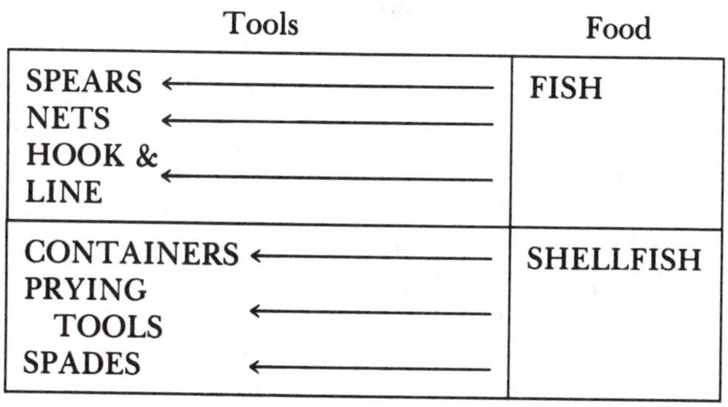

It was very intriguing to hear these third graders use their prior knowledge and transfer it to study of the American Indian. They seemed adroit also as they made the transition from one habitat to a more variable habitat, central Illinois.

From these discussions the class moved to an imaginary dig in which individuals were given an object, from a current plastic "artifact" to older, early twentieth century objects and, finally, some centuries-old flint objects about which they were to infer use. Objects were described on the board along with possible uses. Students were able to make some reasonable guesses about the function of some of the tools from their structural attributes.

While students were making cordage from milkweed fibers, with only minimum aid from the visitor (one student had seen it done on television, so he became the instructor for a time); I spread the collection of artifacts on tables. Students then were allowed to examine artifacts from central Illinois, ask questions and discuss their interests. Students were particularly intrigued with guessing about uses, or functions, from the structural characteristics of various items.

This session lasted from about 8:30 in the morning until noon. The visitor's parting words to the group were "You really knew a lot about American Indians. I'm impressed!"

A prim young lady spoke, "But Dr. West, we've been in school three years!"

As the artifacts were being packed the teacher's assignment for the afternoon was overheard: "After lunch we will go on a field trip into the school yard. Find some objects that you think are human made. Pretend you are an archaeologist hundreds of years from now and make guesses about what you find. We will write essays about these guesses."

We are aware of the fact that there is a theory of culture implicit in this frame. We are also aware that there are options other than this theory. The idea, however, is that a great deal of learning can occur when a good theory or general principle is used in conjunction with a frame.

One other example will be briefly presented before further discussion of characteristics and uses of type two frames. This is the dinosaur frame.

THE DINOSAUR FRAME, TYPE TWO

In the dinosaur frame the guiding principle is: where they lived and what they ate tells a great deal about dinosaurs. Notice that in Figure 4-3 the habitats, the column headings, are very general: water and land. Food categories are plant, animal and either or both. Each food category is subdivided to provide interesting detail. The slots are to be completed with imaginary information about characteristics of imaginary dinosaurs.

In using frames during instruction, slots can be expanded into frames connected to the big picture provided by the original frame. For example, the slot from Figure 4-3—carnivorous, big, swift, terrestrial—could be expanded

FIGURE 4-3

The dinosaur frame, type two.

	Aquatic	Terrestrial
Herbivorous Short Plants		
Tall Plants		
Carnivorous Big, Swift Dinosaurs		
Little, Slow Dinosaurs		
Omnivorous Short Plants and Swift Dinosaurs		
Tall, Tough Plants and Swift Dinosaurs		

into a frame such as that in Figure 4-4. The new column heading can provide more detail which further prompts ideas for slot completion. Many options exist for the column subheadings, but in this example teeth and claws, subdivided by structure and function, are used.

Structure and function are multipurpose organizing strategies which can be very useful especially when combined with type two frames. They provide a rich suggestive format for idea production in writing, discussion and thinking.

We now turn from two examples of type two frames to a more abstract discussion of characteristics and general instructional uses. The two examples provide background and are used illustratively in this discussion.

FIGURE 4-4

A frame within the dinosaur frame, placed in the slot under terrestrial.

| | Teeth | | Legs/Claws | |
	Structure	Function	Structure	Function
Big, Swift Dinosaurs				
Little, Slow				

CHARACTERISTICS AND USES

In this section some similarities and differences between frames, type one, and frames, type two, are discussed. These are discussed in terms of *format* and *uses*. The examples of frames in both this chapter and Chapter 2 aid this discussion.

Format

As has been discussed, the primary *format* difference between the frames, type one, presented in Chapter 3, and frames, type two, is that the latter is based on a general law-like statement. For best use the law-like statement must be a relationship based on two general, well-understood concepts, concepts which are meaningful to the students for whom the instruction is intended.

The general principle and the concepts contained have their origins in the big ideas of a discipline, its theories, its structures and the primary assumptions. Instructional designers and teachers, in order to use frames, type two, must dig into the structures of the discipline. They must know the theories, or learn them.

Use

In frames, type one, the frame is *used* in instruction as a visual arrangement into which students place information in slots. Generally, the information is to be taken from material presented through such media as text, lectures and computers. There is no reason, however, that some of the information could not be supplied from the memory of the student.

In contrast, for frames, type two, substantial portions of the information are supplied from the concepts and the relationship by logical inference. As was stated in the narrative of the American Indian frame lesson, students *inferred* information to be recorded. These inferences proceeded in two ways: from the general principle to specific information, and from specifics to specifics or from slot to slot (see Figure 3-2). Recall also supplies some of the information for the slots.

Just as with frames, type one, frames, type two, may be used in all phases of courses, units or lessons. Frames, type two, provide a very powerful beginning for instruction, by providing the big picture or a spatial learning strategy, and by helping students infer and/or recall prior learning pertinent to information to be later introduced. They also may be designed into the instructional sequence during the lesson or unit as a guide to study, notetaking and discussions. They are also powerful as guides to review and analysis.

Frames, type two, in addition, work well for use by individuals, small groups such as those formed for cooperative learning and in larger intact classes. Individuals may work alone using the frame, type two, as a guide and worksheet in the ways described in the foregoing. When the students are learning cooperatively, the frame, type two, can be used similarly. For a larger group use it is a dandy guide for keeping the discussion focused. This latter use is best for introducing lessons, units or courses and for review.

Often lessons are directed toward problem solving, thinking and/or creativity—those learnings which are going beyond learning facts, concepts and principles into application, synthesis, analysis and criticism, higher levels of learning in the taxonomy of educational objectives in the cognitive domain (Bloom, Hastings, & Madaus, 1971). With these kinds of learning, a frame, type two, can be very powerful. Its use can involve brainstorming both in groups, as was the case in the third-grade class on the American Indian, and with individuals.

Of course, when using a frame as a brainstorming aid, leaders should refrain from evaluating the ideas generated. The objective should be to generate as many ideas as possible because evaluating the ideas as they are presented tends to inhibit participation. Leaders can, after the brainstorming session is complete, work on criticism and evaluation of each idea in its turn.

We have seen that the characteristics and uses of frames, type two, are very similar. The primary difference between the two is that frames, type two, depend on the existence and use of a general, law-like, abstract statement. Most of the difficulty in designing instruction around a frame, type two, arises from the nature of this difference.

PROBLEMS RELATED TO CONCEIVING FRAMES, TYPE TWO

Designers may have difficulty in developing frames, type two. These difficulties originate from (a) the structure or lack of structure of the discipline; (b) ignorance of structure, if it exists; (c) the sense that the target students lack skills or knowledge or motivation to work at this abstract level, and some surely are lacking; (d) the tendency to avoid big ideas, theories and very general principles; (e) reluctance to attend to theory, if the knowledge domain has theory; (f) the tendency to overvalue the concrete and undervalue abstractions; and (g) overemphasis on precision and exactness, especially in early phases of instruction.

Structure of the Knowledge Domain

Perhaps the most basic consideration about whether or not a frame, type two, is possible is the structure of the knowledge. The development of frames, type two, is not possible for ill-structured knowledge. In the absence of substantial logical structure, other cognitive strategies must be used (see Figure 1-5, p. 24). It is not required, however, that the entire discipline be well structured. Some disciplines lack structure for the whole, but have some structure for parts. This is the case for the American Indian example. Archaeology and anthropology are not particularly well-structured knowledge domains on the whole, but one major cultural theory provides some structure for some of its knowledge.

Student Maturation

In order to use frames, type two, students must be intellectually capable of performing the logical operations involved and systematically recalling information. Experience with frames, type two, supports that children as young as eight or nine have this capability. It is probable, then, that students this young and older can benefit from instruction designed around this type of frame.

Researchers are now vividly demonstrating that the cognitive abilities of children (as young as three, certainly as young as six, years) have been grossly underestimated. The *cognitive ability* differences between children and adults are, thus, not nearly as great as has been thought. (Please see Brewer and Samarapungavan. (in press) for an extensive review and analysis of a large number of relevant studies.) Observed differences are, more often than not, differences of information rather than inferencing and abstract thinking abilities.

It seems reasonable, then, to assume that normal children and adults can contend with frames, type two, until any given group demonstrates that it cannot. We urge teachers and designers to attempt the development of frames, type two, without the typical underestimations of abilities of youth. As with all strategies, we commend the process of *tinkering*: attempting the development of frames, type two, and trying them in instruction.

This tinkering extends to the creation of "models" (the typical word used in the research reviewed by Brewer and Samarapungavan) and "microworlds" (Papert's [1980] word) for use during instruction. The "facts" children infer from their own models of the world tend toward consistency with that model and are not necessarily concrete. By having learners themselves (of any age) tinker with their own models and, in the case of frames, type two, the models of the discipline, considerable mastery can be attained.

Avoidance of Theory

In many knowledge domains there exists at least one, and perhaps a few, theories which can provide a basis for one or more general principles upon which a frame, type two, may be based. In the search for this theory or general principle the designer may be guided by the literature in the knowledge domain or may consult an expert.

Of course, there is frustration in trying to design instruction in terms of theories or general principles—trying to organize instruction around these— if there is no theory or general principles in the knowledge domain. This would be misleading. It is an instructional disservice to overstructure ill-structured knowledge. For most knowledge domains, however, at least portions contain general principles, if not theory.

In some knowledge domains there exists applied versus "pure" subspecializations, a distinction more likely to be reflected in higher education than in kindergarten through high school. In the applied subspecializations, students and some faculty may erroneously oppose theory to practice (application) and thus forego benefits accruing from structuring through theory and general principles. At least for learning the practical and designing instruction, nothing can be more practical than knowing theory.

Overvaluing Concreteness

Just as theory is often wrongly eschewed, so also is abstraction. You may recall from Chapter 1 that an important "front" of the cognitive revolution is the emphasis on abstractness. *Learning, when it occurs, is abstraction.* Whatever gets "into mind" is an abstraction: it is coded verbally or imaginally; but in either case it is an abstraction. Prior to the cognitive revolution, it was generally thought that learning best begins with the concrete and proceeds with the concrete. In the new cognitive science, in contrast, there is a continuous transactive relationship during learning between the concrete and the abstract. Learning may proceed from either initially. So also can instructional design. Effective design will not necessarily begin with concreteness. Should the designer overvalue concreteness the formulation of abstractions may be inhibited. Overvaluing concreteness generally precludes the use of the frames, type two, strategy.

Overvaluing concreteness may take the form of dependence on visual media, such as film or videotape, or field experience. Such dependencies may result in the failure of students forming the abstractions inherent in learning. Film or videotape may be no more concrete than print, even though there is the common belief that it is.

This is not to deny categorically the value of using visual media or field experience within the sequence of instruction. These may be very helpful. Their effective use, however, is dependent on the extent to which the students are provided, during instruction, with aid in the abstractive process, with aid in actively cognitively processing the experience. These are at best focal for some form of treatment which abets active cognitive processing. Frames, type two, may provide the aid.

Precision

Another factor inhibiting the use of frames, type two, may be the fear that students may err in the information which they supply through inference and recall and place in the slots in the frames. It is true that this may happen. This is true especially when the frame, type two, is used in the beginning phases of a lesson, unit or course. If so, it should not preclude its use.

It should be remembered that there are three important goals beyond insuring precision. One is to have students use what they know, or what they can infer, in approaching a new topic. Another is to have them develop a big picture into which information can be plotted and which helps students to comprehend relationships among items of information, and among those items and a general principle. A third goal is to insure that they learn the primary general principles in the knowledge domain.

It also should be remembered that learning does not particularly move from parts to wholes. Rather, there is the feedback loop in which learning may begin with parts or wholes; for cognition proceeds by going back and forth among parts and wholes and parts and parts, just as it proceeds with the concrete-abstract continuum.

If the foregoing goals are present, and if the instructional design employs a frame, type two, early in the sequence of instruction, imprecise data supplied in slots in the frame should cause no concern, for the imprecision can be corrected. It can be corrected by revision of the information initially provided in the slots. Students can revise the frame by further study using text and lecture or other sources of information with the original frame as a guide. One way to do this is to expand the frame by creating a frame within the original frame which could be similar to that in Figure 4-5. This example takes the form of a comparison-contrast listing within existing slots. Students could consult references about a specific American Indian tribe or culture to determine features of the climate and habitat and then list them in column one; they could also research materials, food, tools, and so on, and list those in the appropriate slots. In this manner the original inferred or recalled data may be checked.

In this fashion there is systematic correction for checking for misinformation. The value of frames, type two, is retained. Students, especially mature students, should be capable of going through this process of idea and data creation and revision—all guided by the overriding principle.

These systematic activities can involve the three kinds of learning: accretion, tuning and restructuring (Rumelhart & Norman, 1978) or assimilation and accommodation (Piaget, 1952). When students know the general principle and merely generate or recall information, accretion and tuning (assimilation) occur. If, however, the general principle is not known, the learning is restructuring (accommodation). As students revise and correct information they are likely to be either tuning or restructuring. This is an important consideration in that there are few instructional design techniques, or even cognitive strategies, which entail restructuring or accommodation.

FIGURE 4-5

American Indian frame revised.

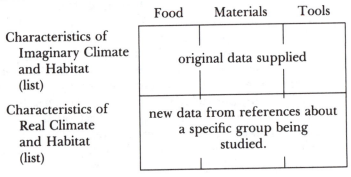

We have discussed some of the design uses of frames, type two, and some of the inhibiting factors associated with their design uses. Now let us turn to a designers' guide to this type of frame.

DESIGNERS' GUIDE TO FRAMES, TYPE TWO

Except for the differences between frames, type one, and frames, type two, presented in this chapter, there are very similar procedures and issues associated with using frames, type two, in instructional design. Thus, it may be helpful for the reader to review the designers' guide to frames, type one, before study of this section.

The conditions for use of frames, type two, as we have seen, are very similar to the conditions of use for frames, type one. That major difference of having a general principle is reflected in Figure 4-6 in which we show that high structure knowledge is a primary specification for using these types of frames. High structure is also a characteristic of expositive chunking.

Perhaps the best beginning point for the development of frames, type two, is to inspect the content to be taught for general law-like statements or theory (high structure). Assumed, however, is that the content exists in the form in which it is to be presented to students. If it does not, and part of the design task is to develop the content, then the content must be developed. It is desirable to begin that development with the general principle as the organizing structure of the content.

We have mentioned that the general principles are likely to be found in the theory of a discipline. This implies that the designer should know the discipline well enough to know the major theories, or be willing to learn, or have access to an expert in the domain of knowledge.

Once the general principle is found or formulated the second step is to develop an associated grid. This grid or matrix development should follow the guidelines in Chapter 2. It is likely that an instructional designer should become proficient with frame, type one, development before trying to develop type two frames.

Remember that the grid (frames, type one) contains concepts or phrases as headings of rows and columns. These concepts and the law-like relationship between them must conform to several conditions in order for the frame, type two, to work. First, concept one must represent a large set of possibilities (living habits). Second, concept two must meaningfully influence concept one (weather or climate influences living habits). Third, ideally, concept one must be divisible into several subcategories that are natural or highly indicative of the concept (tools, food, clothing, shelter, art, religion). Fourth, the subcategories of concept one or two must represent a set of categories (food = fish, shellfish, turtles, waterfowl and seaweed; habitat = desert, plain, forest, mountain and coast). It is, however, desirable, if the frame is to be elaborate, that both concepts be divisible into categories each with a set of possibilities. Fifth, possibilities of concept one should be able to interact with possibilities of concept two. Sixth, the relationships between the two concepts should be

FIGURE 4-6
Specifications chart for frames, type two.

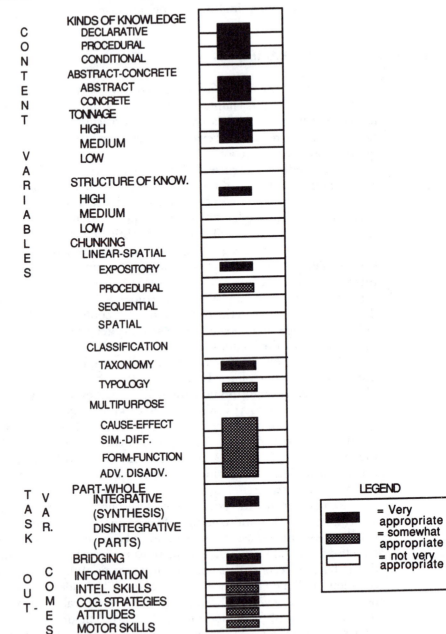

explicitly expressed (that is, one can tell a lot about life patterns by the climates in which they occur).

These steps should be of substantial help in the development of a frame, type two. But, if the steps are followed and attempts at development fail, the designer still has a dandy frame, type one, to use.

Finally, we wish to emphasize that *frames, type two, can be used to manage large information sets just as frames, type one.* The same adjustments can be made on a frame, type two, so that it can serve those vital big-picture functions in instructional or performance augmentation with even more robustness than with frames, type one. (Please review the discussion in Chapter 3 on pp. 72–74).

HYBRIDIZATION

Frames, type two, may be combined with the same cognitive strategies as frames, type one. Appropriate combinations are *imagery, rehearsal* and *mnemonics*. Chunking is inevitable in any type of framing. It is important to remember the simple three-phase model for all spatial strategies which was presented in Chapter 3 (see p. 75): chunking, development of the product (the frame or map) and processing the product (the specific frame or map). It is this third phase in which imagery, rehearsal and mnemonics particularly are used as the students actively intellectually process (study) the product. Since the recall potential and data tonnage of frames, type two, are so high (see Figure 1-3), however, frames, type two, may not require as much supplementation as other cognitive strategies.

SUMMARY

In this chapter we have presented one of the most powerful cognitive strategies. While it has been discussed as the second *spatial learning strategy* it is important to note that it is also a *bridging strategy*. The frame, type two, was defined as a matrix combined with a general theory-like statement. Inclusion of this general statement adds substantial power in terms of recall and data tonnage potential. Two examples were given, one on the American Indian and one on dinosaurs. Uses and a guide to design were included in the chapter. We now turn to the third and last spatial learning strategy, concept mapping.

EXERCISES

1. Write a paragraph entitled "Frames, Type One, and Frames, Type Two: Similarities and Differences." As you prepare for this task and write the paragraph keep a diary of your strategies and activities.
2. What are your names for those strategies or activities? Are these labels similar to names for strategies in this text, or different?

REFERENCES

Bloom, B. S., Hastings, J. T., & Madaus, G. F. (1971). *Handbook on formative and summative evaluation of student learning*. New York: McGraw-Hill.

Brewer, W. F., & Samarapungavan, A. (in press). Children's theories versus scientific theories: Differences in reasoning or differences in knowledge? In R. R. Hoffman & D. S. Palermo (Eds.), *Cognition and the symbolic processes: Vol. 3: Applied and ecological perspectives*. Hillsdale, NJ: Lawrence Erlbaum Associates.

Minsky, M. (1975). A framework for presenting knowledge. In P. H. Winston (Ed.), *The psychology of computer vision*. New York: McGraw-Hill.

Minsky, M. (1986). *The society of mind*. New York: Simon and Schuster.

Papert, S. (1980). *Mindstorms: Children, computers, and powerful ideas*. New York: Basic Books.

Piaget, J. (1952). *Origins of intelligence in children*. New York: International Universities Press.

Rumelhart, D. E., & Norman, D. A. (1978). Accretion, tuning, and restructuring: Three modes of learning. In J. W. Cotton & R. Klatzky (Eds.), *Semantic factors in cognition*. Hillsdale, NJ: Lawrence Erlbaum Associates.

CHAPTER 5

Concept Mapping

In this chapter the third spatial learning strategy, concept mapping, is presented. Concept mapping is a way of graphically displaying concepts and relationships between or among concepts. In concept mapping, concepts are placed in a visual array. Relationships are recorded in spaces between connected concepts. The completed map is a display of those concepts with relationships plotted and reveals a single view of patterns of interrelationships.

The concept map is similar to a terrain or road map (McAleese, 1986). The concepts are roughly analogous to place names while relationships are like roads or streets; that is, relationships (named "links" in some of the literature) between connected concepts are like routes of travel between places. The total concept map is a guide for comprehension, as a road map is a travel guide.

McAleese (1988) also used the metaphor of a wadded net for concept maps. This is a very interesting and apt metaphor especially if one thinks of the knots (concepts) and the connecting cordage (relationships) as representing not just concept maps but knowledge in general. Our knowledge can be thought of as connected ultimately with all other knowledge through concepts and relationships. We select parts for study, but know that those parts of the nets have limitless interconnections. To enrich the metaphor (and mix metaphors), each concept can be a Gordian knot (very complex and intricate)—and a specific concept map is a partial cross section of the infinite net.

INTRODUCTION

In the literature and research on concept mapping there are several factors which create some confusion and which impede its synthesis and integration. One factor is that there are several terms or phrases for concept mapping, four of which are semantic mapping, graphic organizers (Hawk, 1986), information mapping (McAleese, 1986) and networking (Holley & Dansereau, 1984). In this book we have chosen to use the term *concept mapping* for consistency. Another confusing factor is the considerable overlap in the literature and research between framing and concept mapping.

We have sorted these spatial learning strategies into either frames, types one or two, or mapping. Not every scholar would agree with our sorting, but we have been guided primarily by the appearance of the spatial learning strategy and the characteristics of the operations involved. When the strategy involves primarily grid-like arrangements with intersecting slots, we have sorted the strategy as framing. When the strategy involves the highlighting of concepts and specific relations between connecting concepts, we have sorted the strategy as concept mapping. The two strategies do appear to be very different, both structurally and functionally.

The sorting has been complicated and enriched also by the research on text organizations, on story frames (Dreher & Singer, 1980; Whaley, 1981; and others) and intertwined issues such as those raised in van den Broek and Trabasso (1986) on the nature of the narrative and variations of narratives. We have generally attempted to sort this research, again by the suggested operations and by whether a grid or map arrangement is involved. This research on text organizations has been discussed in the second chapter, entitled "Chunking: Organizing Strategies" since that research illuminates various forms of chunking (organizing strategies). Some form of chunking is preparatory to mapping and framing.

For the purposes of instructional design, whether the best strategy is framing or concept mapping depends on numerous variables including the characteristics of the content and the objectives of the instruction. It seems apparent that some material lends itself to framing and some material is best represented in concept mapping. Other material could be displayed with either frames or maps. Of course, in some material designers could use both. The following sections should help designers choose between the two similar strategies.

OVERVIEW OF MAPPING PROCEDURES

Before presenting the research and literature on concept mapping it should be helpful to provide an overview of this strategy. This should supply the reader with a big picture of this strategy. Very generally, concept mapping consists of extracting concepts and their relationships from a text or other content, plotting these concepts on paper or a computer screen and, finally, naming relationships.

For examples of concept maps see Figures 5-1, 5-2 and 5-3 for three types of concept maps identified by Jones, Palincsar, Ogle and Carr (1987). These three types are *spider maps* [labeled by Dansereau (1987) as cluster], *chain maps* and *hierarchy maps*. Each of these represents a different type of

FIGURE 5-1
Spider map: Types of concept maps.

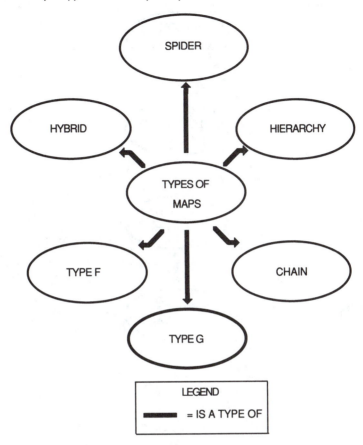

structure of content. These three are common types, but may not be a complete list, so we indicate other possibilities by capital letters. Obviously, hybrids of these types exist. For example, many hierarchical maps contain spider arrangements.

In concept maps, typically, relationships are named and the relationship name is written between concepts or included in a legend as presented with symbols for relationships (as in Figure 5-1). Thus, for the spider map in Figure 5-1 the relationship name "is a type of" is included in a legend. For the chain map in Figure 5-2 the relationship "leads to" or "enables" is also included in a legend, but it could have been written between each of the stages or steps. For the hierarchy in Figure 5-3, "subsumes" is the relationship name.

Having the concepts mapped and the relationships shown enables a third typical emphasis in mapping: that of stating propositions. For example, the user of the map in Figure 5-1 could generate several propositions, one of which is, "Spider is a type of map." The propositions become repetitious unless numerous relationships are contained on the map.

FIGURE 5-2

Chain map: Stages in concept mapping.

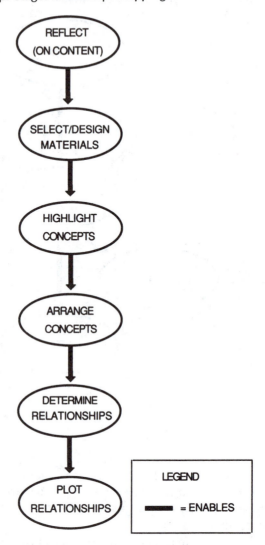

There are applications of mapping in which relationships are neither named nor emphasized. For some instructional purposes it may be adequate, even desirable, merely to present concepts with the information that there are relationships without instruction on those relationships.

RESEARCH AND DEVELOPMENT

In this section the research on concept mapping is discussed. This research has been conducted with a variety of *content* (knowledge domains), several *age* groups and with two *media*: print and computers. This content has

FIGURE 5-3

Hierarchy map: Research on concept mapping.

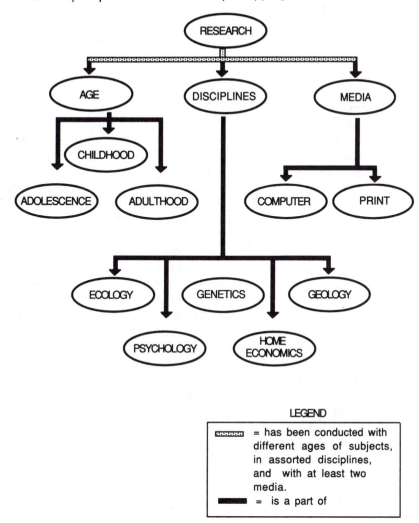

LEGEND

▭▭▭ = has been conducted with different ages of subjects, in assorted disciplines, and with at least two media.

▬▬ = is a part of

included such *disciplines* as ecology, genetics, home economics, geology, psychology, basic college science, middle and high school science and statistics. Age groups include graduate and undergraduate college students, sixth graders, seventh graders, high school students and elementary students.

Holley and Dansereau (1984) report on a series of investigations which they and their colleagues conducted. The first was a study of the effects of mapping with undergraduate college students who were given three two-hour training sessions. The content was two 1,000-word passages from *Scientific American*. Students were tested for immediate and delayed recall. There were no significant effects for the training. It may be that six hours is too little training on mapping for the kinds of materials in this study. Several other studies were conducted by this group in which training and experimental procedures were refined.

After refining training and experimental procedures, Holley, Damsereau, McDonald, Garland and Collins (1979) did a study in which undergraduate students were better trained in the use of mapping. Subjects were given an introduction to mapping, training on connections and relationship names and practice on mapping. Practice was provided on several passages of 500 and 1,000 words provided by the experimenters. In addition, students practiced using material from their general psychology textbooks. Finally the students used mapping to study a 3,000-word passage from a geology text which was unrelated to other materials used in earlier phases of the study. The control group was asked to use their usual study methods on the geology text materials.

After five days students were tested on the geology passage with a long essay question, 10 short essay questions, cloze (fill in the blanks left in brief prose passages) items and 18 multiple-choice items. The networking group recalled significantly more main ideas than did the controls. There was no significant difference between groups on the recall of detail. Another interesting finding is that when subjects were divided into high and low grade-point-average groups, the mapping aided recall of detail for the low grade-point-average group. The mapping group with high GPA, however, performed less well on the detail questions when compared with controls. Holley, Dansereau, McDonald, Garland and Collins (1979) speculate that the high GPA students had efficient study strategies for detail for preparing for multiple-choice tests.

Holley and Dansereau (1984) report two other studies, again with university undergraduates as subjects in geology and science. Both investigations resulted in positive effects for mapping. In one of these studies Dansereau, Brooks, Holley and Collins (1983) combined mapping with concentration management [setting goals, self control of study mood (Dansereau, 1987)] and looked at the order effect of the two with reasonable controls. While training with both orders resulted in performance superior to controls, the group receiving the mapping training first seemed to be superior to the group receiving the concentration treatment first.

Holley and Dansereau (1984) also report that training in mapping has been helpful in graduate statistics courses and independent studies courses. In the statistics course students were provided with maps of chapters, which seems to help students understand the big picture and place detail in perspective. In the independent study the students generated the maps of sections of books and discussed the maps with the instructor.

Other systematic work on mapping has been conducted by Stewart (1980, 1982) and his colleagues (Stewart, Van Kirk, & Rowell, 1979). This research is qualitative rather than experimental—based on Piagetian style interviews with relatively small numbers of students (Stewart, 1980, 1982). Students were interviewed about their knowledge of such topics as genetics, energy and ecosystems. They were asked to develop concept maps in a manner similar to that described in Figure 5-2 (the chain map). Students were able to develop several types of maps representing both declarative and procedural knowledge. As a result of this research, Stewart, Van Kirk and Rowell (1979) consider mapping to have several uses and to be a very flexible tool. These uses include the development of curricula, instructional planning and evaluation.

Hawk (1986) examined the use of concept maps in middle school (sixth- and seventh-grade) life science. There were 455 students from 15 classes in this study. The treatment groups were given seven concept maps developed for use with seven chapters of a life science text. These concept maps were presented to the treatment groups and explained as study guides at the beginning of instruction on each chapter. The experimental groups scored substantially higher than controls on the achievement test at the conclusion of the experiment.

Another study with adolescents (Novak, Gowin, & Johansen, 1983) combined concept mapping with a technique called Vee diagrams (Novak & Gowin, 1984). In this study students of high, middle and low ability learned to use both techniques in existing science programs. The investigators report that the techniques were helpful in both learning and problem solving.

In another study at the high school level (Alvermann, 1981), the researcher gave students two passages for study, one which compared and contrasted material and the other which was a description of main ideas about a topic. Both passages were presented with a concept map. The number of ideas recalled was measured both immediately and with a one-week delay. The concept maps aided recall only for the less organized, merely descriptive condition on both immediate and delayed recall measures. This finding held for all students regardless of reading level. Presumably, the map was not necessary for learning the material which was structured around a comparison-contrast organization.

With another tenth-grade class, mapping in world history was investigated (Bean, Singer, Sorter, & Frazee, 1986). Students were taught a mapping technique which involved the emphasis of cause-and-effect relationships. Students were also provided a list of options which a major historical figure might have available for an important event in history. The cause and effect map and the list of options were used by the students to make predictions about outcomes of revolutions and other events. These predictions were later checked for accuracy with historical sources. Training in the mapping and the use of the options enabled students later to make predictions without the options guide.

In a study of mapping (Boothby & Alvermann, 1984), fourth-grade students participated in a training session lasting three months. Students in the concept mapping training condition practiced three times a week using maps with typical fourth-grade material. Students in the control group were given the same instructional contact time, read the same material and took the same tests. The groups seemed equivalent on reading level and background. The number of idea units recalled was tested immediately following the experimental treatment, with a 48-hour delay and with a delay of one month. There were significant differences in favor of the mapping group for both immediate and 48-hour delay, but not for the longer delay.

Other research has demonstrated that elementary students can learn mapping (Hauf, 1971; Symington & Novak, 1982; Wandersee, 1983). These studies, and those discussed in the preceding paragraphs, have been conducted with textbooks or similar material.

There have also been successful attempts to use computers as an aid in concept mapping. In mapping, computers are particularly useful for classroom and design uses for several reasons. The concept names can easily be placed on the screen and moved around. This allows greater flexibility than using gummed labels which can be removed, placed in one spot and then moved as some investigators have done. Using the computer is as flexible as using cards with concepts on each card, and often the map can be done more quickly, for concept names do not have to be rewritten from the cards. Another possible advantage, depending on the program, is that the concept map, once completed, may be reduced and placed in a window on the screen while other instructional material is present. Relationship cues can also be placed in a window for quick reference (McAleese, 1985, 1986). Students then have the capability of quickly glancing from the other material on the screen to the window.

Cammelot (1987) used a microcomputer as an aid for concept mapping with students from the sixth, seventh and eighth grades. The content was material from a home economics textbook. Students initially practiced concept mapping with paper and gummed labels, then plotted them on the computer screen. Students were able to accomplish this with varying amounts of help from the investigator and reported that they enjoyed doing it.

McAleese (1985, 1986) developed a sophisticated computer-based intelligent interactive video system for use in study of the structures of knowledge. Concept mapping is an important component of his work. Concept maps are constructed from the knowledge of authors (experts). From the maps displayed on the screen, students can obtain material for study by "pulling down" concepts, which activates this associated material for study. Work such as this is important for further understanding of underlying structures of knowledge and how to represent those structures, as well as learning and instructional design. Similar work is being done by Fisher (1988).

Another development in mapping with computers is that of Learning Tool, a software program (Kozma & Van Roekel, 1986) created for friendly use with the Macintosh 512K, the Macintosh XL and the Macintosh Plus. Users outline notes, texts or other materials from which concept maps are automatically produced. The outlines and the concept maps may then be used for study and review.

In this research and development literature there is ample evidence that concept mapping is a useful spatial learning strategy. It seems especially useful when students construct concept maps after or during the study of content, and when knowledge of concepts and relationships is the primary goal of instruction (Moore & Readence, 1984). It is useful in a variety of disciplines, for students from middle childhood into adulthood. It is useful with text material. Concept mapping is also an aid in computer-based learning and instruction.

SPECIAL ISSUES

In this section we discuss several issues. These include assessment and mapping, implications of type of knowledge for mapping and comparisons between frames and mapping and between mapping and outlining. Of central importance is the variety of kinds of relationships in mapping.

Kinds of Relationships

In the concept mapping literature a substantial amount of the material in the experiments is declarative and, more specifically, propositional. These propositions receive careful attention in most of the mapping research. That is to say, the propositions can be considered as important for study and learning as the concepts and relationships. A proposition consists of the concepts connected and the relationships or "links" and can be generated by using the connected concepts and their relationship in a sentence. For example, from Figure 5-4 nine typical propositions can be generated, one of which is "Categorizing is a type of relationship."

FIGURE 5-4

Spider map: Kinds of relationships.

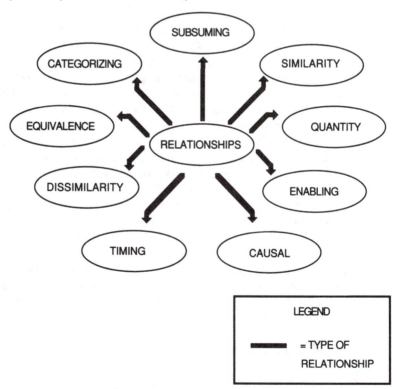

Source: See Armbruster and Anderson (1984), Huang (1988) and McAleese (1985, 1986) for further details.

Several investigators have contributed to the identification of several kinds of relationships mapped in Figure 5-4 (Armbruster & Anderson, 1984; Huang, 1988; McAleese, 1985, 1986, 1988). The relationships identified so far in the mapping literature consist of a small number of types, but further research and infusion from other knowledge domains could readily expand the understanding of the nature of these relationships, their number [for example, Wartofsky (1968) has identified 16 types of causal relationships] and the number of types. Most types of relationships, as currently conceived, are observed in most knowledge domains, so that they have some utility in aiding understanding of the nature of knowledge in a variety of domains.

These kinds of relationships include, first, such statements as *A is an instance of B*. This is essentially a categorization link. This consists of placing instances into types or categories. Some examples of key words in material include *for example, type of, kind of* and *for instance*.

A second kind of relationship is *A is a property of B*. This is a subsuming and/or defining link. Some key words or examples in text are *is a feature of, is a characteristic of, is called* and *is defined as*.

A third kind of relationship is *A is identical to B*. This is essentially an equivalence relationship. Some examples include *is, is identical to* and *is the same as*.

A fourth type is *A is similar to B*. This highlights a similarity relationship. Some examples are *like, is similar* and *in a similar manner*. Its opposite is the fifth type, *A is not similar to B*. Examples are *is different, is unlike* and *in contrast*.

A sixth type is *A is greater than (less than) B*, a quantity relationship. Examples in content are *is more, is larger* and *is less*.

A seventh kind of relationship is that of *A occurs before B*, obviously one of time. Examples consist of *and then, before, after, followed by* and *earlier*. This relationship is sometimes confused with that of causing and enabling.

The eighth class of relationship is *A causes B*. This is reserved for events in which A is both necessary and sufficient for B. Example statements are *causes, produces, because* and *consequently*. A third cousin is the ninth type, *A enables B*. This is the necessary but not sufficient condition. Example statements are *enables, requires* and *allows*.

Figure 5-5 is a frame, a summary of these nine relationships. The discussion of these relationships and Figure 5-5 are based primarily on the work of Armbruster and Anderson (1984), Huang (1988) and McAleese (1985, 1986).

The emphasis on types of relationships should not be taken to mean that all of those in mapping research and development advocate the emphasis on relationships for all instructional purposes and for all students. Some instruction may be quite adequate under certain conditions if it is mentioned that a relationship exists.

Mapping and Outlining

Some have noted that concept mapping is similar to the traditional outline. Outlining is a traditional study strategy and has been recommended as one method of study in the literature on studying. Similarities between con-

FIGURE 5-5

A frame showing relationship type, essential operation and examples.

Relationship Type	Essential Operation	Examples in Text
A is an instance of B	classification	for example, type of, kind of, for instance
A is a property of B	subsuming, defining	is a feature of, is characteristic of, is defined as, is called
A is identical to B	showing equivalence	is identical to, is the same as
A is similar to B	shows similarity	like, is similar,
A is not similar to B	illustrates difference	is different, unlike, in contrast
A is greater (less) than B	quantity	is more, is larger, is less
A occurs before	time sequence	then, before, after, follows
A causes B	causal, necessary and sufficient	causes, produces, because
A enables B	necessary, but not sufficient condition	enables, allows

cept mapping and outlining include the fact that both are structured representations. Also both *can* be hierarchical and linear. But only one kind of concept map is hierarchical, whereas all outlines are. Recursion cannot be shown on a traditional outline whereas it can on a concept map. Finally both techniques involve isolating and organizing concepts.

Another similarity is the requirement of training. Students must learn mapping techniques and the literature is clear that they can. Outlining, however, at some point in education must be learned also, if it is to be used. At least U.S. children are not born knowing outlining. Teachers who consider that outlining is the primary study strategy or prewriting strategy report that outlining must be taught.

It should be emphasized, however, that there are also several differences between concept mapping and outlining. Concept maps are more visual than outlines so that maps are more easily imaged. Concept maps can be encoded both verbally and imaginally, whereas outlines are, for most people, coded verbally. Maps provide a total big picture which can be more coherently scanned, while this would be true only of short outlines. Concept mapping can more readily display numerous interrelationships among concepts (please see Figure 4-3, for an example) and the concepts are not displayed in isolation. The linking can be more elaborate than in outlining (Ault, 1985).

From this comparison it follows that, if material lends itself to mapping, it would be *best to have students map rather than outline* when the intention is one of remembering material. In one pilot study reported by Lehman, Carter and Kahle (1985), minority high school students actually recalled more on a biology test when mapping was used when compared with outlining. Again, the decision of whether or not to use mapping instead of outlining should be made on the bases of characteristics of content, its stage of development and the instructional objectives.

Bean, Sorter, Singer and Frazee (1986) compared outlining with mapping in a study of tenth-grade world history instruction over a period of 14 weeks. Two groups were taught mapping and another group received instruction in outlining. One of the mapping groups had had previous instruction on summarization and question generation (rehearsal techniques). The group which learned mapping alone was not superior to the outlining group in recall, but the group which had had the earlier rehearsal training learned more than the outlining group.

In addition, the students in the mapping groups reported more positive attitudes toward the strategy learned than the outlining group. A third dependent measure in this study revealed that the mapping plus rehearsal group transferred their strategic study skills to learning a new challenging passage.

Frames or Concept Mapping

For the instructional designer no clear and easy answer can be provided as a guide to deciding between frames and mapping. Much depends on whether the designer is planning instruction around existing material or developing the material from scratch. If the designer is using existing materials, it should be relatively easy to inspect the material to determine if it lends itself to a frame arrangement or mapping and, if so, what type. If, however, the designer is developing the material, it may be wise to choose the spatial strategy before that development. Then, the big picture becomes a powerful determinant or a reflection of the inherent structure of the material. That big picture then has the chance of permeating the material in obvious and powerful ways.

One other idea may help in this decision. Frames have the capability of including, not only concepts and principles, but also facts, details, examples and principles. Concept mapping, on the other hand, at least in the pristine and uncluttered form in which it is presented in this book, is primarily appropriate for instruction and learning of concepts, propositions and relationships, but not for all factual detail. You may wish to inspect and then compare the kinds of information contained in Figures 5-4 and 5-5. Note the similarity and differences in the information contained.

If the material is clearly conceptual in nature, and if the instructional objectives are primarily conceptual learning, either framing or mapping should be very helpful. If, however, the focus of content and objectives is other than conceptual, framing is likely to be more fruitful.

Declarative, Conditional or Procedural Knowledge?

Mapping lends itself to "knowing that," "knowing how" and "knowing when," but the kind of map used depends partially on the type of relationship. When the material to be mapped is declarative, either spider maps or hierarchical maps may be used. In addition, if the relationship is one of timing (time sequence), chain maps may also be used. On the other hand, if the knowledge is procedural, the relationship will be either timing, causal or enabling and thus chain maps must be used. We have found no research and development efforts in which conditional knowledge is mapped. It seems plausible, however, that the hybrid map would be most appropriate.

Mapping and Large Information Sets

Just as framing has considerable potential for the management of large information sets, so also has mapping. On this point McAleese's (1988) metaphor of the concept map as a wadded net with all knowledge somehow interconnected is particularly felicitous. While this use of mapping is not restricted to the machine medium, the computer with its power and flexibility as found in such applications as HyperCard, hypertext and hypermedia is notably fitting.

Think of the possibility of mapping this entire text. There are many possible beginnings but, for the major concepts, one might begin with schemata. Off that concept might be structure, function and the two types which include process, then from process to the families of strategies and so on. Then the major concepts in each chapter could be mapped off the name of each strategy. Such a large map of our text would be, of course, hybrid, a combination of the other three types. The first author has created a skeleton of such a map for this text on HyperCard for use with an overhead panel for presentations.

Such maps not only function as a learning aid but also could function as external intellectual waldoes, in performance augmentation as discussed in Chapter 3 for use in extremely complex performance situations. On a computer such a map provides—as does a frame—a convenient, meaningful, not necessarily hierarchical, *access* device. It provides a big picture, as do frames, within which one can "zoom" from the whole to parts and from parts to parts with the capability of rapid scanning and retrieval.

Such scanning and retrieval can work by programming the machine so that "tapping" a concept can bring to the screen either greater detail such as text, examples, illustrations or a large, but perhaps miniaturized, version of a piece of the map. The miniature version could be kept in one corner of the screen, for example, to retain a partial big picture while detail is being inspected or studied. Precisely what applications and what computers are capable of such uses is not known by these authors at this time. We know that some of these uses are currently in place and more are possible with current technology.

In books, maps and parts of maps could be presented with miniatures somewhere on the pages or as figures at the beginning of sections. We have demonstrated some of this potential of maps as the big, continuing picture for Chapters 11 and 12.

Mapping and Testing

There is some interest in the implications of mapping for testing or assessment, and diagnosis of strengths and weaknesses (Surber, 1984; Huang, 1988). Surber (1984) rightly notes that a primary weakness of traditional test formats such as teacher-made multiple choice is insensitivity to the structures of knowledge and that mapping-based tests can be made to remedy this. For mapping based testing he recommends taking the map developed for the instructional material (the *master map*) and deleting some of the concepts and relationships. Students then, for the test, supply the missing portions. The test cues, of course, are in the master map supplied for completion. Errors allow diagnosis of weaknesses, not only about concepts, relationships and propositions, but also about the knowledge structure as represented in the map. Students, as one would expect, need training before this kind of testing is implemented; and such testing should typically be used only if the material was mapped during instruction.

Huang (1988), in a very systematic developmental effort, trained middle school students to use concept mapping. The focus of this effort was to investigate mapping as an assessment device and to investigate students' reactions to mapping. There were 170 eighth-grade subjects from seven intact classes. Some groups were trained briefly by being given a training package and listening to an oral presentation, and some were trained more intensively by practice on the linkages (relationships) and map drawing. Huang gave students a mapping test on pairing concepts, providing linkages and supplying directions of relationships. She also gave an essay test and an attitude questionnaire.

There are several interesting findings. Training in mapping did increase the performance on the tests. Learning to map did not seem to be determined by general ability. Map testing did not seem to require more time than other types of teacher-made tests. The test appears to be valid and reliable. The attitude questionnaire responses were not particularly favorable, however.

From these developmental efforts it is clear that map-based tests have some potential, especially for assessing students' structural knowledge. At this point in the development, *if map-based tests are to be given, the instruction should be designed at least partially around mapping.* Students will generally do poorly and dislike such tests until they become accustomed to and practiced in mapping.

One point in favor of this test format, however, is that teachers and instructional designers may not have the training necessary to design multiple-choice tests which detect knowledge of structure or the big picture. With much less training they can detect structure with mapping tests.

In the preceding sections we have explained mapping, discussed the research, and presented some of the issues related to mapping. How is one to design instruction using this spatial learning strategy?

DESIGNERS' GUIDE TO MAPPING

Before selecting mapping as the spatial strategy to use in a design, the specifications included in Figure 5-6 should be reviewed. Please notice that we have columns for the four common types of maps. Each type of map has its own conditions for use. Should you not understand these you may wish to review portions of this chapter.

In this section we provide a step-by-step guide (procedural) to concept mapping for the instructional designer, similar to that of Ault (1985) and reminiscent of rules developed by Kintsch and van Dijk (1978) for abstraction, integration and retention of concepts. Figure 5-2 is a concept map for this guide. An initial step is to reflect on the instructional materials and the objectives for the instruction. If the primary objective is concept learning, materials should be developed or selected in which concepts are emphasized.

In this reflection it is important to consider the nature of concepts. A *concept* is a class name for objects (events, things) of awareness together with its meaning. The name of the class is a referent for objects and events which share similar characteristics. The referent is inherently abstract.

The material must be read carefully in preparation for the subsequent step of highlighting the concepts, or in some manner making the most important concepts obvious. To do this the concepts must be reviewed carefully for their meaning. This is complicated by the fact that concepts inevitably will be embedded in text in propositions and principles. Also, often the meaning of the concept is dependent on knowledge of a seemingly limitless number of other concepts.

A common problem with this step in mapping is isolating a concept. If, for example, one were attempting a chain map for a new operating room procedure for an existing staff, one would have to select and highlight the central concepts from the written procedure. There is a temptation to write or highlight a phrase or even a sentence and try to use this as a concept. This is the most common problem in learning to map. *Remember to place the concept name on the map rather than a long phrase or sentence.* Definitions of concepts must be presented elsewhere, unless the definitions are to be themselves mapped. In defining concepts, other concepts known (hopefully) by the student are used. It may be helpful for some instruction to map definitions.

One way to deliver supplemental instruction on the definitions is to use a frame similar to that in Figure 5-7. This framing capitalizes on the very traditional sequence in teaching of naming concept, defining concept and

FIGURE 5-6
Specifications for concept maps.

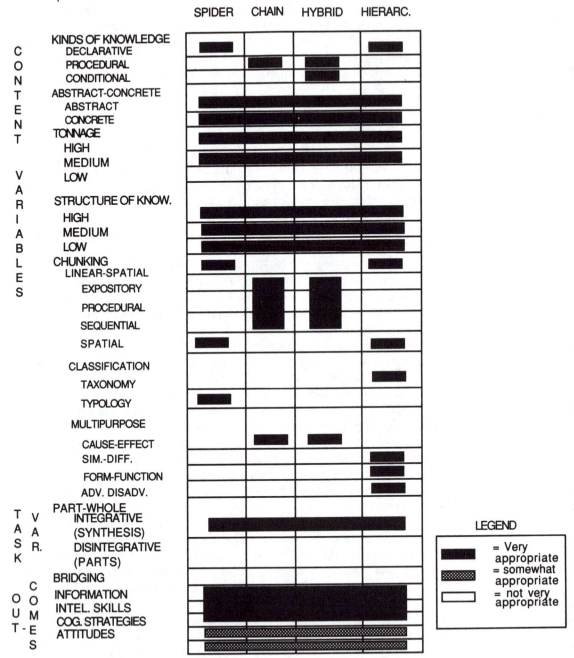

FIGURE 5-7

A frame for teaching definitions of concepts.

| | Definition | | Example | |
	Text	Paraphrase	Text*	Student's*
Concept #1				
Concept #2				
Concept #3				
Concept #4				

* For some content it may be helpful to further subdivide these into columns for positive and negative examples.

giving example. Notice that in Figure 5-7 the rows are concept names (concept #1, #2, etc.); that is, the names of the concepts are written as row headings while definitions and examples are the column headings. In the first slots students record (or the teacher provides) the definitions from sources such as a text or lecture, and in the next slots students record their paraphrasings of the definitions. In subsequent slots the students record (or the teacher provides) an example, then the students supply examples which they conceive. Such a frame provides a systematic routine for concept learning which could be deployed to complement the use of concept maps when instruction on the definitions of concepts is vital. Systematically obtaining paraphrasings and examples from students can be very helpful for we usually feel that students do understand when they can paraphrase and create their own examples.

Next, the primary concepts must be arranged on a page or screen, which provides the big picture. Each concept should be used only once. The most important or central concept must be selected and placed in a central position on the medium. If the medium is paper, it will be helpful to use removable gummed labels so that different arrangements may be tried quickly. If the medium is a computer screen, the software should permit transportation of concept names around on the screen. The details of this step depend greatly on the choice of whether the mapping is to be developed and provided by the designer or developed by the students. Along with this step, during the arrangement, the type of map must be selected—or the arrangement of the concepts will determine the type. Remember that there are three basic types: spider, chain and hierarchy. (Please refer to Figures 5-1, 5-2 and 5-3 and accompanying sections in this chapter.)

This arrangement, or map type, it should be remembered, depends partially on whether the knowledge is declarative or procedural, each of which contains specific relationships, of course. Declarative knowledge may be mapped with the three map types, but procedural knowledge is restricted to chain maps. This is complicated further by the nature of the relationships involved. Remember that if the knowledge is procedural, the relationship will be either causal or enabling, and thus the appropriate map is chain. (Please see Figure 5-5 and accompanying material.)

Thus the type of map interacting with the type of relationship determines the arrangement of the concepts on the map. Concepts are arrayed in a superordinate to subordinate order. Often clustered arrangements occur in hierarchy maps, and if one were to break off one of these clusters it would be a spider (as in Figure 5-3 in which five kinds of disciplines are clustered around the concept discipline). The page or screen layout should be as uncluttered as possible, and there should be space for the placement of the relationships.

The concept arrangement enables the next step, that of drawing and naming relationships. Directions of relationships are indicated by arrows. Relationship names may be used more than once. Directions of relationships can be one-way or two-way (one could point the arrow toward the cause from the effect and from the effect to the cause, for example). The manner of indicating the relationships may be seen in some of the figures in this chapter. There are at least two options in the literature for naming relationships. McAleese (1985, 1986) provides a window on the machine screen for a legend of relationship names and symbols, so that the direction and label of the relationship is represented with a lined symbol. This option is helpful, especially for complicated maps or maps which might otherwise be cluttered. This option could also be used with print. Another way of representing the relationships is to "break" the arrow and record the label of the relationship in the break.

So far in the designers' guide, we have written of the concept and the relationship. The third important feature of mapping is the proposition. *While propositions do not appear on the map itself, it helps to remember that students' benefits derived from use of the map will depend partially on whether or not they generate the propositions in the manner discussed earlier.*

HYBRIDIZATION

It is likely that the use of concept mapping also entails substantial time spent in rehearsal. The designer will wish to plan time and opportunity for students to inspect maps and the explanatory passages on which the maps are based. Time and opportunity must be planned for such rehearsal activities as reviewing, abstracting, asking questions, answering questions, thinking about meaning and predicting meaning, many if not all of which are necessary for the student to map. Paraphrasing is particularly critical in stating the propositions derived from the map.

Concept mapping can also be combined or supplemented with frames when both are appropriate, particularly as in Figure 5-7. Since concept mapping is a spatial learning strategy, it is also likely that it could be combined with imagery. For some students and some content, mnemonics could also be helpful.

The use of concept mapping is dependent on some type of classification or chunking. It is probable that, in most instructional material, this classification will have been done by the author of the material. If not, the designer must plan for classification to be completed prior to the use of concept maps. Here, again, remember the simple three-phase model, presented originally in Chapter 3 ("Frames, Type One,") of chunking, building the product (the specific map or frame) and planning for the processing (study) of that product.

SUMMARY

In this chapter we have presented the third spatial learning strategy, concept mapping. We have provided an overview of the research in which it is illustrated that concept mapping is appropriate for students from childhood to adulthood, that it is appropriate for a variety of disciplines and that it can be done in print and on computers. We have also presented a guide for designers in the implementation of mapping.

In the following two chapters a new "family" of cognitive strategies is discussed: the strategies which help students remember what they know and apply that knowledge to new material. These strategies are advance organizer and metaphor.

EXERCISES

1. Select material from the first five chapters and create and complete a concept map incorporating the main concepts. You may wish to review the section entitled "Designers' Guide" before attempting this task.

2. Study that concept map carefully. Name in your own words the strategy or strategies you used during that study. Be sure to emphasize the statements of propositions.

3. Is the material in this concept map declarative, procedural or conditional?

4. Look at Figure 1-3 (p. 12). Would a frame or a concept map be best for this material? Why? What kind of chunking is present in that figure?

REFERENCES

Armbruster, B. B., & Anderson, T. H. (1984). Mapping: Representing informative text diagrammatically. In C. D. Holley & D. F. Dansereau (Eds.), *Spatial learning strategies: Techniques, applications, and related issues.* Orlando, FL: Academic Press.

Ault, C. R. (1985). Concept mapping as a study strategy in earth science. *Journal of College Science Teaching, 15,* 38–44.

Alvermann, D. E. (1981). The compensatory effect of graphic organizers on descriptive text. *Journal of Educational Research, 75,* 44–48.

Bean, T. W., Singer, H., Sorter, J., & Frazee, C. (1986). The effect of metacognitive instruction in outlining and graphic organizer construction on students' comprehension in a tenth-grade world history class. *Journal of Reading Behavior, 18,* 153–169.

Bean, T. W., Sorter, J., Singer, H., & Frazee, C. (1986). Teaching students how to make predictions about events in history with a graphic organizer plus options guide. *Journal of Reading, 29,* 739–745.

Boothby, P. R., & Alvermann, D. E. (1984). A classroom training study: The effects of graphic organizer instruction on fourth graders' comprehension. *Reading World, 26,* 325–339.

Cammelot, J. A. (1987). *Design and evaluation of software for computer-based concept mapping.* Unpublished masters thesis. University of Illinois at Urbana-Champaign.

Dansereau, D. F. (1987). Technical learning strategies. *Engineering Education, 77,* 280–284.

Dansereau, D. F., Brooks, L. W., Holley, C. D., & Collins, K. W. (1983). Learning strategies training: Effects of sequencing. *Journal of Experimental Education, 51,* 102–108.

Dreher, M. J., & Singer, H. (1980). Story grammar instruction unnecessary in intermediate grade students. *The Reading Teacher, 33,* 261–268.

Fisher, K. M. (1988). SemNet: Software for student or faculty construction of large relational networks of concepts. Paper presented at the annual meeting of the American Educational Research Association, New Orleans, LA.

Hauf, M. B. (1971). Mapping: A technique for translating reading into thinking. *Journal of Reading, 14,* 225–230.

Hawk, P. P. (1986). Using graphic organizers to increase achievement in middle school life science. *Science Education, 70,* 81–87.

Holley, C. D., & Dansereau, D. F. (Eds.). (1984). *Spatial learning strategies: Techniques, applications, and related issues.* Orlando, FL: Academic Press.

Holley, C. D., Dansereau, D. F., McDonald, B. A., Garland, J. C., & Collins, K. W. (1979). Evaluation of a hierarchical mapping technique as an aid to prose processing. *Contemporary Educational Psychology, 4,* 227–237.

Huang, J. (1988). Assessing knowledge structure: The development and try-out of a mapping technique. Unpublished doctoral dissertation. University of Illinois at Urbana-Champaign.

Jones, B. F., Palincsar, A. S., Ogle, D. S., & Carr, E. G. (Eds.). (1987). *Strategic teaching and learning: Cognitive instruction in the content areas.* Elmhurst, IL: North Central Regional Laboratory and the Association for Supervision and Curriculum Development.

Kintsch, W., & Van Dijk, T. A. (1978). Toward a model of text comprehension and production. *Psychological Review, 85,* 363–394.

Kozma, R. B., & Van Roekel, J. (1986). *Learning tool.* Ann Arbor, MI: Arborworks.

Lehman, J. D., Carter, C., & Kahle, J. B. (1985). Concept mapping, vee mapping, and achievement: Results of a field study with black high school students. *Journal of Research in Science Teaching, 22,* 663–673.

McAleese, R. (1985). Some problems of knowledge representation in an authoring environment: Exteriorization, anomalous state metacognition and self confrontation. *Programmed Learning and Educational Technology, 22,* 299–306.

McAleese, R. (1986). Computer-based authoring and intelligent interactive video. In C. W. Osborne & A. J. Trott (Eds.), *International yearbook of educational and instructional technology.* New York: Kogan Page.

McAleese, R. (1988). From concept maps to computer-aided instruction: Is it possible using Notecard? Paper presented at the annual meeting of the American Educational Research Association, New Orleans, LA.

Moore, D. W., & Readence, J. E. (1984). A quantitative and qualitative review of graphic organizer research. *Journal of Educational Research, 78,* 11–17.

Novak, J. D., & Gowin, D. B. (1984). *Learning how to learn.* Cambridge: Cambridge University Press.

Novak, J. D., Gowin, D. B., & Johansen, G. T. (1983). The use of concept mapping and knowledge vee mapping with junior high school science students. *Science Education, 67,* 625–645.

Stewart, J. (1980). Techniques for assessing and representing information in cognitive structure. *Science Education, 64,* 223–235.

Stewart, J. (1982). Two aspects of meaningful problem solving. *Science Education, 66,* 731–749.

Stewart, J., Van Kirk J., & Rowell, R. (1979). Concept maps: A tool for use in biology teaching. *The American Biology Teacher, 41,* 171–175.

Surber, J. R. (1984). Mapping as a testing and diagnostic device. In C. D. Holley & D. F. Dansereau (Eds.), *Spatial learning strategies: Techniques, applications, and related issues.* Orlando, FL.: Academic Press, Inc.

Symington, D. J., & Novak, J. D. (1982). Teaching children how to learn. *Education Magazine, 39,* 13–16.

van den Broek, P., & Trabasso, T. (1986). Causal networks versus goal hierarchies in summarizing text. *Discourse Processes, 9,* 1–15.

Wandersee, J. H. (1983). The concept of "away." *Science and Children, 21,* 47–49.

Wartofsky, M. W. (1968). *Conceptual foundations of scientific thought.* New York: Macmillan.

Whaley, J. F. (1981). Story grammars and reading instruction. *The Reading Teacher, 34,* 762–771.

CHAPTER 6

Advance Organizer

During instruction there is often a chasm, sometimes vast, between what is to be taught and what is known by the student. Students often appear to have no knowledge about a topic, and the instructional designer or instructor has no insight about how to introduce a topic in ways which help students remember and transfer the knowledge the student may have to the new topic.

Two cognitive strategies are available which have the capability of helping students recall what they know and transfer that knowledge to new topics. These two strategies are the advance organizer and metaphor. We have called these *bridging* strategies. We discuss the advance organizer in this chapter.

Often it seems that instruction proceeds from unit to unit, course to course or lesson to lesson with little or no connection, or bridging. Every topic is seemingly approached as an unexplored territory with nothing known by the student which is pertinent or helpful for comprehension; or, there is little effort made during instruction to help students retrieve and apply prior knowledge which may be pertinent.

When there is no obvious connection between topics, students must most often approach a new topic relatively mindlessly with no attempt to reflect on what they might know which could help them bridge the chasm between what they know and what they must learn. Without these connections, learning, if it occurs at all, may be rote and forgotten quickly. Perhaps students have been presented with so much which appears so new, or which has been represented as new, that they are "programmed" to ignore possibilities of connections.

Occasionally, however, very good students on their own and without prompting may try to remember material which bridges this chasm. Anderson, Armbruster and Kantor (1980) and Kantor, Anderson and Armbruster (1983), in a study of "unfriendly text," have an imaginary protocol of an exceptional elementary student desperately trying to make sense of selected passages in a widely used elementary text. She struggles through sentence after sentence. There is both humor and pathos in her attempts to understand the material, for she periodically exits the text, expresses her frustration, but valiantly dredges from memory and restates information which helps her comprehend the main ideas.

Students should not routinely be required to go through the kinds of processes described. Friendly text, or other media of well-designed instruction, provides help. How does the instructional designer manage this momentous and stirring design challenge? How does one help students remember pertinent information and apply it to a new topic or unit or course? The significance of prior knowledge must first be recognized. Then advance organizers can be developed to bridge the chasm between the known and the unknown.

It is basic that the instructional designer know that the two most important variables in instructional design which can be systematically, if sometimes partially, managed are what the student already knows (Ausubel, 1968) and how that knowledge is organized. The development of advance organizers is a major way to capitalize on students' prior knowledge about the material in lessons being planned. Advance organizers *may* capitalize on how the student has previously mentally organized the knowledge or may capitalize on reorganization. Either approach is based on prior knowledge of students.

We wish to emphasize that the advance organizer is different from the other strategies in this text in that *students are not ordinarily likely to be able to create them.* The use of the advance organizer in teaching and instructional design is restricted to helping the students learn. The other uses of the other strategies, (1) teaching the strategies while teaching content and (2) activating the strategies, are *not appropriate for the advance organizer.* Generally, one would not have the objective of teaching this as a strategy to students along with content. There is, however, one exception to this: we can teach this strategy to others for their use in teaching and design.

Following are paragraphs and sections on features of the advance organizer, a guide to their development which includes steps in the analysis of prior knowledge and several examples. Also included is a section on research on the topic.

FEATURES OF THE ADVANCE ORGANIZER

The advance organizer is like a bridge which can be constructed and used with material presented in written and oral form. The advance organizer is a brief prose passage, usually about a paragraph in length. It introduces, comes before a lesson or a unit of instruction, before the main body of presentation. It is a rich and powerful transition statement.

More than an ordinary introduction or transition, the advance organizer is based on the students' prior knowledge. It is brief and abstract. It also organizes the material to be presented later by outlining, arranging, logically sequencing or patterning the main points, ideas or procedures.

FIGURE 6-1

Features of the advance organizer.

1. It is a brief, abstract prose passage.
2. It is a bridge, a linking of new information with something already known. The foundation is *similarities* between the old knowledge and the new. Without substantial similarity, the advance organizer is not possible.
3. It is an introduction of a new lesson, unit or course.
4. It is an abstract outline of new information *and* is a restatement of prior knowledge.
5. It provides the students with a structure of the new information.
6. It encourages students to transfer or apply what they know.
7. It consists of content having considerable intellectual substance, material which is more than common knowledge.

There has been a tendency for any introductory statement, or even pictures or illustrations, to be called advance organizers. Neither ordinary introductions nor illustrations, however stimulating or motivating they may be, are advance organizers. It is crucial to remember that advance organizers have *all* the features listed in Figure 6-1. The seventh feature, that of intellectual substance, is difficult to gauge. As we discuss examples of advance organizers, we attempt to provide further information on this feature.

While the use of the advance organizer is restricted to verbal material, it can be used for declarative, procedural and conditional learning. When either "knowing that," "knowing how" or "knowing when" is to be taught, advance organizers can aid learning.

EXAMPLES OF ADVANCE ORGANIZERS

Suppose that a unit of instruction had been completed on the U.S. government and that the next unit to be designed and taught was a unit on the government of the United Kingdom. Assuming appropriate coverage in the two units, an advance organizer such as that in Figure 6-2 could be de-

FIGURE 6-2

Advance organizer for unit on the United Kingdom.

In our unit on the U.S. government we learned that there are three branches in the federal government: the executive, the legislative and the judicial. The primary function of the executive branch is the enforcement of laws. The primary function of the legislative branch, the Congress, is the passage of laws; whereas the major task of the judicial branch is the protection of citizens' rights under the national Constitution. In this next unit on the United Kingdom we will learn that there are also these three branches: executive, legislative and judicial, with similar functions.

FIGURE 6-3

Advance organizer for causes of war.

Remember in our unit on World War I we studied several causes of that war. Among those causes studied were economic forces, political upheaval, internal strife and boundary disputes. Also we learned about several important events which occurred just before the declaration of that war. In this next unit we will learn that the causes of World War II are much the same and that there were very similar events which happened before each war.

signed and presented at the beginning of unit two. Notice that the statement is abstract and brief and that the main ideas about the three branches of government in the two systems—executive, legislative and judicial—are mentioned.

In Figure 6-3 is another example of an advance organizer which bridges units on World War I and World War II. It is based on the idea of a few similar factors contributing to warfare, such as immediate precipitating events, economic factors, political factors, internal strife in the warring nations existing just before the war and boundary disputes among or between nations.

Figure 6-4 contains an example of an advance organizer for an adult lesson reviewing the operation of different types of engines. It is based on first having a lesson on piston engines, in which students learned the basic operations of that type of engine. Three general ideas from that lesson are restated in the organizer, and the lesson on turbine engines will be organized around those ideas about similarity of operations. Figure 6-5 gives another example of an advance organizer, this one in biological science.

To return for a moment to the seventh feature listed in Figure 6-1 (intellectual substance), notice that each of the examples included as Figures 6-2 through 6-5 contain content with considerable intellectual substance. For a negative example, a statement with little intellectual substance, suppose we

FIGURE 6-4

Advance organizer for a science unit: Engines.

In our last lesson we learned about *piston engines*. For our next lesson we will study *turbine engines*. Piston engines and turbine engines have one important feature in common: combustion of fuel produces hot gases at high pressures. In our last lesson we learned that for piston engines to operate, *first*, a fuel must be burned at high pressure. *Second*, this burning or combustion creates hot gases under high pressure. This high pressure occurs in a restricted chamber. *Third*, under this pressure the hot gases expand and push against pistons. In this next lesson on turbine engines we will see that turbine engines work in very similar ways, but with one major difference. In this next lesson we will examine the operation of turbine engines by tracing these three similar operations, then investigate the major difference between the piston engine and the turbine engine.

FIGURE 6-5
Advance organizer for a science unit: Evolution.

Mammals, with their highly developed nervous systems and ingenious adaptations, represent the most highly evolved group in the animal kingdom. Their position was achieved by improvements along several key lines of development. As we studied in the preceding unit, reptiles offer a good example for showing the ways in which evolution occurs. For one, reptiles show significant *structural* changes such as tougher skin, better limb design and the forming of copulatory organs. These structural improvements lead to better *functionality*, including being able to survive away from water longer, move about faster, and reproduce more efficiently. Finally, from these structural and functional characteristics there developed many new *behavioral* adaptations, such as borrowing to maintain necessary body temperatures, playing dead to ward off predators and mating rituals for attracting the most desirable mates. Viewing improvements as either *structural, functional or behavioral* adaptations offers a helpful classification scheme for the kinds of changes that commonly take place. In the next unit we will see how mammals developed along very similar evolutionary lines.

had begun this chapter with a paragraph containing this: "In the last chapter we discussed concept mapping by presenting sections including 'overview,' 'research and development,' 'designers' guide,' 'hybridization' and 'summary.' As we present the advance organizer here in Chapter 6 we will follow the same format." Rehashing main entries such as these does not meet the standard of intellectual substance.

BACKGROUND AND RESEARCH

In this section we discuss the background and research on the advance organizer. Research on organizer effects on learning has been conducted in several knowledge domains including social studies, science, mathematics and religion. Subjects in these studies range from third graders through college graduates. Also the research has been done with high, average and low ability levels.

David P. Ausubel, one of the more influential scholars in applied cognitive psychology, developed a theory of meaningful verbal learning (Ausubel, 1968; Ausubel & Robinson, 1969). Called *subsumption theory*, its main ideas are concerned with how a person's prior knowledge and its organization determine learning. During meaningful learning the person organizes, or "subsumes" or incorporates, the new knowledge into old knowledge. The advance organizer operates as a schema.

Within Ausubel's theory, *if* there is previously relevant knowledge held by the learner, *if* the material is logical and *if* the person intends to learn the material in a meaningful way, then meaningful learning will occur. If these conditions are not met, learning will be very difficult, usually rote and of short duration. When these conditions are not met, students typically memorize in an unmeaningful way, make few attempts to incorporate the material into their schemas and usually forget quickly what they do learn.

The primary practical implication of subsumption theory has become the use of the advance organizer, originally reported in Ausubel (1960). In this study college students were given material on the metallurgical properties of steel. The advance organizer had material on the similarities and differences between metals and alloys and their advantages and disadvantages. The material was general and abstract. The advance organizer was presented before the instruction. Recall of the material was apparently aided by the presentation of the advance organizer.

Reviews of Research

Since this original study there have been dozens of research efforts. Some experimenters have found that advance organizers do improve learning, and some have found that advance organizers do not. It is fortunate that there are a meta-analysis (Luiten, Ames, & Ackerson, 1980) and two very substantial and systematic reviews of this research, one by Barnes and Clawson (1975) and a more recent one by Mayer (1979). Barnes and Clawson (1975) reported that, of 32 studies conducted between 1960 and 1974, 12 found significant effects on learning and 20 found no significant effects. In a search for patterns among the studies which might reveal reasons for the inconsistency among findings, these reviewers categorized studies by length of treatment (one day to more than ten days), by ability level of students (high, average and low), by age of subjects (elementary through college graduates) and by subject areas (social studies, mathematics and science). There were no discernible patterns of effects for studies within these categories.

Barnes and Clawson concluded their review with a number of recommendations for further research. The most important of these include more attention to possible long-term effects, examination of possible effects on learning at all levels of the cognitive domain (e. g., fact learning, applications, problem solving, analysis and synthesis), greater fidelity to the features of the organizer espoused by Ausubel, improved operational definitions, extensions into more subject matter areas and more research with all grade levels. These recommendations seem to be based on the idea that the advance organizer did have some potential for meaningful learning and the belief that the characteristics of advance organizers as stated by Ausubel (see Figure 6-1)—abstraction, generality and inclusiveness—may not have been reflected in all of the studies reviewed. Their review helped to stimulate debate (Lawton & Wanska, 1977; Ausubel, 1978), further review (Mayer, 1979) and research which has, on balance, revealed the strengths and weaknesses of the advance organizer. Further research has shown the conditions under which advance organizers can improve learning.

Further debate and clarification make it apparent that an abstract introduction meeting the characteristics of an organizer will not act as an advance organizer *unless students have the prior knowledge necessary.* Possible effects attendant to subsuming or assimilation could not occur. Many of the studies in the literature, therefore, may not be adequate tests of organizer effects.

In his review (Mayer, 1979) adds several other conditions for adequate experimental control and testing of the effects of organizers. Among these conditions are whether or not students in the experiments had other subsuming strategies available to them and whether or not those students actually used those available. This availability/use of other subsumer aids is especially important when the new material is difficult to relate to the existing knowledge of the student. In other words, advance organizers should aid learning for difficult-to-assimilate (relate) new information for students who have no other or use no other subsuming strategy (Mayer, 1975). Without adequate control of the availability/use of other subsumer aids by subjects it is impossible to determine organizer effects.

Another condition highlighted by Mayer (1979) is that many of the studies, perhaps because they were not conceived in close harmony with Ausubel's subsumption theory, were not sensitive to what was learned in the experiment. In many of the studies the amount recalled was measured with no sensitivity to the fact that *the strength of the organizer is in long-term recall and transfer of general concepts.* Mayer (1979) cites several studies in which general concept recall was measured, and in these studies organizers did have significant effects.

For their meta-analysis Luiten, Ames and Ackerson (1980) examined 135 published and unpublished studies of the advance organizer. Meta-analysis, a recently developed technique of averaging effects across studies and attending particularly to studies with powerful effects, is a robust supplement to the logical analysis, synthesis and criticism of studies typically done in other types of reviews. These scholars conclude that there is a small but facilitative effect of the advance organizer on learning and memory. Furthermore, this effect extends across age of subjects and subject matter fields. In addition, they conclude that the organizer effect increases with time; that is, when the instruction in the experiment extends to several days or weeks as compared to a few hours, the retention effects are stronger.

Research

In a series of investigations particularly designed in terms of the features of the organizer, including its subsuming effects and its strengths as an aid to the learning of general concepts, Mayer and his colleagues (Mayer, 1975; 1976; Mayer, Stiel, & Greeno, 1975; Mayer & Bromage, 1978) demonstrated positive effects on learning. In Mayer (1975) college freshmen studied a ten-page text on computer programming. The experimental group had an advance organizer while the control group did not. The experimental group did better on *far transfer,* recall of items not in the text; but the controls did better on *near transfer,* recall of items in the text. Similar findings were noted by Mayer (1976) and Mayer and Bromage (1978).

In these two studies the experimental groups received the organizer before reading the text while the control groups read the text first and then received the organizer. Again, as in Mayer (1975), the experimental groups did better on far transfer, and the control groups did better on near transfer. Thus the problem of double exposure was controlled because both experimentals and controls read both the organizer and the text. Other data in the Mayer and Bromage (1978) study revealed that the before-text (experimental) group was superior in idea units recalled and in relating the material to new ideas. These investigators believe that the organizers presented before the text provided aid for encoding general principles which resulted in breadth of transfer that extended beyond merely recall of immediately following instructional material.

In a test of this belief Mayer (1978) varied the text presented by giving one group a randomly ordered (unfriendly) text and another group the same text, logically ordered. The organizer aided recall for the group which read the randomly ordered text, but not for those who read the logically ordered text. Apparently the organizer provided the schema needed for assimilation, while the friendly (logically ordered) text provided its own schema for these undergraduate students. These undergraduate students perhaps did not need the help that an organizer might otherwise have provided. Mayer inferred that, when a text has logical order, students do not need the kind of help provided by an advance organizer. This could be true of subjects at the level of those in that specific study.

Other studies addressed to this question of possible effects of the advance organizer when the text is varied (orderly vs. random) and when more is known about subjects' prior knowledge and relevant schemas suggest an increasingly complex picture about effects of advance organizers on different students and for different kinds of text (subject matter) (Siu, 1986; Mannes & Kintsch, 1987). Siu (1986) did control for subjects' prior knowledge, but failed to find positive effects for what was labeled an advance organizer. That organizer, however, was presented *after* the experimental materials; furthermore, Siu speculates that organizers which are beyond students' comprehension are distracting.

The series of studies by Mannes and Kintsch (1987) is more on the mark of advance organizer by text organization interaction and a better test of organizer effects, because the organizer was presented before the lesson and care was taken that subjects knew the material in the organizer. In experiment one, subjects studied an outline which provided background knowledge before reading the experimental material. One group studied an organizer (outline) which was consistent with the text and another group an organizer which was inconsistent with the order of the text. Recall of textual materials was measured in a variety of ways: a written summary of the article, true-false items, reproduction of a paragraph from the text, a problem-solving task, and ranking of the adequacy of some alternative solutions to that problem. Half the students in each group were tested immediately on these five subtests, and half were tested two days after the materials were studied. Students who had the organizer which was consistent with the text did better on the subtests of the written summary, the true-false items and the paragraph reproduction. Students who had the inconsistent outline performed better on the problem-solving task and the ranking of alternative solutions.

These findings show interaction between organizers and text. A second experiment was done to determine possible effects of the organizer alone: subjects studied one or the other of the outlines used in experiment one. The subtests were the same as in experiment one. The pattern of results was very unlike those of experiment one, so the experimenters conclude that studying a text which is inconsistent with a student's background induces kinds of processing that are different from those induced by consistency. Inconsistency produces the kinds of processing which aids problem solving whereas consistency induces processing which aids recall.

To check effects of the text alone, a third experiment was conducted which was similar to experiment one with only the outline omitted. Performance on the subtests was substantially lower as was the case in experiment two (outline only). The investigators could conclude, therefore, that the findings attendant with experiment one are attributable to the interaction between the forms of the outlines and the text. Having text consistent with organizers induces different intellectual processing than does having inconsistent organizers.

Thus it seems that similar material organized in two different ways (organizer plus text structure) increases the probability of retrieving information necessary for inference and problem solving. Consistency of organizer and text, on the other hand, helped students to understand the text more easily and remember it better.

Two additional points about this series of experiments may help to clarify some of the inconsistencies in the advance organizer research. First, care was taken that the organizer contained relevant background knowledge. Second, the material was sufficiently difficult to challenge the subjects so that strategic aid in the form of an organizer had the possibility of making a difference. Both are basic to any possibility of organizer effects on learning.

The findings of Mannes and Kintsch (1987) and those of Mayer (1976, 1978) and Mayer and Bromage (1978) are very difficult to reconcile. Mannes and Kintsch varied the organizers, while Mayer (1978) varied the text (random vs. logical), which contributes to the difficulty of comparison. Different organizers, different subjects and different texts may contribute to the problem of reconciliation of these mixed findings.

In addition to research on advance organizers which are paragraph-length passages designed and intended for prose learning, there is research on preorganizers (sometimes labeled advance organizers) which are pictorial or lists of ideas (Arnold & Brooks, 1976; Bransford & Johnson, 1972; Dean & Enemoh, 1983; Dean & Kulhavy, 1981; Lane, Newman, & Bull, 1988; Tajika, Taniguchi, Yamamoto, & Meyer, 1988). We feel that such preorganizers, while they may be very effective, are more precisely thought of as framing (Lane, Newman, & Bull, 1988) or illustration studies (Arnold & Brooks, 1976; Bransford & Johnson, 1972; Dean & Enemoh, 1983; Dean & Kulhavy, 1981; Tajika, Taniguchi, Yamamoto, & Meyer, 1988). Efforts such as these may lead to types of preorganizers that are effective for learning and retention of subject matter which is other than verbal.

Research Summary

Ausubel's (1968) subsumption theory and subsequent research on the advance organizer has revealed much about the characteristics of organizers, the conditions under which they can be expected to aid learning and the instructional purposes toward which they should be directed (provision of schema or conceptual basis for assimilation, aiding recall of unfriendly text and aiding recall and transfer of general concepts). Researchers have also revealed that whether or not the advance organizer does aid learning is dependent on a number of variables. These variables include the particular learner (whether the student knows the material in the organizer and whether the learner already has an alternative schema which is used to assimilate the subject matter which follows the advance organizer) and the specific attributes of the text to be learned (such as whether or not the text is structured along the same lines as the organizer). Each of these seems to be very important, and all probably interact. Further research may resolve the inconsistencies of findings, but at this time it is highly probable that positive effects will likely occur when an advance organizer is developed according to the recommendations in the following section; when it is designed with precision in terms of the features stated in Figure 6-1, which are harmonious with Ausubel's subsumption theory; when the material is difficult for the target students; and when students are thought not to have other schemas which may better serve their learning.

DESIGNERS' GUIDE

In this section we review the conditions under which advance organizers are appropriate (please see Figure 6-6) and discuss the development and use of advance organizers. In the first section procedures are presented which, if implemented, should capitalize on the strengths of the organizer. In the second subsection we present a supplementary mechanism which, if used during instruction, should mitigate the primary weakness of the organizer.

Before getting into the development of advance organizers please examine Figure 6-6. Notice that there are only a few important specifications, such as abstractness and medium to low data tonnage. Discussions throughout the chapter are explanations of these specifications. Readers may wish to review some of these discussions.

How to Develop Advance Organizers

The advance organizer can typically only be developed (see Figure 6-7 for a list of steps) after deciding on the content of the lesson or unit, outlining the major ideas and developing the major objectives for the lesson or unit, if

FIGURE 6-6
Specifications for advance organizer.

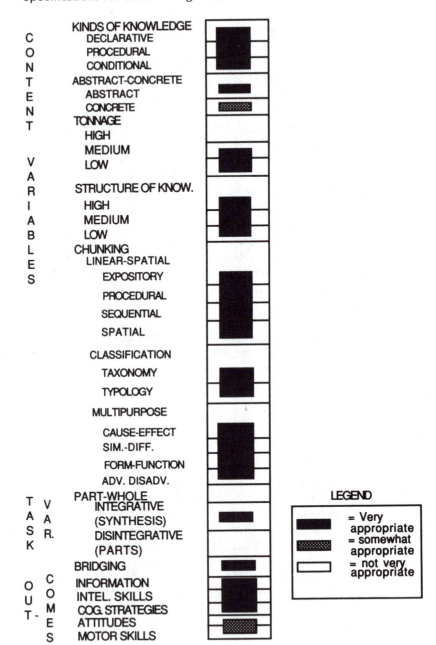

FIGURE 6-7

Procedures for developing and using advance organizers.

1. Examine the new lesson or unit to discover necessary prerequisite knowledge. List.
2. Find out if students know this prerequisite material.
3. Reteach* if necessary.
4. List or summarize the major general principles or ideas in the new lesson or unit (could be done first).
5. Write a paragraph (the advance organizer) emphasizing the major general principles, *similarities across old and new topics*. Examine examples in this text. Use them as models.
6. The main subtopics of the unit or lesson should be covered in the same sequence as they are presented in the advance organizer.

* Because teachers have more complete access to students than experimenters do, this step is more likely to occur in actual instruction than in experimentation and, thus, the organizer is likely to aid learning.

objectives are considered necessary. The initial step should be carefully examining the content of the lesson to determine what knowledge is prerequisite to comprehension of the main ideas, facts, procedures, concepts or principles. List these.

The second step is to find out whether the major ideas, facts and so forth which are prerequisite to the lesson are known by the students. This analysis can be based on the content of previous lessons and associated materials and prior test performance. This may be the important missing piece contributing to the inconsistency of findings in the research. Researchers have not always determined if students had the prior knowledge. Should the designer not have access to tests taken by the students, a pretest may be necessary.

If most students do not have the prior knowledge, that knowledge should be taught before presentation of the new lesson or unit. A brief review may suffice. This knowledge is a prerequisite for advance organizer use. It is important to recognize that designers and teachers have more opportunity to be aware of their students' prior knowledge than the typical researcher. In continuing education, for example, the knowledge an existing staff would have about an old procedure or system could be easily determined and used as the basis for the organizer. *The failure of the learner to possess the prior relevant knowledge has been a major variable in many failures of advance organizers.*

In a brief abstract statement, summarize or list the main ideas known which are pertinent to the new lesson. Be sure to review the features of the organizer listed in Figure 6-1. These main ideas, common general principles or concepts can then be written in a paragraph form which will be presented to students as the advance organizer. Remember to present it before the main body of the lesson or unit.

The main ideas in the subsequent unit or lesson should follow the same sequence in which the ideas are presented in the advance organizer. Remember that the advance organizer is the bridge between what the students know and what they are learning!

Supplementation of Organizers

We believe that the advance organizer is likely to work best when used to introduce units and lessons subsequent to some instruction in a topic because this increases the probability that students will use what they know about a topic. Remember that one of the primary conditions for an advance organizer to work is that learners must know the abstract ideas within the organizer.

In the final analysis, an advance organizer depends on the existence of similarities from something known to something new. Notice that, for examples, each of the illustrative organizers in this chapter (Figures 6-2 to 6-5) lists similarities about governments (Figure 6-2), wars (Figure 6-3) and science topics (Figures 6-4 and 6-5). Because the new topic contains new knowledge about similarities, because there will also be differences between the old topic and the new topic and because these similarities and differences will be elaborated, a designer will need a strategy for supplementation.

For this purpose we recommend a multipurpose frame which can be used in the body (as opposed to the introduction) of the unit or lesson. Notice that in Figure 6-8 there are slots for completion in which similarities and differences could be recorded. These similarities and differences may be subdivided into attributes, relationships or functions. Such a spatial display will be a helpful device for recording and organizing the subtle differences and the elaboration of similarities and differences which are the substance of further instruction on a topic.

The use of this frame may also bolster retention of minor details and technical facts which may be "obliterated" by sole reliance on advance organiz-

FIGURE 6-8
A frame to be used to supplement advance organizers.

	Old Topic	New Topic
Similarities Attributes		
Relationships or Functions		
Differences Attributes		
Relationships or Functions		

ers. It is likely that the strength of organizers is aiding learning and recall of general concepts (Merrill & Stolurow, 1966; Grotelueschen & Sjogren, 1968; Scandurda & Wells, 1967), but the weakness may be the masking of detail. When organizers "work" to aid assimilation, *obliterative subsumption* may occur; that is, minor detail and technical facts may be lost during assimilation. Using this multipurpose frame enables reemphasis and further processing of detail through rehearsal so that detail adjudged to be important will not be lost. Such a frame may also provide yet another "organizer" (but not an advance organizer) in addition to the advance organizer and the text structure itself which can further aid learning, transfer and problem solving. If two organizers can be desirable (Battig, 1979; Mannes & Kintsch, 1987) perhaps three can be even better. It is generally thought that multiple processing is very desirable, particularly for such outcomes as far transfer, problem solving, analysis and synthesis.

HYBRIDIZATION

The advance organizer is "naturally" hybridized with a number of other cognitive strategies. It will inevitably be combined with rehearsal when students study it carefully. Some of the content of the advance organizer may lend itself to imagery, although the content is by definition abstract. Some students may use mnemonics although the material is expected to be so meaningful that mnemonics should not be necessary.

Should the designer follow the recommendations here about the generic frame, in which similarities and differences of the old (known) topic to the new topic are spatially displayed, framing is obviously combined. Then, of course, the frame as a product must be studied by some form of rehearsal.

SUMMARY

In this chapter we have discussed the bridging strategy, advance organizer. While the literature contains mixed findings about its instructional effectiveness, researchers have established that advance organizers are powerful design tools when definite conditions are met. It should not be surprising that there are such conditions for there are probably no "design tools" which are free of constraints, no cognitive strategies which work for all materials under all conditions.

In the discussion of the design uses of the advance organizer we have used the metaphor of "spanning a chasm" from what a student knows to new knowledge. Even the idea of a family of bridging strategies is a metaphor. In the following chapter we present explicitly the research and design uses of the other member of that family, metaphor.

EXERCISES

1. Carefully review Figures 6-1 and 6-7. Try writing an advance organizer which could be used for Chapter 4. It should be based on the similarities between a matrix type of frames, type one, and frames, type two. Use the examples of advance organizers in Figures 6-2, 6-3, and 6-4 as guides.

OR

2. Do you think that an advance organizer (meeting all the features in Figure 6-1) for Chapter 4 is possible? Why or why not? How about the next chapter?

REFERENCES

Anderson, T. H., Armbruster, B. B., & Kantor, R. N. (1980). How clearly written are children's textbooks? Or of bladderworts and Alfa. (Reading Education Report No. 16). University of Illinois at Urbana-Champaign, Center for the Study of Reading.

Arnold, D. E., & Brooks, P. H. (1976). Influences of contextual organizing material on children's listening comprehension. *Journal of Educational Psychology, 68,* 711–716.

Ausubel, D. P. (1960). The use of advance organizer in the learning and retention of meaningful verbal material. *Journal of Educational Psychology, 51,* 267–272.

Ausubel, D. P. (1968). *Educational psychology: A cognitive view.* New York: Holt, Rinehart & Winston.

Ausubel, D. P., & Robinson, F. G. (1969). *School learning.* New York: Holt, Rinehart & Winston.

Ausubel, D. E. (1978). In defense of advance organizers: A reply to critics. *Review of Educational Research, 48,* 251–257.

Barnes, B. R., & Clawson, E. U. (1975). Do advance organizers facilitate learning? Recommendations for further research based on an analysis of 32 studies. *Review of Educational Research, 45,* 637–659.

Battig, W. F. (1979). The flexibility of human memory. In L. S. Cermak & F. I. M. Craik (Eds.), *Levels of processing in human memory.* Hillsdale, NJ: Lawrence Erlbaum Associates.

Bransford, J. D., & Johnson, M. K. (1972). Contextual prerequisites for understanding: Some investigations of comprehension and recall. *Journal of Verbal Learning and Verbal Behavior, 11,* 717–726.

Dean, R. S., & Enemoh, P. A. C. (1983). Pictorial organization in prose learning. *Contemporary Educational Psychology, 8,* 20–27.

Dean, R. S., & Kulhavy, R. W. (1981). The influence of spatial organization in prose learning. *Journal of Educational Psychology, 73,* 57–64.

Grotelueschen, A., & Sjogren, D. D. (1968). Effects of differentially structured introductory materials and learning tasks on learning and transfer. *American Educational Research Journal, 5,* 191–202.

Kantor, R. S., Anderson, T. H., & Armbruster, B. B. (1983). How considerate are children's textbooks? *Journal of Curriculum Studies, 15,* 61–72.

Lane, D. S., Jr., Newman, D. L., & Bull, K. S. (1988). The relationship of student interest and advance organizer effectiveness. *Contemporary Educational Psychology, 13,* 15–25.

Lawton, J. T., & Wanska, S. K. (1977). Advance organizers as a teaching strategy. *Review of Educational Research, 47*, 233–244.

Luiten, J., Ames, W., & Ackerson, G. (1980). A meta-analysis of the effects of advance organizers on learning and retention. *American Educational Research Journal, 17*, 211–218.

Mannes, S. M., & Kintsch, W. (1987). Knowledge organization and text organization. *Cognition and Instruction, 4*, 91–115.

Mayer, R. E. (1975). Different problem solving competencies established in learning computer programming with and without meaningful models. *Journal of Educational Psychology, 67*, 725–734.

Mayer, R. E. (1976). Some conditions of meaningful learning of computer programming: Advance organizers and subject control of frame sequencing. *Journal of Educational Psychology, 68*, 143–150.

Mayer, R. E., Stiehl, C. C., & Greeno, J. G. (1975). Acquisition of understanding and skill in relation to subject's preparation and meaningfulness of instruction. *Journal of Educational Psychology, 67*, 331–350.

Mayer, R. E. (1978). Can advance organizers counter the effects of text organization? Paper presented at the annual meeting of the American Educational Research Association, Toronto, Canada.

Mayer, R. E., & Bromage, B. (1978). Effects of advance organizers on the pattern of recall protocols. Paper presented at the annual meeting of the American Educational Research Association, Toronto, Canada.

Mayer, R. E. (1979). Can advance organizers influence meaningful learning? *Review of Educational Research, 49*, 371–383.

Merrill, M. D., & Stolurow, L. M. (1966). Hierarchical preview vs. problem oriented review in learning an imaginary science. *Journal of Educational Psychology, 3*, 251–261.

Scandura, J. M., & Wells, J. N. (1967). Advance organizers in learning abstract mathematics. *American Educational Research Journal, 4*, 295–301.

Siu, P. K. (1986). Understanding Chinese prose: Effects of number of ideas, metaphor, and advance organizers on comprehension. *Journal of Educational Psychology, 78*, 417–423.

Tajika, H., Taniguchi, A., Yamamoto, K., & Mayer, R. E. (1988). Effects of pictorial advance organizers on passage retention. *Contemporary Educational Psychology, 13*, 133–139.

Metaphor, Analogy and Simile

In this and the preceding chapter we discuss two cognitive strategies which serve as bridging mechanisms between prior knowledge and new knowledge. In Chapter 6 on the advance organizer we saw how one can design a prose passage which, because it is abstract, may serve this bridging function. In this chapter metaphors will be discussed.

There are interesting similarities and differences between advance organizers and metaphors. Functionally, as we have said, both are strategies which help learners transfer prior knowledge to another topic. Both are based on similarities across topics. Major differences are:

1. *Inclusiveness*: Advance organizers generally supply more information explicitly than metaphors.

2. *Denotation*: Advance organizers signify similarities explicitly, whereas metaphors usually signify via connotation. Without metaphor subtle, connotative meanings are not emphasized adequately (Baldwin, Ford, & Readence, 1981).

3. *Origins of the prior knowledge*: Most often advance organizers are designed after instruction on a topic to achieve the bridging effect to new information, so that the designer or teacher is more confident that students have at least had the opportunity of learning the similarities on which the advance organizer is based. In contrast, metaphorical familiarity is often based on general background knowledge.

4. *Definitiveness*: Similarities are stated in advance organizers for the bridging, subsuming effect, and differences are left for emphasis during the instruction which follows. In metaphor, in the absence of elaboration or

systematic instructional design, students may be aware of only one of many similarities and may mentally focus on differences, to the detriment of bridging.

5. *Imageability*: Good metaphors, good in the sense of effectiveness in instructional design and quality literature, are *often* rich in imagery (Ortony, 1975) and concreteness. Advance organizers are verbal, abstract and, thus, less likely to lend themselves to imagery. This is not to say that imagery is not possible with advance organizer use.

6. *Figurative-literal language*: Advance organizers most often consist of literal language, whereas metaphors consist of figurative language.

In this chapter we present further material which will expand on these attributes of metaphor. In the section immediately following, examples of metaphor are presented along with some definitions which are critical to understanding the place of metaphor in instructional design.

INTRODUCTION

The extensive use of metaphor in Western prose and poetry has delighted untold generations of literature professors and sometimes, because of the subtlety or datedness of the metaphor, profoundly confused as many generations of their students. An obscure or dated metaphor does not aid comprehension. Indeed, an obscure metaphor may interfere with learning by becoming yet another complex idea to study in an already challenging array. On the other hand, metaphors which are chosen and presented specifically to aid intellectual processing are among the more useful cognitive strategies (Royer, 1986). More than a trope, more than literary "icing" and more than a primary device in poetic expression, metaphor may be intrinsic to comprehension. At least it is seen so by some modern cognitive scientists (Lakoff & Johnson, 1980).

Cognitive psychologists generally have not researched differences among metaphor, analogy and simile but rather have treated them as a unity. These are each figures of speech in which partial meaning in the form of similar attributes of one thing is transferred to something else. This common feature and the intellectual power of these figures of speech is such that, at this time, cognitive scientists as a rule are not yet intrigued by differences (Ortony, 1975). This is not to imply, however, that, as researchers continue, they will not discover some specific and unique functions for these close cousins.

Even though most cognitive psychologists have not researched differences among these types of figures of speech, some have recognized those differences (for example, Baldwin, Luce and Readence, 1982) so it may be helpful to distinguish among these close cousins. To promote understanding about glacial movement and its effects on the land, for example, Farb (1963, p. 10–12; please see Box 7-1) explains the movement of glaciers as flowing like batter on a griddle and that the glacier was a "monumental plow upon the

Although temperatures plummeted during the glacial epochs, extraordinary cold is not necessary for the formation of a glacier. All that is required is that more snow fall during the winter than is melted during the summer. Seen under a microscope, a fresh snowflake has a delicate six-pointed shape. At first the flakes collect in fluffy masses, separated from each other by their points. But as the water of which they are composed evaporates, these points are lost. The flakes become rounded and thus fit together more closely, in the same way that *marbles fit more closely into a jar than do jagged pieces of rock*. As additional snow falls, the flakes become packed together. The flakes begin to merge, first into clusters, then into chunks, until under the weight of additional snow they are all compressed into ice.

Thus year by year, inch by inch, a towering mound of ice several miles high was built up. Eventually, a time came at which the mound began to spread outward, *flowing in much the same way as a thick batter dropped on a griddle*. Under its own massive weight, the ice mound behaved rather more in the manner of a liquid than of a solid. As the ice kept accumulating, the mound went on spreading outward; it radiated over North America.

The moving wall of ice, which at times pushed forward at the speed of a foot a day, altered everything in its path. It ripped out immense boulders and used them as *sandpaper* to scrape off the thin veneer of soil. The glacier was like a *monumental plow* upon the land . . .

From Peter Farb, *Face of North America*. New York: Harper & Row, 1963, pp. 10–12. Reprinted by permission of Evelyn Singer Agency. (Italics added.)

land." If Farb had written, "The glacier is flowing potato pancake batter," the statement would be a metaphor. Written as they are, ". . . flowing in much the same way as a thick batter dropped on a griddle" and ". . . like a monumental plow upon the land . . .," the statements are similes. If he had stated, "The glacier gouged as if it were a monumental plow upon the land," it would be an analogy. Thus, metaphor is a figure of speech in which there is more equivalence between the known and the supposedly unknown than is true of the analogy and the simile. This equivalence is expressed as "is": the glacier *is* a plow. In the analogy the relationship is typically expressed as an "as if" or "is to" relationship: glaciers are to terrain as plows are to farmers' fields, whereas in the simile, the relationship is expressed with "is like" or "is similar to" statements.

Notice the richness of the metaphors contained in the brief passage in Box 7-1. Most are relatively *concrete* and thus lend themselves to imagery. Many readers would be familiar with marbles, rocks, batter on a griddle and plows; so the metaphors are likely to be *meaningful*. When Farb writes of glaciers moving like batter on a griddle, it may elicit from memory observations and other experiential content from days long past when hungry youths peeked over edges of skillets sizzling with potato pancake batter.

Such evoked memories frequently extend beyond recall and transfer of mere information about attributes which are similar. Ortony (1975) states that experiences may be reconstructed mentally by the metaphor. This reconstruction includes shared characteristics rich with detail and, perhaps, emotions connected with the reconstructed experience. Ortony (1975) is probably correct in arguing that metaphor is more than an interesting but often weak or, worse, confusing substitute for literal explanations, and that, in specific instances, metaphors can often convey more cognitive and affective meanings than could literal language. That is, there are occasions when figurative language is more powerful than literal language—both intellectually and emotionally. The use of metaphor in poetry, fiction and other literary forms is testimony to this power and to the strategic cognitive sophistication of those who write successfully in those forms.

Continuing with the use of the Farb excerpt, two important concepts in the instructional uses of metaphor are topic and vehicle. The *topic* is the new material or concept. The *vehicle* is the supposedly known material or concept. Thus the topics in the excerpt by Farb are the fitting together of round pieces of snow, glacial flow and boulders reshaping terrain. The vehicles, in respective order, are fitting together like marbles, batter on a griddle and sandpaper combined with plow. For a metaphor to aid communication or comprehension, obviously, the listener or student must have knowledge of the vehicle in order to transfer the knowledge to the topic.

Other concepts which are important in the literature on metaphor are figurative and literal. *Figurative language or meaning* is hypothetical and nonstandard in that it is a violation of accepted categories or concepts. Often based on secondary definitions, figurative expression is elaborative, connotative and associative. *Literal language or meaning*, by contrast, is based on primary definitions and adheres to ordinary constructions: it is based on denotative, exact or conventionally accepted classes and concepts.

These definitions help to distinguish between metaphors and literal statements, but the difference between figurative and literal and what is a metaphor and what is not is sometimes unclear. Sometimes it is difficult to be certain if a statement is to be taken in the metaphorical, or figurative, sense (Rumelhart, 1979) as opposed to the literal. As an example of lack of clarity consider the use of the word *veneer* in the Farb passage. "A thin covering" is one of the secondary meanings of the word *veneer*, but does this fact determine that it is used in a metaphorical sense? That is a difficult question. For the purposes of this text, perhaps it is best to recognize that the boundaries between figurative speech and literal speech are fogged (Vosniadou, 1987).

This lack of clear boundaries between some metaphorical and literal usages on which adults cannot agree has caused some problems for researchers. One such problem is knowing whether children are using metaphor or is it that they just do not know the literal, conventional speech and categories so that what may appear to be a juxtaposition is really ignorance of standard meanings and categories.

While cognitive scientists are rightly more concerned with the similarity of metaphor, analogy and simile—because of their intellectual power as devices to aid comprehension—than they are with the differences; they also, as a rule, are not concerned with the issue of the truth or falseness of any particular metaphor, analogy or simile. In logic the truth of an analogy is an issue. In cognitive science a more important issue is: Does it aid comprehension? By contrast, in logic, often the analogy is used in argument so truth is critical. In cognitive science the metaphor or analogy is to be judged as theory is to be judged in science: Does it function? Does it aid understanding?

As we have emphasized, one of the most important problems in instruction is how to get students to be aware of what they know and then apply or transfer that knowledge to something new. A major strategy is metaphor or analogy or simile. A substantial research effort has been mounted within the last decade or so to construct how these are used in learning and how to use them systematically during instruction (Ortony, 1979; Santostefano, 1985; Vosniadou, 1987). We now turn to a discussion of this research.

RESEARCH ON METAPHOR

In this section we discuss developmental research on the onset and relative consolidation of the figurative abilities. Following that is a discussion of some of the experiments on the instructional uses of metaphor.

For uses in instructional design there are at a minimum two important considerations about metaphor which are critical. First, *metaphors can often convey meaning of some material as well and as rapidly as literal language*. Second, *metaphor is a cognitive strategy shared across age; certainly its strategic use extends from the middle years of elementary age children through adulthood*. In the following two subsections some of the research on these considerations is discussed.

Development

In a recent review Vosniadou (1987) discussed the research on children's use of metaphor. According to her analysis of a considerable body of research, evidence exists for use of metaphor by children as young as four years of age (Vosniadou & Ortony, 1983; Vosniadou, Ortony, Reynolds, & Wilson, 1984), five years of age (Malgady, 1977), six years of age (Winner, Engel, & Gardner, 1980), and seven years of age (Reynolds & Ortony, 1980; Nippold, Leonard, & Kail, 1984; Honeck, Sowry, & Voegtle, 1978). It should be understood, however, that exactly when metaphorical abilities emerge is contentious, and that there are likely to be considerable individual differences in the age at which they develop to the point that they can be observed.

Assuming that metaphorical abilities emerge during ages four to eight, when may instructional designers and teachers expect that these abilities become relatively well developed? Some research on this question (Billow, 1975; Cometa & Eson, 1978) provides mixed evidence. Billow (1975) places well-developed metaphorical ability prior to the concrete operations period (age seven) of Inhelder and Piaget (1964). Cometa and Eson (1978); Marsh, Desberg and Cooper (1977); and Marsh, Friedman, Desberg and Saterdahl (1981) believe it is developed during the concrete operations period (ages 7–12). Any exact answer to this question is not possible at this time.

Not only are there individual differences in the pace of the development of metaphorical skills, there are also differences within the same individual as to which metaphors may be comprehended (Vosniadou, Ortony, Reynolds, & Wilson, 1984; Billow, 1975; Cometa & Eson, 1978). While these experiments are with preadolescents, individual differences may be expected across age.

Some of the contention about development, as Vosniadou (1987) states, is that it can be difficult, particularly for judging metaphorical use by children, to determine whether an utterance is an instance of metaphor or a crossing of conventional meaning boundaries by ignorance or mistake. The determination is made even more difficult when adults, who make the judgment, cannot agree in those foggy instances such as the use of *veneer* in Box 7-1. These difficulties create problems in the determination of when the development of metaphorical skills becomes apparent and when the skills are more or less fully developed.

Vosniadou's primary thesis in her review (1987) is that metaphorical competence is based on ability to perceive similarities among objects. This ability is not only critical for categorization, but also for metaphorical production. Since metaphors are the crossing of conventional categories based on one or more similarities, the user must perceive the similarities in both conventional categories and be aware that the objects or events belong to different conventional categories.

There are several reasons for contention about when figurative abilities appear and when they are relatively complete. These include individual differences within age, the individual differences across age and a number of technical issues which are involved in the measurement of other abilities and traits. Some of the technical problems entail sampling. Most of the studies are with a small number of nonrandomly chosen, intact groups. The context varies across the studies; the specific metaphors used vary, with some requiring more logical and more abstract operations than others; the relative difficulty of the metaphors used varies; knowledge of vehicle varies; and the response format varies. All these factors contribute to the contention.

Given these sources of difficulty, it is impossible to be exact about the developmental appearance and relative completion of figurative abilities. Large-scale testing of representative samples with carefully developed items would be necessary to resolve this. Inferences about IQ, however, are already being made in some of the standardized tests based on figurative items.

Despite these problems we believe that the development of both literal language skills and metaphorical language skills is interactive, gradual and coordinative. As children gradually learn both of these language skills, so much of which is category based, they "play" with both literal and metaphorical uses. They observe the communicative effects of both forms. They observe others using both forms. Progress in one promotes progress in the other. The social and intellectual climate contributes substantially to that growth.

This interactive, gradual and coordinative development should make it possible for instructional designers to use metaphors in systematic and cautious ways during the early elementary years. Gradually the complexity of metaphors used could increase during early adolescence, until during mid-adolescence, when figurative skills seem to be relatively well developed for most students.

Research Using Metaphor in Instruction

A primary assumption is that existence and knowledge of similarities between the vehicle and the topic are essential to correct interpretation of metaphor. This assumption was investigated by Baldwin, Luce and Readence (1982) with fifth- and sixth-grade students for both metaphor and simile. According to their results, knowledge of similarities is critical to the correct interpretation of both metaphor and simile.

Having the specific background knowledge is necessary for comprehension of metaphor, particularly when, as in the Baldwin, Luce, and Readence (1982) study, several metaphors are serially presented without context. That is, in that study there was no narrative or prose passage which set the background and from which readers might infer similarities basic to any metaphor contained in the passage. It is likely that context reduces to a degree the need for prior specific knowledge of similarities. While the following study is not a direct test of this, it does emphasize the importance of context.

Can children interpret and recall stories equally well when one version of a story has only literal statements and another version of the same story contains a metaphor? An experiment by Waggoner, Meese and Palermo (1985) provides insight into this question. The answer depends on a complex set of variables including age and context. In this study second-, fourth- and sixth-grade students heard some stories with and some without metaphor. The stories, while brief, set the context for both the literal statements and the metaphorical statements.

Having a complete story or other context, these authors (Waggoner, Meese, & Palermo, 1985) believe, is helpful if not essential to the comprehension of metaphor. They, therefore, provided the complete stories which established the background. (As an aside, it should be mentioned that even the meaning of literal statements is often gleaned or predicted from the context.) There were no significant differences between recall of literal and metaphorical counterparts in each grade; but there were differences among the grades in accuracy of recall, with older students recalling more than younger students.

Other studies have further established the importance of context and time in the interpretation of literal and metaphorical material (Ortony, Schallert, Reynolds, & Antos, 1978; Inhoff, Lima, & Carroll, 1984). With similar materials these researchers tested the role of time and context. The hypothesis in these studies is that when short, perhaps inadequate, context is provided, interpreting a metaphor takes more time as compared with a literal interpretation. Providing more extensive context results in no significant differences between the time taken to interpret literal and metaphorical passages.

It may be that comprehension of a metaphor isolated from context takes more time because the learner is more accustomed to literal text and thus has a set for literality for most material presented in academic situations. Or it may be that context is as important for literality as it is for figurative material but that the existing studies have inadequate controls for context with both types of material. Perhaps it takes a moment to break a set for literality—if the set is actually present. Further, when the metaphor is isolated, additional time is used in searching long-term memory for knowledge of similarities. When context is present, the context is searched more rapidly than is long-term memory. Furthermore, that search of context of metaphor may take no longer than a search of context of literality.

The question of metaphoric comprehension taking longer than literal comprehension was also investigated by Pollio, Fabrizi, Sills and Smith (1984). This study is also an investigation of the related idea that metaphorical comprehension is a multistep process. If the comprehension of metaphors takes more time, it is likely that it is a multistep process. That is to say, many steps should take more time than few steps.

According to Pollio, Fabrizi, Sills and Smith (1984), prior models of comprehension of literal and figurative language include four stages. First, a reader or listener attempts to interpret a message as containing new literal information—the aforementioned "set for literality." Should the message fail the test for new literal information a second stage is attempted, that of redundancy or analysis. (Is the message a repetition or a breaking into parts?) If the message does not pass this "test" the student moves to a third stage of interpretation of "Is this contradiction or nonsense?" Finally, if all these tests of the message fails, the fourth-stage attempt is made to interpret the message metaphorically.

Again, if the comprehension of figurative messages is a multistep procedure, it ought to take more time than the comprehension of literal statements. Pollio, Fabrizi, Sills and Smith (1984) researched this with reaction time in a series of six experiments with 20 undergraduate students in each experiment. Experimental messages consisted of five different types of sentences: synthetic, analytic, contradictory, anomalous and metaphoric. The results were interpreted to mean that metaphorical interpretation generally is not a multistage process and that interpretation of metaphor takes no longer than most literal material, except contradictory statements. The contradictory sentences were responded to most rapidly of all and were the least confused with other sentence types.

These studies allow the inference that, given reasonable context, metaphors can be processed as rapidly as literal material. Other research, such as Hayes and Henk (1986), discussed later in this chapter, has established that metaphor can have powerful effects on long-term recall.

Research Summary

In the preceding subsections we have established that metaphoric comprehension abilities extend from the early elementary school years through adulthood. We have also established that, given a reasonable context, metaphorical language can convey meaning as rapidly as several types of literal language. Obviously, further research is needed on many of the issues raised by the research discussed in this section. In the following section we discuss some of the special issues in instructional uses of metaphor.

SPECIAL ISSUES

As is the case with most of the research and literature on instructional uses of other cognitive strategies so also are there several interesting and complex issues on the use of metaphor, many of which are not adequately researched. In the following subsections we discuss briefly the issues of assimilation and accommodation (tuning and restructuring) types of metaphor; declarative, conditional and procedural knowledge; the seductive analogy; bridging; metaphor as a top-down strategy; and the relationship between imagery and analogy.

Assimilation and Accommodation

We have seen in Chapter 1 that most formal learning is assimilative learning rather than accommodative learning and that, when accommodative (Piaget, 1952) or reconstructive (Rumelhart & Norman, 1978) learning does occur, it is thought usually to proceed slowly. Petrie (1979), Carey (1985) and Vosniadou (1987), however, assign to metaphor a role that allows rapid accommodative learning. This accommodative role of metaphor may provide one of the most rapid forms of this type of learning. By using an appropriate metaphor to *create* an organized set of similarities in the minds of students, it may be that relatively large portions of information (similarities) may be juxtaposed from prior knowledge to a new area of knowledge, that is, an area of knowledge which is new to the student. Examined in the view of schema theory, this juxtaposition may induce a substantial and relatively rapid revision of a schema in a student's knowledge.

Suppose that, for example, a student had fair knowledge about the workings of a mechanical pump, but very limited and largely erroneous knowledge of the human heart. Further suppose that both sets of knowledge were organized into a bundle to the point that it would be permissible to think of knowledge of both the pump and heart as schematic knowledge. If the simile were used, "The human heart is like a pump," and if it were understood, the schema associated with the heart might be reconstructed (accommodation) quickly. Carey (1985) found that the metaphor of the human body as a machine worked in this restructuring fashion.

Are All Metaphors the Same?

Some of the complexities in the research may be attributable to wide variation within the category of communication traditionally lumped as figurative. It may be that there is as much variation in the figurative utterance as there is thought to be in the literal. There has been a temptation to sort figurative language by imageability, that is, some figures of speech have high imageability and others low; but that sorting is made complex by the recognition that the entire figurative statement may be rated on imageability. So also in metaphor the vehicle and topic may be rated separately for image value (Fainsilber & Kogan, 1984; Marschark & Hunt, 1985). These investigators have also examined several other attributes or dimensions of metaphors which reveal considerable variation within figurative language.

Cueing on other attributes, Petrie (1979) (see also Black, 1979; Levin, 1979; Searle, 1979) notes that there are two types of metaphor, comparative and interactive, distinguished seemingly in part on students' prior knowledge of similarities. According to Pietrie the *comparative metaphor* is an implicit statement that two apparently dissimilar objects do have common features. The comparative metaphor informs of similarities already known by extending similarities from vehicle to topic. The *interactive metaphor creates* similarities in the mind of the student between the vehicle and topic. It is the interactive metaphor, according to Pietrie, which allows accommodation or reconstruction, because it creates new cognitive structures around the topic.

One could also sort metaphors by their content, not by prior knowledge of students (Vosniadou, 1987; Gentner, 1983). These researchers distinguish between attribute metaphors and relational metaphors. *Attribute metaphors* are those which are based on physical or perceptual similarities. An example is "Pancakes are nickels." *Relational metaphors* are those which are based on abstract connections of a logical or natural character. An example is "The mind is a computer." Of course, a metaphor may be both, as in "Plant stems are drinking straws."

It seems that all metaphors are not the same. They could be chunked in a variety of ways. If it is true that some of the complexities in the research are caused by variation within figurative language, more systematic examinations of this variation would be helpful.

Declarative, Conditional and Procedural Knowledge

Metaphors may convey all three kinds of knowledge. Whether a metaphor is about declarative, conditional or procedural knowledge depends on the specific metaphor. For example, if it were said that Simon Bolivar was the George Washington of Venezuela, the knowledge would be declarative. If it were said that one organizes for a lab experiment as one arranges for baking in a kitchen, the knowledge would be procedural.

The "Seductive" Analogy

By their very nature analogies are likely to be oversimplifications and at best represent partial understanding of the topic (Spiro, Feltovich, Coulson, & Anderson, 1988). Their use may leave the student with the feeling that the topic is correctly understood, when in fact it is not. This is one of the dangers of instructional use of metaphors, a danger which is sufficient for some (for example, Green, 1979) to be unenthusiastic about metaphor as an instructional strategy.

It is true that there is some danger in the use of metaphor; but the utility of metaphor far outweighs the pitfalls. There are so few available bridging strategies that avoiding the systematic use of metaphor leaves the designer with too narrow a set of instructional tools. Since the dangers can be eluded through the systematic use of metaphor as recommended in the section following, the *Designers' Guide*, there are ample reasons to consider metaphor as an invaluable, often irreplaceable instructional tool.

Metaphor as the Multipurpose Bridging Strategy

One reason that metaphor is such a valuable cognitive strategy and instructional tool is that the other bridging strategies, advance organizer and frames, type two, require extensive designer preparation primarily because of their nature. There are also knowledge domain constraints. For the advance organizer, in most situations, the use is restricted to structuring similar material to follow material already covered, and hopefully known, by the target students. It lends itself to sequenced topics which contain several similarities. For frames, type two, a rich, complex array of prior knowledge is brought to bear—if it is being used and if it works for bridging. Also, it is important to remember that frames, type two, require well-structured knowledge.

In contrast, the metaphor is amenable to more uses in more knowledge domains. Most instructional material contains figurative language which may be adopted for use in design. While there is no all-purpose specific metaphor suitable across domains, each domain probably contains numerous metaphors from which designers can choose.

Metaphor is a Top-Down Strategy

One of the emphatic features of the cognitive revolution is that learning is usually top down (whole to part) as opposed to part to whole. Metaphor can generally be considered as a top-down strategy in that a set of connected ideas, concepts or propositions in the guise of similarities is juxtaposed from the vehicle to the topic. As lessons develop, however, some of the parts—the similarities—must be examined for further instructional processing.

Metaphors and Imagery

Is imagery necessary for comprehension of metaphor? While it is true that many metaphors contain vehicles and topics which are rich in evoking imagery, it is not true that all metaphors necessarily are, or that imagery is essential to the comprehension of metaphor.

Some insight into this question may be provided by investigation into the aesthetic *quality* of metaphors. Fainsilber and Kogan (1984) had college students rate with a six-point scale 75 metaphors on appropriateness, novelty and imageability. There seems to be a complex interaction among these three components of metaphoric quality. Novelty and imagery are negatively correlated. So also are novelty and appropriateness. Appropriateness and imagery, however, are positively correlated. Analyses other than simple correlation reveal that subjects do not describe quality in terms of imageability, but that imagery is critical to appropriateness. According to these authors quality is predicted best by appropriateness and novelty, rather than imagery.

Since the subjects in the Fainsilber and Kogan study rated a large number of metaphors (75) among which there was variability, some insight is provided on characteristics of metaphor which are rated highest and lowest on imagery. In those metaphors rated highest on imagery, both the vehicle and topic seem to be highly imageable, in contrast to those rated lowest, which seem to be more conceptual in nature. This finding lends support to the idea that metaphors may be intellectually processed either through imagery or verbally, depending partially, of course, on the characteristics of the specific metaphor.

Other research has been conducted on comprehension and recall. Marschark and Hunt (1985) conducted a series of three experiments on how metaphors are represented in memory and their influences on recall. Among ten dimensions or characteristics of metaphor which they consider important for comprehension and recall of metaphor are: imagery of vehicle, imagery of topic, imagery of metaphorical sentence, ease of interpretation, number of interpretations, semantic relatedness and familiarity. Recall was measured in two ways: free recall, in which subjects were asked to write the metaphor or any ideas or parts recalled (experiments 1 and 2) and free recall in addition to cued recall, that is, supplying the vehicle when the topic was given for some of the metaphors and supplying the topic when the vehicle was given for other metaphors (experiment 3).

The number of interpretations and the imageability of the topic were the most consistent predictors of recall. The imageability of vehicles was not a reliable predictor of recall. A large number of possible interpretations resulted in better free recall and worse cued recall as compared with few possible interpretations. The authors infer that when a variety of interpretations for a metaphor is available, the probability is increased that at least one can be recalled in a free recall task. In cued recall, however, the variety of interpretations causes interference.

It would be convenient, tidy and intellectually undemanding to believe that imagery and analogy are (or involve) separate encoding processes; each a single purpose tool for comprehension which learners select for appropriate tasks or materials to be learned. As tidy as it would be, it is not apparently true. Hayes and Henk (1986) examined the possible interactive effect of pictures (imagery) and text with and without analogy on immediate and delayed

FIGURE 7-1

Specifications for metaphor.

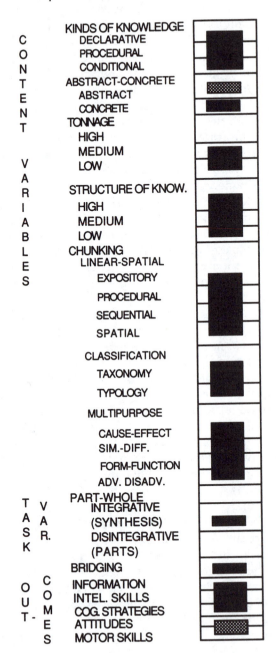

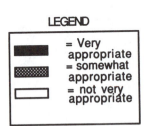

recall. The task of 102 high school subjects was to learn a procedure, tying a bowline knot. Analogy combined with imagery produced the highest mean delayed recall score of all treatments, but literal prose combined with imagery produced superior short-term recall. Incidentally, the analogy-only treatment produced better short-term and delayed recall than the literal-only treatment. Thus we see a complex interaction between literal versus figurative language and imagery.

While it is difficult, if not impossible, to integrate these findings, metaphor can be expected to interact with imagery, although the nature of the context and the material are critical. Depending on the specific metaphor, comprehension may or may not require imagery.

Despite the complexity, we have seen that metaphor has considerable potential as a strategy around which instruction can be designed. For accommodation, metaphor may accelerate what is normally very time consuming. Metaphor is one of few bridging mechanisms. It is less knowledge-domain constrained, and it seems to work for both procedural and declarative knowledge.

In the following section we present a *designers' guide*. In this section we attempt to draw practical inferences from research and emphasize implications for instructional design.

DESIGNERS' GUIDE

In this section we present a summary of the conditions under which metaphors are appropriate in Figure 7-1, and a designers' guide organized around a six-step procedure contained in Figure 7-2. In Figure 7-1 notice that an important specification is concreteness, although abstract metaphors are possible. Also note that metaphorical use generally extends across all types of knowledge and all types of chunking.

Into Figure 7-2 we attempt to incorporate ideas from the research and sequence those ideas in a reasonable order. The following subsections are explanations of the steps in this procedure.

FIGURE 7-2
A procedure for using metaphor in instructional design.

1. Select metaphor(s).
2. Emphasize metaphors(s).
3. Insure context is established.
4. Provide imagery instructions for vehicle and/or topic if appropriate.
5. Emphasize similarities/differences between topic and vehicle.
6. Provide opportunity for rehearsal of similarities/differences.

Select Metaphor(s)

This first step in the procedure is made easy if the instructional content chosen for instruction contains an appropriate metaphor. Metaphors contained in available material may or may not be appropriate. If the material does not contain a metaphor, or if the metaphor is judged inappropriate, the designer should provide the metaphor to be used. There is no substitute for broad training and reading in the liberal arts and sciences during this selection stage.

In judging and selecting metaphors there are a few ideas from the literature which may help. Perhaps the most important standard is *goodness of fit between topic and vehicle* (Fainsilber & Kogan, 1984). This is based on the quality and number of similarities of attributes and/or relationships between the topic and the vehicle. This standard may be similar to that of *number of interpretations*, an attribute investigated by Marschark and Hunt (1985).

In general, more relational and/or attributional similarities increase the instructional quality of a metaphor, perhaps by making more interpretations possible. While this is generally true, it is important to realize that one or a few shared similarities can make a good analogy. On this point Gentner (1983) shares the example of "Batteries are reservoirs." Typically, attribute differences include size, shape, color and substance. What makes this metaphor good is that both store energy, and the energy can be released to provide power.

Shared similarities may also be important for the standard of *familiarity*—the extent to which the target students are aware of the vehicle. *Imagery of topic* is another standard of quality (Marschark & Hunt, 1985), but this depends on the nature of the topic and vehicle and the novelty of the metaphor.

Another candidate for a standard of quality is *novelty* (Fainsilber & Kogan, 1984). It seems, however, that there is a tenuous balance between novelty, familiarity and appropriateness: very novel metaphors may sacrifice

FIGURE 7-3
A generic similarity/difference frame for use with metaphor.

	Vehicle Name	Topic Name
Similarities Attributes Relations		
Differences Attributes Relations		

goodness of fit and those metaphors whose vehicle and topic have very close fit have little novelty and viturally no "power to surprise." There is also the possibility that metaphors high in novelty are difficult to image.

By way of summary, judging the quality of metaphors is difficult. The standards for conceiving or selection of quality metaphors for instructional use should include goodness of fit, imageability, novelty and familiarity. It is, however, not possible to "pack" all these standards into any one metaphor because some preclude others.

It may be useful for the designer to complete a frame similar to that in Figure 7-3. Listing similarities and differences and being alert for both attributes and relations should aid the selection of a metaphor and evaluating its instructional potential. If too many differences exist, one should select another metaphor.

Emphasize the Metaphor(s)

Once the metaphor is selected and presented in the instruction, it must be emphasized. The metaphor used to convey relatively large amounts of information for the lesson or unit, the primary metaphor, may be critical to the lesson or unit; so efforts must be made to underscore the attributes of the vehicle in order to insure that all students have the prior knowledge necessary for transfer of that knowledge to the topic (Sticht, 1979).

There is also the problem that some students may have the expectation that the metaphor presented is to be interpreted literally. It may, therefore, be necessary to alert those students to the need to interpret figuratively.

Insure Context Is Established

The research has established that context is critical in the interpretation of metaphor, especially when students lack the background knowledge of the vehicle. Using a metaphor in isolation (without context) would be rare during instruction, so it will probably be provided incidentally during the lesson or unit. It is more likely that metaphor would be presented in isolation in experiments than in instruction, but the caution about the need for context is still valid.

Provide Imagery Instructions

Many of the more helpful metaphors for comprehension are those which involve meanings about materials which are concrete, so that the metaphor, or parts of it, may be imaged. When the vehicle in a metaphor is image rich, one should provide instructions to image. These instructions should be similar to "Form a mental picture of this in your mind." Otherwise some students will fail to benefit from imagery. More will be presented on this in Chapter 9.

Emphasize Similarities/Differences

Given that metaphor is the juxtapostion of similarities about one known object, event or procedure to another, the use of metaphor at some point in the sequence of instruction should involve the emphasis of similarities and differences between the known (the vehicle) and the topic (the new material). If these similarities *and* differences are not emphasized, misconceptions may remain or even develop. Spiro, Feltovich, Boulson and Anderson (1988) label these misconceptions *overextensions of analogy* and have found them common in advanced instruction. This is also called *seduction*. Seduction in metaphor probably functions in ways similar to the ways obliterative subsumption functions in the advance organizer. In other words, seduction is to metaphor as obliterative subsumption is to the advance organizer. To counter these overextensions Spiro et al. (1988) recommend, as we do, that instructors emphasize similarities and differences between the vehicle and topic.

For this emphasis we suggest a generic frame, type one, for use when metaphors are employed in instruction (please see Figure 7-3). Notice that rows and columns are labeled for the similarities and differences which are to be listed. Notice also that there are slots for *shared relations* and *attributes*. Some metaphors are based on attributes, some on relations, and some both. The slots should be completed as are other frames, during instruction, either by students or by the instructor.

In Figure 7-4 we provide a skeletal example of a specific frame for use with the metaphor, "A plant stem is a drinking straw." This metaphor is from Gentner and Stuart (1983). Notice the slots for similarities and differences which are to be completed during instruction.

Provide Opportunity for Rehearsal

The frame developed as a result of the foregoing suggestions becomes a *product* which must be studied by the students. As is the case for all spatial

FIGURE 7-4

A skeletal similarity/difference frame for use with the metaphor, "A plant stem is a drinking straw."

	Drinking Straw	Plant Stem
Similarities Attributes		
Relations		
Differences Attributes		
Relations		

learning strategy products, rehearsal strategies may be the most appropriate for processing the frame produced.

HYBRIDIZATION

As with most of the other cognitive strategies, the design use of metaphors may be combined with practically any of the strategies. Since many of the useful metaphors contain concrete vehicles and/or topics, it may be expected that imagery will often be employed by students without conscious effort by the designer. To increase the use of imagery in metaphor-driven instruction, however, the designer may wish to include instructions to image. From the preceding section it is obvious that we recommend the use of a generic frame, type one, along with primary metaphors for lessons, to counter the ever-possible overextension of the metaphor beyond the actual similarities between the vehicle and the topic.

As with other frames, the generic frame, once the slots are completed, becomes a product for further processing by students. The information in the slots may be processed (studied) with bottom-up strategies such as mnemonics or rehearsal.

SUMMARY

In this chapter we discussed the third bridging strategy, metaphor. Metaphor and the other bridging strategies, frames, type two, and advance organizer, comprise the known list of top-down strategies which designers may use to aid students as they apply prior knowledge to new knowledge. We have seen from this chapter that metaphors occupy a unique place in the cognitive "tool box" for students and instructional designers. We have also seen that metaphorical skills develop early during elementary years so that their instructional use extends through the years of formal education.

In the next chapter we discuss a miscellaneous set of cognitive strategies which we lump together as rehearsal. These are the first group of the fourth family of cognitive strategies, the multipurpose family.

EXERCISE

1. Complete the following frame by placing information in the slots. We have provided the row headings for you. The row headings consist of metaphors used in this text.

Metaphor	Name of Topic	Name of Vehicle	Context	What Was Intended to be Conveyed?	Personal Feelings Engendered?
Advance organizers are bridges across chasms (p. 115).					
Instructional design is like surfing in a crosscurrent (p. 26).					
Some schemata are like computer programs (p. 7).					

REFERENCES

Baldwin, R. S., Ford, J. C., & Readence, J. E. (1981). Teaching word connotations: An alternative strategy. *Reading World, 21,* 103–108.

Baldwin, R. S., Luce, T. S., & Readence, J. E. (1982). The impact of subschemata on metaphorical processing. *Reading Research Quarterly, 17,* 528–543.

Billow, R. M. (1975). A cognitive development study of metaphor comprehension. *Developmental Psychology, 11,* 415–423.

Black, M. (1979). More about metaphor. In A. Ortony (Ed.), *Metaphor and thought.* London: Cambridge University Press.

Carey, S. (1985). *Conceptual change in childhood.* Cambridge, MA: MIT Press.

Cometa, M. S., & Eson, M. E. (1978). Logical operations and metaphor interpretations: A Piagetian model. *Child Development, 49,* 649–659.

Fainsilber, L., & Kogan, N. (1984). Does imagery contribute to metaphoric quality? *Journal of Psycholinguistic Research, 13,* 383–391.

Farb, P., (1963). *Face of North America.* New York: Harper and Row.

Gentner, D., & Stuart, P. (April, 1983). Metaphor as structure mapping: What develops? Paper presented at the biennial meeting of the Society for Research in Child Development, Detroit, Michigan.

Gentner, D. (1983). Structure-mapping: A theoretical framework for analogy. *Cognitive Science, 7,* 155–170.

Green, T. F. (1979). Learning without metaphor. In A. Ortony (Ed.), *Metaphor and thought.* London: Cambridge University Press.

Hayes, D. A., & Henk, W. A. (1986). Understanding and remembering complex prose augmented by analogic and pictorial illustrations. *Journal of Reading Behavior, 18*, 63–76.

Honeck, R. P., Sowry, B. M., & Voegtle, K. (1978). Proverbial understanding in a pictorial context. *Child Development, 49*, 327–331.

Inhelder, B., & Piaget, J. (1964). *The early growth of logic in the child*. London: Routledge & Kegan Paul.

Inhoff, A. W., Lima, S. D., & Carroll, P. J. (1984). Contextual effects on metaphor comprehension in reading. *Memory & Cognition, 12*, 558–567.

Lakoff, G., & Johnson, M. (1980). *Metaphors we live by*. Chicago: University of Chicago Press.

Levin, S. R. (1979). Standard approaches to metaphor and a proposal for literary metaphor. In A. Ortony (Ed.), *Metaphor and thought*. London: Cambridge University Press.

Malgady, R. G. (1977). Children's interpretation and appreciation of similes. *Child Development, 48*, 1734–1738.

Marschark, M., & Hunt, R. R. (1985). On memory for metaphor. *Memory and Cognition, 13*, 413–424.

Marsh, G., Desberg, P., & Cooper, J. (1977). Developmental strategies in reading. *Journal of Reading Behavior, 9*, 391–394.

Marsh, G., Friedman, M. P., Desberg, P., & Saterdahl, K. (1981). Comparison of reading and spelling strategies in normal and reading disabled children. In M. P. Friedman, J. P. Das, & N. O'Connor (Eds.), *Intelligence and learning*. New York: Plenum.

Nippold, M. A., Leonard, L. B., & Kail, R. (1984). Syntactic and conceptual factors in children's understanding of metaphors. *Journal of Speech and Hearing Research, 27*, 197–205.

Ortony, A. (1975). Why metaphors are necessary and not just nice. *Educational Theory, 25*, 45–53.

Ortony, A., Schallert, D. L., Reynolds, R. E., & Antos, S. J. (1978). Interpreting metaphors and idioms: Some effects of context upon comprehension. *Journal of Verbal Learning and Verbal Behavior, 17*, 465–477.

Ortony, A. (Ed.). (1979). *Metaphor and thought*. London: Cambridge University Press.

Petrie, H. G. (1979). Metaphor and learning. In A. Ortony (Ed.), *Metaphor and thought*. London: Cambridge University Press.

Piaget, J. (1952). *Origins of intelligence in children*. New York: International Universities Press.

Pollio, H. R., Fabrizi, M. S., Sills, A., & Smith, M. K. (1984). Need metaphoric comprehension take longer than literal comprehension? *Journal of Psycholinguistic Research, 13*, 195–214.

Reynolds, R. E., & Ortony, A. (1980). Some issues in the measurement of children's comprehension of metaphorical language. *Child Development, 51*, 1110–1119.

Royer, J. M. (1986). Designing instruction to produce understanding: An approach based on cognitive theory. In G. D. Phye & T. Andre (Eds.), *Cognitive classroom learning*. New York: Academic Press.

Rumelhart, D. E., & Norman, D. A. (1978). Accretion, tuning, and restructuring: Three modes of learning. In J. W. Cotton & R. Klatzky (Eds.), *Semantic factors in cognition*. Hillsdale, N. J.: Lawrence Erlbaum Associates.

Rumelhart, D. E. (1979). Some problems with the notion of literal meanings. In A. Ortony (Ed.), *Metaphor and thought*. London: Cambridge University Press.

Santostefano, S. (1985). Metaphor: Integrating action, fantasy, and language in development. *Imagination, Cognition and Personality, 4*, 127–146.

Searle, J. R. (1979). Metaphor. In A. Ortony (Ed.), *Metaphor and thought*. London: Cambridge University Press.

Spiro, R. J., Feltovich, P., Coulson, R., & Anderson, D. (1988). Multiple analogies for complex concepts: Antidotes for analogy-induced misconception in advanced knowledge acquisition. In S. Vosniadou & A. Ortony (Eds.), *Similarity and analogical learning*. New York: Cambridge University Press.

Sticht, T. G. (1979). Educational uses of metaphor. In A. Ortony (Ed.), *Metaphor and thought*. New York: Cambridge University Press.

Vosniadou, S., & Ortony, A. (1983). The emergence of the literal-metaphorical-anomalous distinction in young children. *Child Development, 54*, 154–161.

Vosniadou, S. (1987). Children and metaphors. *Child Development, 58*, 870–885.

Vosniadou, S., Ortony, A., Reynolds, R. A., & Wilson, P. T. (1984). Sources of difficulty in children's comprehension of metaphorical language. *Child Development, 55*, 1588–1606.

Waggoner, J. E., Messe, M. J., & Palermo, D. S. (1985). Grasping the meaning of metaphor: Story recall and comprehension. *Child Development, 56*, 1156–1166.

Winner, E., Engel, M., & Gardner, H. (1980). Misunderstanding metaphor: What's the problem? *Journal of Experimental Child Psychology, 30*, 22–32.

Rehearsal: General-Purpose Study Strategies

In this chapter we discuss the first set of strategies in the fourth and large family of multipurpose cognitive strategies. We label this first set *rehearsal*, as do Mayer (1987), Slavin (1988) and Gagne (1985). We present rehearsal skills and their definitions and discuss how to plan instruction in ways which students can use these strategies. Rehearsal is usually defined as *activities which help process material into short-term memory by keeping material active in consciousness so that it can be more deeply processed for recall for long periods* (Mayer, 1987, p. 11). Rehearsal strategies include activities labeled repetition, or practice, and studying. As can be seen from Figure 8-1, this is a relatively large list of various kinds of activities so rehearsal is a potpourri.

This set of rehearsal strategies is similar to the other strategies in this text in that most are activities which students perform. A difference for some of the strategies is that some do not require text preparation, product development or special presentation by the designer or teacher. Another difference is that these rehearsal strategies are virtually unlimited by the characteristics of the knowledge domain or task to be learned. While specific design implications are presented later in this chapter, the primary tasks for designers and teachers in the context of rehearsal are to provide time and opportunity for rehearsal to occur, to encourage students to rehearse if they have the skills and to train students in improving rehearsal skills. The primary task for students is to become actively intellectually engaged through these activities.

This set of strategies discussed in this chapter, which we have chunked into the family named "multipurpose," is so diverse that it even includes some which are not only multipurpose but also belong to the second strategic family named "bridging." Paraphrasing and clarifying, as named and defined in Figure 8-1, have this dual family membership because not only are they comprehension aids for learning in practically any knowledge domain, but they

FIGURE 8-1

A list of rehearsal activities and definitions.

Repetition and Cumulative Rehearsal	Students repeat a sequence of motor movements, a list of words or steps in a procedure. More typically, however, each "pass" consists of repeating part of the list with other items added during subsequent passes.
Questioning and Answering	Students form questions about material. Teachers, text writers or designers ask questions. Students answer the questions posed.
Predicting and Clarifying	Students predict questions to be asked by the teacher. Students try to predict meaning of the content. Students guess about intentions of text writer or teacher. Students, after identifying concepts, ideas or propositions which they understand poorly, study with the goal of better understanding. This often involves prior knowledge.
Restating or Paraphrasing	Students put concepts, ideas and propositions in their own words, thereby relating the new material to their prior knowledge.
Reviewing and Summarizing	Students "pass" through material to reflect on its meaning and to think about what they recall. Students create an overview of the gist of the material.
Selecting	Students decide on or are informed about which information is important and concentrate on it, spending less effort on information adjudged to be less important. This often entails *prediction*.
Notetaking	Students write ideas, definitions, propositions, etc. At its best, note taking involves *selecting* (importance) and *predicting*.
Underlining	Students mark important material, thus reducing the amount to be more deeply processed. It includes *selecting* and *predicting*.
SQ3R	A study system proposed by Robinson (1941), now most recently in Robinson (1970). The letters and numbers in the acronym stand for *survey* (Examine headings in a chapter to find out the big points and read the summary paragraph if there is one.); *question* (Turn the heading into a question.); *read* (Study or read to answer the question.); *recite* (After reading to answer the question, recall the answer and paraphrase, then cite an example. Continue questioning, reading for answers and reciting

FIGURE 8-1 (continued)

	throughout the chapter or assignment. Make notes.); *review* (After completing the study as described in these steps, check recall of main points by remembering and restating them.). Obviously SQ3R includes many of the specific rehearsal strategies listed in this figure.
PQRST	A study system which is very similar to SQ3R which may be found in Thomas and Robinson (1982, pp. 162–173). The acronym stands for *preview, question, read, self-recite, test (review)*. As in SQ3R this study system includes many of the specific rehearsal strategies listed in this figure.

also entail relating new material to prior learning. They may be designated as bottom-up, as opposed to top-down, bridging strategies because they are driven by parts of the content rather than holistic mental constructs.

With the exception of paraphrasing and clarifying, the rehearsal strategies are primarily partistic as opposed to holistic strategies. When compared with the spatial learning strategies, for example, the rehearsal strategies are means of learning "parts of the forest: the trees, the ferns, the shrubs, etc." as opposed to getting the big picture of the forest which can be provided by the frame or concept map. Another way of saying this is that the rehearsal strategies are means of dividing and conquering. While the spatial learning strategies provide and are instances of integration of rich items of knowledge present, and while the bridging strategies provide and are instances of integration of prior knowledge with present knowledge, rehearsal strategies typically are disintegrative—they divide and conquer; they allow the mastery of manageable chunks. Good students, of course, have at their disposal both integrative and disintegrative strategies.

Research on some of these rehearsal strategies has been conducted for many decades, and thus some predate the cognitive revolution. Predating or not, they are vital and proven strategies which cannot be ignored in learning and instructional design. During the cognitive revolution, however, there has been heightened interest in these strategies. Figure 8-1 is a list of strategies which we include in this chapter together with their definitions.

These strategies include a wide variety of activities performed by students as they study using methods such as SQ3R. The SQ3R method is as follows:

1. The students first survey (or preview) the material to be studied to get an overall idea of what is covered.

2. Students examine the topics and subtopics and formulate them into questions.

3. The first reading is to answer those questions.

4. The second reading is for the purpose of adding detail, facts and concepts to main ideas.

5. The final "R" is review.

There are several forms of this five-step study method in the literature; another is the PQRST method (Thomas & Robinson, 1982). Rehearsal as a category of activities includes the activities of the SQ3R and PQRST methods, and such activities as predicting possible questions, predicting material to follow a sentence or passage, paraphrasing main ideas, summarizing, note taking and underlining.

Good students have a number of the rehearsal strategies listed and defined in Figure 8-1 and use them for study. Poor students, on the other hand, appear to have few such strategies. Contrast the list of activities in Figure 8-1 with the answers provided by a poor student who had failed a major examination well into a course. The student visits the professor for some help. The professor asks, "Did you study for this test?"

"Yeah."

"Please tell me how you studied."

"I read every chapter."

"What else did you do?"

"I read every chapter again."

"Anything else?"

"No."

It is amazing that a student could progress academically through high school into a university with such a limited set of study skills. Nonetheless it happens. Many student service offices in universities provide some help with study skills. Learning those skills and using them often improves performance. Knowledge about those skills has emerged from a long tradition of recognition of the problem of poor study skills and research in rehearsal strategies.

RESEARCH ON REHEARSAL STRATEGIES

In this section we discuss research on the strategies. That research will be discussed in the same sequence in which the strategies are listed in Figure 8-1. Because there is so much research on many of these strategies we rely on published reviews in those cases in which we could locate those reviews. This research has been conducted with subjects from childhood into adulthood (college-age) in a wide variety of knowledge domains.

It is important for us to emphasize that the *rehearsal strategies, while in use, are not typically static, separate or easily predicted in sequence; but rather more likely fluid and interdependent with considerable variation, both within students and between students, in sequencing and subsequencing.* For example, to have an effect on learning, questions must be answered; but doing so is often based on selecting important ideas or portions of the material. Repetitive sequences with many subsequences may be established around surveying–selecting–questioning–answering–cumulative rehearsal. Material such as text or pictures will be surveyed for the purpose of answering questions. Then, unless verbatim answers are to be given, restating or paraphrasing becomes involved. Thus, while these strategies may be discussed somewhat separately, in actual use by students and often in the research and development efforts, they are interdependent. Generally speaking, the more naturalistic and field-based the research and development effort, the more interdependence and fluidity are observed.

Repetition and Cumulative Rehearsal

In learning material such as sequential motor movements, lists of words and steps in a procedure, students often adopt the rote strategy of merely repeating the sequence or list. When this repetition reproduces the exact wording, in the case of prose learning, it is called rote learning, which is generally thought neither to be a very sophisticated strategy nor, among rehearsal strategies, the most productive one. Verbatim or rote learning via repetition is generally not as effective as repetition using one's own words—in verbal material. A more sophisticated and productive strategy is called cumulative rehearsal in which the first few items in the sequence are recited or practiced in the first few "passes," with one or more items added for subsequent passes through the sequence (Hagen & Stanovich, 1977; Ornstein & Naus, 1978; Pressley & Levin, 1983).

Questioning and Answering

Much research exists on questioning and answering. That research can be subdivided into two categories: one on teacher- or text-posed questions and the other on student-generated questions. Questions posed in text have been called adjunct questioning, inserted questioning (Sefkow & Myers, 1980) and priming questioning.

What are some of the effects of questions? For research on the effects of adjunct questioning on learning there is a relatively recent review (Hamilton, 1985) of dozens of studies. The reviewer notes that questions asked before or after text passages can aid retention. There is a general pattern of this positive effect on learning and retention when the questions are to be answered with verbatim information as well as more meaningfully processed (encoded) material in which paraphrasing typically occurs. There are patterns of effects not only for immediate recall but also for delayed recall and transfer.

Where should questions be placed? Hamilton (1985) compared the effects observed in the research of questions posed before text with those asked after text passages. For questions calling for verbatim answers, the placing of the question before or after seems to be equally helpful, but, for more meaningful or higher-level questions about applications or synthesis, the best placement is *before* text.

There is another option in addition to placing questions before or after text, that of placing them within text between sections. Palmere, Benton, Glover and Ronning (1983) repeated for three times a sequence of eight paragraphs then one question. There was also a sequence of eight paragraphs and no questions. The paragraphs in each sequence were different and the questions varied from inquiry about three, two and one items of information which appeared in the text. The more items necessary to answer the question, the greater the effect on recall.

What is a "good" question? This implies that one attribute of a "good" question is one that calls for information embedded across paragraphs. It should be mentioned that apparently these questions were inquiries about factual information, but not just one item of information per question. It is also important to note that subjects also had opportunity to read the question and return to text to scan for the answer. When this opportunity is available, and when students do scan, where questions are placed becomes less important in design.

A considerable body of research also exists on teacher-posed questions (Gall et al., 1978; Dunkin & Biddle, 1974). Much of this research occurred in classrooms in which teachers were observed while teaching. Records are kept of the number of questions asked by the teacher and the quality of those questions. In many of these studies the quality, or type, of questions was determined by correspondence with the taxonomy of educational objectives, the cognitive domain (Bloom, 1956). That is, were the questions inquiries about low-level knowledge of facts or definitions or high-level knowledge such as problem solving, analysis or evaluation (judging merit, validity, etc.)?

Gall et al. (1978) report that recall is aided by questions calling for lower-level answers, whereas the effects of higher-level questions on recall are not clearly established. Furthermore, as one might expect, the aiding of recall was manifested more on test items about which there was focus of study (intentional learning) to answer the questions than on items about which there was less focus (incidental learning).

Text writers and teachers can pose questions. So also can students themselves. In a recent review Wong (1985) discussed studies on training question-generating skills and effects of those self-generated questions. Wong (1985) found ample evidence that children and adolescents can be trained to ask questions about instructional material with a variety of techniques, such as modeling, reinforcement and the presentation of ambiguous and inconsistent text. Based on 27 investigations with subjects ranging from elementary school through college, Wong concludes that self-generated questions aid learning. These helpful effects depend on the quality (usually, but not always, thought of in terms of correspondence with Bloom's taxonomy of objectives, cognitive domain) of the question, the questioning skills of the student, the number of questions generated (generally, a few are better than many) and the match of questions with the content and tests used to measure retention. Obviously then, the effects of self-questioning are not a simple issue.

Why do questions aid recall? There are several possible explanations as to why both presented and self-generated questions aid learning. The reasons are not necessarily independent, and some of these explanations entail rehearsal strategies other than questioning. Questions noted by students or generated have the possibility of, first, inducing more active and deeper cognitive processing than might occur in the absence of those questions. Second, as students learn to attend to questions or learn to generate questions themselves, they add these skills to their repertory of cognitive strategies and become increasingly metacognitively sophisticated. Third, those questions signify important topics, facts, ideas or concepts and aid in selecting important material for active processing which can involve review, predicting meaning, predicting answers and predicting further questions. Fourth, self-initiated questions may help activate relevant prior knowledge and help to integrate that prior knowledge with new information. These reasons why questioning aids learning are thus connected to predicting, reviewing, clarifying and selecting.

Predicting and Clarifying

As an integral part of their research and development on reciprocal teaching, Palincsar and Brown (1984) included training in several rehearsal activities including clarifying and predicting. Their work on other rehearsal strategies in this study and other investigations is included in the reviews discussed in the foregoing section and subsequently. Subjects in this particular study were seventh-grade low achievers. Adult tutors guided students in these activities. As is the case in metacognitive and reciprocal research and development in general, the intention was to teach strategies and content. In this study the content consisted of passages from standard seventh-grade texts. Results of this effort were very positive in that comprehension improved substantially, and the strategies were found to be durable and transferable.

Prediction in this study included students' forecasting content to follow, questions which may be asked on exams and forming hypotheses about the intents of the teacher and the author of the text. For examples, after summarizing a section just studied or inspected, students were asked to predict what might follow; or, after noting or formulating a question, the students forecasted the material to follow; or prediction was attempted when students or teachers recognized cues which hinted about material to follow, but there is no compelling reason that prediction should be limited in this way. Nonetheless, that is a good departure point for prediction training. Such activities as these increase the probability that the students will be intellectually engaged with the material and help students remember and apply prior knowledge.

When there was confusion in the material or in the students' interpretation of it, clarifying was attempted. Initially the tutor provided help, but as training proceeded, students themselves became better at scanning text or memory for aid in resolving the confusion or lack of clarity and emitting clarification statements.

Restating and Paraphrasing

There is evidence that, if students paraphrase or restate ideas, definitions or examples, recall is aided. The plausibility of this rests at least in part on the fact that it would be difficult to restate in one's own words without having committed gists of the material to memory in some manner. It is also likely that there will have been some use of prior knowledge.

Coomber, Ramstad and Sheets (1986) compared effects on recall of three common forms of teaching vocabulary—use of definitions, examples and sentence composition. Students chose among alternatives for the definitions and examples, whereas in the sentence composing task they were to write a sentence using the word. The sentence composing group was superior in recall.

Reviewing and Summarizing

Based on a review of dozens of studies on summarizing, Hidi and Anderson (1986) conclude that student-produced summaries lead to better retention. They further conclude that related skills vary greatly, particularly during childhood and adolescence; that students often need training to develop proficiency; and that such training is not easy.

From this research Hidi and Anderson (1986) offer a set of instructional recommendations which, if followed, should enable teachers and designers to train students in this strategy. First, the training should begin with short segments of material and gradually increase the amount of material. A paragraph is an operative length for beginning, with the students choosing topic sentences and/or stating the main idea. Paraphrasing or stating main ideas in one's own words can be important for at least two reasons: the paragraph may not have an obvious topic sentence, and summaries are best indicators of meaningful learning when they are stated in the student's own words. A second recommendation is that students should summarize simple narratives initially and phase gradually into other more complex genres because young children particularly find the narrative genre easier. Since texts vary greatly in complexity and "reader considerateness," summarization training should begin with less complex and more considerate text. Students must have feedback about the quality of their summaries which can be provided through group discussion or teacher comments. The feedback can help students reflect on the quality of their summaries. A third recommendation consists of beginning with the material present and phasing to summarizing with the text or other material not available for scanning. All through the training students should be encouraged to paraphrase instead of copying exact wordings.

This recommended training procedure actually involves several rehearsal strategies, including selecting and paraphrasing main ideas. These are, of course, important components in the SQ3R and PQRST methods of study.

It is very important to recognize that summarizing, as a rehearsal strategy, is a student activity. While author-, designer- or teacher-generated summaries are important components in "considerate" text and instruction, and while they may aid comprehension, student-produced summaries of comparable quality may be expected to be a better aid for comprehension. Summaries produced for students may or may not be actively processed for a number of reasons, only one of which is that there is no guarantee that students will attend to them or actively process them.

Dwyer (1985–1986) compared comprehension effects in adults among four treatments: no rehearsal, author-prepared summaries, student-generated summaries consisting of filling in the blanks and student-generated summaries consisting of coloring parts of a drawing. The latter treatment resulted in superior comprehension, probably because both verbal and visual encoding were intrinsic to this specific task of identifying parts of the human heart and coloring those parts of the drawing. It is assumed that subjects reviewed both the prose and the illustration prior to coloring the parts. This visual coding hypothesis, of course, is pertinent to imagery.

Selecting

Instructional materials often contain massive amounts of information. Perhaps the most basic rehearsal strategy is selecting the important information so that the important information can be further and more deeply processed. The more students are left to their own devices during instruction, the more important skills related to this strategy become.

The simple definition of *selecting* is: searching arrays such as text, lecture and illustrations to adjudge which portions are critical or important. There are a number of sources for this judgment, including the statement of objectives (Hamilton, 1985) or other in-text highlightings by authors, teachers or designers and students themselves. This judgment can reduce the amount of material to be further processed or studied. It can be based on forecasts about what will be included on tests or what transfer tasks are predicted or what the intentions of the instructors or students are for the learning.

There are also a number of text or task cues which provide information about importance. Among them are inserted questions, stated objectives, variations in print in the case of prose learning and use of topics and subtopics in prose. Advanced students often base their judgments on their own diagnoses of gaps in their knowledge. We have already presented the research on questions and now turn to the research on objectives.

An excellent review of research on the effect of objectives in learning was made by Hamilton (1985), who included both questioning and objectives research. Hamilton subdivided objectives into two areas: learning goals and instructional objectives. *Instructional objectives* are those which meet the standards specified by Mager (1962) of identifying behaviors which will be accepted as evidence that the objective has been accomplished, of defining conditions within which the behavior should be expected to occur, and of identifying standards of acceptable performance. Learning goals are those which often are more general mentionings of topics to be learned about, or those which are missing one or more of Mager's three components of instructional objectives.

Based on his review and analysis of the research on objectives, Hamilton concludes that both instructional objectives and learning goals consistently produced positive effects on learning verbatim information. For more meaningful learning of concepts and principles, however, learning goals have produced more consistent effects; but instructional objectives have not had consistent effects on learning concepts and principles. Hamilton did not locate sufficient research on transfer effects for either instructional objectives or learning goals for estimations of consistency.

Another in-text cue for selecting is adjunct questions. We have already discussed the research on the design value of questioning but here note that one of several advantages of adjunct questions is the provision of cues about important items of information in rich and dense arrays.

As we have written, teachers, tasks and texts can provide cues for selecting, but the self-selection of important parts of texts or tasks is itself a critical and learned skill. Brown and Smiley (1977) found that adults and seventh-grade subjects could select important parts of prose passages. Furthermore, the two age groups displayed considerable agreement in ratings of relative importance of parts. In contrast, third- and fifth-grade students were less able to differentiate parts in terms of their importance. A very tidy developmental progression in rating skills was observed.

Recall of information was influenced significantly by these ratings across all ages, but the influence was much greater for the seventh graders and the adults. Items rated as less important on a four-point scale tended not to be remembered, while those rated high on the scale were almost always recalled, particularly for the two older groups. Such a finding is powerful testimony for selecting as a powerful, basic metacognitive strategy.

Note Taking

In a review of approximately 40 note-taking research efforts, Anderson and Armbruster (in press) have found ample evidence that note taking by students can improve learning. As one would expect, most of the research reviewed involved students listening to lectures or audio tapes. Anderson and Armbruster discuss this research in terms of encoding and external storage hypotheses. Research on encoding in this context is the examination of the extent to which note taking helps students to process or learn the material relatively immediately during its presentation by quickly deciding what is important, perhaps paraphrasing the important fact, concept or idea, and then writing it down—all accomplished during the lecture or presentation. Thus note taking is not a single activity. As a rehearsal strategy it actually involves several activities within the potpourri called rehearsal.

Another substantial set of investigations are tests of note taking as external storage. As the phrase implies, note taking may aid learning and recall because students use the notes to record facts, concepts, and ideas which they think are important so that later they can study those notes. Further study, of course, involves encoding, which implies a dual function—both storage and encoding.

Experimentally, separating these two functions attendant with the two hypotheses is very difficult since isolating encoding effects would necessitate testing recall immediately after note taking. Anderson and Armbruster found 24 studies in which there were attempts to isolate encoding from storage by typically having at least one group listen to a presentation without taking notes and another listen and take notes. Students are tested before they can review the notes. If those who take notes recall more, this is taken to mean that note taking is not only advantageous but also supports this encoding function. Of the 24 studies, 10 provide support for encoding and 14 do not.

Rather than discard the possibility of encoding outright based on a tally of findings, it is reasonable to conclude that under some conditions note taking is better than merely listening and that encoding does occur under those conditions. One condition is the qualitative difference in what is recalled. In some of the studies the test items called for transfer and some did not. Note takers did better on the transfer items. Another condition favoring note taking is that notes which are brief aid recall more than detailed notes. Other qualities of notes which aid encoding and recall are the recording of main ideas (those adjudged by the students to be important) and the matching of main ideas adjudged by the presenter and the student to be important. Other conditions in these experiments consist of characteristics of the presentation. These include presentation rate and amount of information (density). Rapid presentation of large amounts of information reduces the possibility of efficient note taking and encoding. Breaks in presentation, another important condition, seem to aid better note taking and more efficient encoding, particularly when presentations are rapid and dense.

Another significant condition is that good notes taken by the students are better than listening alone as compared to presenter-provided notes. This is a favorable finding for the possible encoding effect since instructor-prepared notes would not entail the students' actively processing what they hear.

When note taking is examined in terms of external storage functions as compared to encoding, other important implications about conditions were drawn by Anderson and Armbruster. Fifteen studies were reviewed on external storage, all of which provided evidence of helpful effects on recall. A typical design in these studies is to have groups, one of which listens only and is provided with notes; a second group which listens, take notes and reviews their notes (or provided notes); and a third which takes notes but does not review before a test on the material. Typically, also, designs include a delay between the presentation and reviewing for the test. Following the logic of this typical design, if the main function of notes is external storage, the group that listens and reviews provided notes should do better on the test of recall.

Anderson and Armbruster conclude that all 15 studies reviewed provided support for the external storage hypothesis.

These reviewers emphasize several variables which are critical to the value of note taking as an external storage device. First, there should be congruence between the notes and the test; that is, notes are most helpful for test performance, obviously, when they contain the material on the tests. Second, the more complete the notes, the more notes aid recall. Since instructor-provided notes are often more congruent with tests and more complete than notes taken by students, there are some situations in which instructor-provided notes are a better aid for learning.

Whether or not to provide notes is not a simple issue. The decision partially depends on whether a designer is expecting immediate encoding or is expecting students to use notes for external storage. For relatively immediate encoding, students should take notes themselves. This decision is made more complex by the density and pace of the presentation, the summarization and selection skills of students and availability of the presentation for review.

Providing notes for students is a reasonable beginning for the development of note-taking skills. Students may need these as a model of notes which an instructor deems appropriate for the task, the knowledge and any tests over the instruction.

Underlining

Prose and other visual arrays are often rich and dense. The problem becomes one of highlighting portions which are, for one reason or another, adjudged to be important. One rehearsal technique associated with this problem with a modest amount of research support is underlining. The basic strategy foundational for underlining is selecting, since parts of the array must be selected.

McAndrew (1983) reviewed a few studies on underlining. In essence, it aids recall of the material underlined to the detriment of recall of material not underlined unless the students underline more general sentences. For the most part, if students underline detail they tend to recall detail. Underlining general statements aids recall of both general statements and supporting detail.

Another important idea is that excessive underlining reduces helpful effects. McAndrew (1983) recommends that students mark no more than one general statement per paragraph. Obviously, if the student underlines large proportions of the material, helpful selective effects are lost.

Underlining can be viewed as quite similar to note taking in that judgments about importance are crucial, and recall effects could be attributable to both encoding and external storage. (Please see the section on note taking.) That is, as students go through material and underline it, some processing occurs about what is and what is not important, and attempts may be made to rehearse/encode that which was underlined. As for external storage the material underlined can be revisited for later study, just as notes can be.

Just as there are parallels between underlining and note taking for selection, for encoding and for storage, so also are there parallels between them for *who* underlines. Teachers, authors, designers or students may underline or highlight in several ways, with color and font variations, for examples. The primary difference in effect of who underlines is surely due to whether or not there is benefit to the student for going through the personal selection of important portions of the material.

Of course, benefits for personal selection cannot accrue if students lack selection skills. These skills, as we have seen, are very important and can be trained. These skills are departure points for training in both note taking and underlining.

SQ3R and PQRST

These study systems have been used for many decades. Not much research exists on them as systems, but they are in widespread use. Adams, Carnine and Gersten (1982) located six studies with adolescents and adults which were intended to assess the effectiveness of SQ3R. They state that there were mixed results in those studies.

In their own study Adams, Carnine and Gersten (1982) researched the effect on recall of the SQ3R method with fifth graders who tested as having adequate reading skills but inadequate study skills. Using standard fifth-grade social studies material, they provided a four-day (30 to 40 minutes daily) training period on the system as one condition. There were two control conditions: one, independent study with feedback and, two, students remaining in their classroom. While it is clear that both the training group and the independent study group studied the same materials, it is not clear whether or not the students remaining in their classroom studied the same materials. All three groups were tested immediately and with a two-week delay. Students who received training in the SQ3R system performed better than the other groups on both the immediate and delayed short-answer tests, but their performance was not significantly better on free recall tests.

This positive finding is important especially since the training session was only over four days with a maximum of 160 minutes. One might expect that fifth graders who lack effective study skills would need more extensive training. The fact of better recall after such a short training session constitutes good support for the system.

These systems generally do not have the extensive research and development background of the other strategies presented in this chapter. In view of the fact, however, that these two systems incorporate many if not most of the well-researched rehearsal strategies, one can be confident of their utility. These two systems also have the advantages of being memorable as codes and appearing sequential, simple and orderly.

Appearances, however, can be deceiving. In execution the five steps in the SQ3R system can be very complex, and the sequence of the entire routine, as well as the subsequences, can vary greatly within and among students. For example, Anderson (1979) found that a large number of varied, convoluted and involved activities appeared to characterize just the first step (survey or preview), and this with skilled readers at the graduate level.

This is not to be taken as a criticism of these study systems. Indeed their complexity and the opportunities within the systems for individual differences with materials which can vary greatly are the strengths of the systems. While the systems are complex, they have great potential for the development of metacognitive sophistication.

TRAINING REHEARSAL STRATEGIES ACROSS AGES

Substantial research and development exists which has resulted in ample evidence that rehearsal strategies can be trained. This evidence exists for ages across the years of formal instruction. There is also evidence that low-achieving students can be trained in rehearsal strategies. Pressley and Levin (1983) have edited a volume in which much of this research and development is discussed. Included in this training research is the exciting and fruitful work of Palincsar and Brown (1984) and many others in their recent research on reciprocal teaching presented in the initial chapter of this book.

COMPARATIVE RESEARCH

Several efforts have been made to determine how one or more rehearsal strategies compare among themselves and between one or more rehearsal strategies and one or more of the more elaborate strategies covered in other chapters of this book. These we have included in other chapters as we discuss the other strategies.

The comparisons of rehearsal with the more elaborate bridging and spatial learning strategies have generally resulted in favor of the other, more elaborate strategies. This comparative research constitutes part of the basis for our relative ratings for recall potential and power in the initial chapter of this book. This general result, in our opinion, is due to two factors. First, the other strategies involve rehearsal and some additional processing so that multiple processing occurs. Second, other strategies provide a big (spatial) or integrative (bridging) picture while the strength of rehearsal strategies is largely in their promoting the learning of the little picture. In other words, this latter factor suggests a metaphor of rehearsal in general helping to explore and comprehend the moss, the weeds, the trees, the leaves *in* the forest, whereas other, and more elaborate, strategies aid exploration and comprehension of the forest *itself*.

DESIGNERS' GUIDE

The primary tasks for instructional design associated with rehearsal strategies are *providing time and opportunity for rehearsal to occur* and *developing those skills*. These are consistent with our emphasis throughout this text on two equally important outcomes for instruction: improved instruction on content via the cognitive strategies and developing cognitive strategies.

There are, however, specific techniques which teachers and designers can use to prompt or initiate rehearsal activities. Many of these are listed in Figure 8-2. This list, the ideas contained within the discussion of the research and development, and trial and error on the part of the teacher and designer will provide an impressive battery of techniques for use. While we have mentioned the provision of feedback for only several of the entries in Figure 8-2, designers could provide feedback in most of these activities *after* students engage in the activities.

There remains, however, the decision as to which of these multipurpose strategies to use or encourage students to use. In Figure 8-3 we provide again

FIGURE 8-2

A frame display of rehearsal strategies with associated designer and student activities.

	Designer Activity	Associated Student Activities
Repetition and Cumulative Rehearsal	Cue	Practice by repeating Repeating, but adding items
Questioning and Answering	Adjunct questions	Answering, predicting Form own inquiry
Predicting and Clarification	Cue, include transition statements Inquire about (see right)	Forecast meaning and questions Resolve misconceptions, conflicts, confusions
Paraphrasing	Provide feedback	State meaning in own words
Reviewing and Summarizing	Provide feedback	
Selecting	Objectives stated before material, particularly for verbatim learning	Attend to written objectives
Note Taking	Instructor prepares notes (see text for desirable conditions)	Take and study notes

FIGURE 8-3

Specifications for rehearsal.

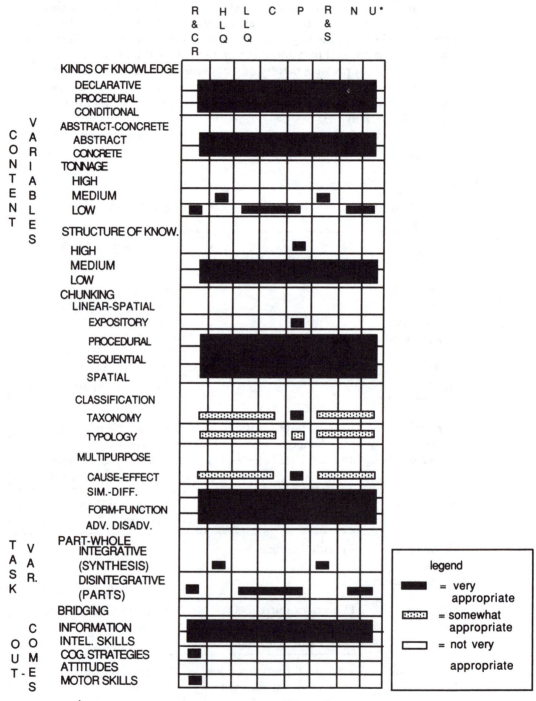

R = repetition   LLQ= lower level question   R & S= reviewing &
CR= cumulative rehearsal   P= predicting   summarizing
HLQ= higher level question   C= clarifying   N = notetaking
                                                             U = underlining

a specification chart to aid that decision. This chart, however, because of space limitations does not contain all rehearsal strategies. It should be obvious from the figure that rehearsal strategies are indeed multipurpose. The primary restrictions are on tonnage and structure of knowledge. On outcomes, notice that repetition and cumulative rehearsal is an option for motor skills. We have noted that there are only a few cognitive strategy choices for this outcome.

HYBRIDIZATION

Throughout the text, in most if not all discussions of the various strategies, we presented the idea that rehearsal strategies are to be combined with other strategies. For the spatial learning strategies, for example, we noted that, after a frame or map (a product) is developed, further processing typically involves rehearsal. This further processing almost inevitably will entail some form of rehearsal. We have also recommended the use of a multipurpose frame for elaborations when advance organizers and metaphors are used in instruction. Processing those multipurpose frames, of course, entails rehearsal.

While it is true that framing or mapping entails rehearsal, it is also true that framing and mapping are wondrous mechanisms for guiding several forms of rehearsal. For example, prediction can be greatly aided by frames because of the multiple pathways via rows and columns. Rehearsal is, of course, intrinsic to our modest model of using the spatial strategies. (See the discussion in Chapter 3.)

It is very difficult to imagine any design technique, based on any of the cognitive strategies, which would not involve one or more of the rehearsal activities. Inspection of the hybridization section in every chapter will reveal the ubiquity of this strategy.

SUMMARY

In this chapter we presented a potpourri of strategies in the category of rehearsal. We summarized the research on these strategies and presented several ideas about how teachers and designers, by using techniques which activate these strategies, can increase comprehension. Remember that in the spatial strategies we have the power of knowing the forest, but in the rehearsal strategies we have mechanisms of exploring the trees, the bark, the twigs, the fern and the shrubs. In the next chapter we present another strategy, imagery, in this fourth family of multipurpose strategies.

EXERCISES

1. Review the list of rehearsal activities in Figure 8-1. Which of these, if any, have been aided by characteristics of this text?

2. From the same list, which have you used as you have studied this text?

3. Rehearsal has often been thought of as practically synonymous with study. Have you adopted any new study strategies as a result of this book and this chapter? Which, if any?

REFERENCES

Adams, A., Carnine, D., & Gersten, R. (1982). Instructional strategies for studying content area texts in the intermediate grades. *Reading Research Quarterly, 18*, 27–55.

Anderson, T. H., & Armbruster, B. B. (in press). The value of taking notes during lectures. In R. F. Filippo & D. C. Caverly (Eds.), *Teaching reading and study strategies at the college level*. Newark, DE: International Reading Association.

Anderson, T. H. (1979). Study skills and learning strategies. In H. F. O'Neil, Jr. & C. D. Spielberger (Eds.), *Cognitive and affective learning strategies*. New York: Academic Press.

Bloom, B. S. (Ed.). (1956). *Taxonomy of educational objectives—the classification of educational goals—handbook I: Cognitive domain*. New York: McKay.

Brown, A. L., & Smiley, S. S. (1977). Rating the importance of structural units of prose passages: A problem of metacognitive development. *Child Development, 48*, 1–8.

Coomber, J. E., Ramstad, D. A., & Sheets, D. (1986). Elaboration in vocabulary learning: A comparison of three rehearsal methods. *Research in the Teaching of English, 20*, 281–293.

Dunkin, M. J., & Biddle, B. J. (1974). *The study of teaching*. New York: Holt, Rinehart & Winston.

Dwyer, C. A. (1985–1986). The effect of varied rehearsal strategies in facilitating achievement of different educational objectives as measured by verbal and visual testing modes. *Journal of Experimental Education, 54*, 73–84.

Gagne, E. D. (1985). *The cognitive psychology of school learning*. Boston: Little, Brown.

Gall, M. D., Ward, B. A., Berliner, D. C., Cahen, L. S., Winne, P. H., Elashoff, J. D., & Stanton, G. C. (1978). Effects of questioning techniques and recitation on student learning. *American Educational Research Journal, 15*, 175–199.

Hagen, J. W., & Stanovich, K. G. (1977). Memory: Strategies of acquisition. In R. V. Kail, Jr., & J. W. Hagen (Eds.), *Perspectives on the development of memory and cognition*. Hillsdale, NJ: Lawrence Erlbaum Associates.

Hamilton, R. J. (1985). A framework for the evaluation of the effectiveness of adjunct questions and objectives. *Review of Educational Research, 55*, 47–85.

Hidi, S., & Anderson, V. (1986). Producing written summaries: Task demands, cognitive operations, and implications for instruction. *Review of Educational Research, 56*, 473–493.

Mager, R. F. (1962). *Preparing instructional objectives*. Palo Alto, CA: Fearon.

Mayer, R. E. (1987). *Educational psychology: A cognitive approach*. Boston: Little, Brown.

McAndrew, D. A. (1983). Underlining and notetaking: Some suggestions from research. *Journal of Reading, 27*, 103–108.

Ornstein, P. A., & Naus, M. J. (1978). Rehearsal processes in children's memory. In P. A. Ornstein (Ed.), *Memory development in children*. New York: Wiley.

Palincsar, A. & Brown, A. (1984). Reciprocal teaching of comprehension-fostering and comprehension-monitoring activities. *Cognition and Instruction, 1*, 117–175.

Palmere, M., Benton, S. L., Glover, J. A., & Ronning, R. R. (1983). Elaboration and recall of main ideas in prose. *Journal of Educational Psychology, 75*, 898–907.

Pressley, M., & Levin, J. R. (Eds.). (1983). *Cognitive strategy research*. New York: Springer-Verlag.

Robinson, F. P. (1961). *Effective study*. New York: Harper & Row.

Sefkow, S. B., & Myers, J. L. (1980). Review of effects of inserted questions on learning from prose. *American Educational Research Journal, 17,* 435–447.

Slavin, R. E. (1988). *Educational psychology: Theory into practice.* (2nd ed.). Englewood Cliffs, NJ: Prentice-Hall.

Thomas, E. L., & Robinson, H. A. (1982). *Improving reading in every class: A source book for teachers*. Boston: Allyn & Bacon.

Wong, B. Y. L. (1985). Self-questioning instructional research: A review. *Review of Educational Research, 55,* 227–268.

CHAPTER 9

Imagery

In this chapter we discuss the research on imagery. In this discussion we include the characteristics of this strategy and how to use imagery as a technique in instructional design. One of the rousing success stories of the cognitive evolution/revolution is that of the renewed interest in imagery and the systematic research efforts which have resulted in many applications. There is extensive research in how imagery can aid recall. Sport psychologists have used imagery enthusiastically. Administrative/management theorists have adapted imagery. Psychological therapists now employ imagery in clinical settings (Sheehan, 1972).

In supercomputing currently, a metaphorical turnover from "The mind is like a computer," to "The computer is like the mind," is driving fascinating developments in computer imaging (Ward, 1989). At the University of Illinois National Center for Supercomputing Applications, at least one mathematician believes that he has achieved more complete comprehension of differential equations via computer imaging. There and at other sites, complex events such as weather, flight, insect epidemics and neutron stars colliding are imaged in drama and detail.

In sport psychology the use of imagery is widespread. Is it possible that professional sports franchises wax and wane in terms of collective imaging prowess? Each spring, at professional football training camps across the country, players practice imaging themselves maiming, pillaging, destroying, gouging and tackling.

"Victory!" they image.

"Pass with spirals and perfection!" quarterbacks picture in their minds.

"My hands are covered with glue!" visualize receivers.

"Block and tackle with brutal vigor!" image linemen.

Even on campuses, in the early winter and mid-spring during final examinations, professors notice that students occasionally pause over test booklets, close their eyes and wrinkle their foreheads. There are several plausible hypotheses for this. Perhaps the students are bored and are escaping into brief fantasy. Or perhaps they are religious and seeking intercession. Perhaps they are tired and merely resting for the moment. But, some, surely, are dredging for the image, the mental picture they formed to help them remember.

Imagery is the second member of the multipurpose family of cognitive strategies. Its uses are legion for several reasons. First, it is not bound by the structure of the knowledge domain; that is, it can be used to aid recall of information of high and low structure. Second, it can be deployed for declarative, conditional and procedural knowledge. Third, it is not restricted to verbal material, particularly when that material is representative of concrete ideas and concepts. Finally, there is general agreement that there are at least two encoding systems existing in mind: verbal and imaginal (Pavio, 1971), and much can be encoded both verbally and imaginally.

There are, however, three restrictions on the use of imagery. Imagery works best for concrete information and less well for abstract information. It is relatively easy to form a picture in mind of an isosceles triangle or a proper body position while serving tennis, but it is very difficult to visualize the meaning of ideas such as "truth" or "hypothesis." A second restriction is that there are substantial individual differences in imagery skills. Some persons have grave difficulty forming images while others are very skilled. Third, there are some restrictions which are developmental. Despite these restrictions, imagery can be used in many ways to improve instruction and to make learning more efficient.

The many uses of imagery attest to the seemingly "natural" place it has in human cognition. Most persons have developed some capacity to process and remember in image form. Some have developed visualization skills to a high degree and use those skills routinely. When something new must be learned, some persons may consciously form a mental picture. Others visualize seemingly unconsciously.

While it may be a natural skill for many, the popularization of various applications are a result of renewed interest in imagery within the past 20 years or so. This renewed interest and rebirth of research is a substantial component in the cognitive evolution.

RESEARCH: REPRESENTATIVE STUDIES

Imagery was one of the first topics to be investigated in the beginnings of empirical psychology in the nineteenth century, but the history of its use extends back in time to 500 B. C. (Higbee, 1979; Yates, 1966). Interest and research waned, however, during the first 60 or so years of this century, particularly in U.S. empirical psychology and particularly during the hegemony of behaviorism. It is said that John B. Watson, the father of behaviorism, claimed that he never imaged, daydreamed or dreamed (Ahsen, 1986)—one implication being that he thought images were not a valid object of research. As the cognitive evolution solidified, however, imagery once more became a topic of interest and research.

Since the mid-1960s a great deal of research has been conducted. Two outstanding reviews of this research exist (Higbee, 1979; Pressley, 1977). In this section we will discuss a few representative studies. This discussion is organized in the following order: imagery-aided recall of words in pairs (paired-associates), sentences, longer prose passages, motor learning, complex nonverbal arrays (pictures, illustrations, maps) and very complex skills, some of which are procedural.

Pairs of Words

In an investigation by Bower and Winzenz (1970), subjects were asked to learn concrete nouns in pairs. There were four treatment groups: a repetition group (repeating or rehearsing silently); a sentence-reading group (reading a sentence aloud containing the two nouns, with the subjects instructed to use the sentence to associate the two nouns); a sentence-generation group (creating a sentence to connect the two nouns in a reasonable way); and an imagery group (forming an image to associate the two nouns in a vivid, elaborate, bizarre and interacting manner). Subjects were asked to reproduce 15 pairs and recognize another 15 pairs. The recall of the 15 pairs on the recognition task was so high that there were no significant differences among groups, but for the 15 items to be reproduced there were significant differences in favor of the imagery group. The relative order of recall in ascending order was repetition, sentence provided, sentence creation and imagery. Thus, as was discussed in the last chapter on rehearsal, the three rehearsal strategies provided some aid, with sentence creation the most helpful of the rehearsal strategies, but the imagery strategy was superior.

Sentences

Anderson and Hidde (1971) extended the research from learning paired-associates to learning sentences. Engaging subjects in an innocuous deception, Anderson and Hidde asked subjects to "norm sentences for use in a future experiment" (p. 527). Half the subjects were asked to form a mental image of the event in the sentence and then rate the vividness of the image. The other half was asked to repeat the sentence aloud three times and rate the pronounceability of the words in the sentence. All subjects were exposed to 30 sentences for seven seconds per sentence; then the sentence was removed from sight, and the subjects were given three seconds to rate the sentence for imagery or pronounceability. Subjects were given a surprise recall test after presentation and rating. The test consisted of a list of sentence nouns, and subjects were asked to supply the remainder of the sentence. Subjects in the imagery group recalled three times as many verbs and objects as the other group. There was a slight effect for vividness in that sentences rated as more vivid were recalled more frequently.

Prose Passages

Intrigued by possibilities of imagery for extended prose passages, Anderson and Kulhavy (1972) presented high school seniors with a 2,000-word text similar to those in typical textbooks. Experimental subjects were instructed to form mental images while reading and the controls were instructed to study carefully. After being tested for recall, all subjects completed a questionnaire on their use of imagery while reading the passage. The imagery instructions had no significant effect on recall; but, of the experimental group, two-thirds reported using imagery through most of the passage, and one-half of the controls reported using imagery. When the researchers looked at recall in terms of reported use of imagery, visualization did have significant effects on recall.

From this study it can be concluded that just because instructions to visualize are given does *not* mean that students will image. Furthermore, students may image in the absence of instructions. The latter is further testimony to the naturalistic status of imagery in human cognition.

In a similar study Giesen and Peeck (1984) found helpful effects on retention for a 2,300-word story. They compared an imagery-instructed group with a group which was asked simply to read the story carefully. The imagery group performed better on a test composed of questions about concrete, explicit, contradictory and spatial information. Imagery had no effect on the retention of abstract information. Subjects in the imagery group reported using more images while answering questions than the control group.

Psychomotor Skills

The representative studies discussed previously in this section are on prose learning. Research has also been conducted on motor skills. As an example of these studies, Koslow (1987) looked at the possibility that imagery instructions could improve acquisition of a complex motor skill. He used a mirrored drawing procedure in which subjects manipulated a photoelectric stylus within a three-centimeter border of a six-pointed star drawing. Subjects could not directly see the drawing and their hand, but could view them with a mirror. Subjects were given one trial to practice and were limited to ten more trials. After the practice trial, experimentals were instructed to use mental imagery and controls were not. Those in the experimental group were given ten minutes to practice imaging the star shape and movements. Then the experimentals had their ten trials. The imagery treatment had a significant effect on performance.

The possibility of "mental practice" through imaging without actual performance having such an effect is intriguing. This is an important key to the use of imagery in sport psychology and psychomotor learning. This possibility has been researched extensively especially during the 1960s and early 1970s. Before 1983, 98 such studies had been located by Feltz and Landers (1983) in preparation for their review and meta-analysis.

Research located and analyzed by Feltz and Landers (1983) included effects for imagery (mental practice) on a large variety of tasks in numerous motor and sport areas with subjects from elementary schools, high schools and colleges. Tasks and/or sports comprised dart throwing; serving in badminton, tennis, volleyball and handball; passing in football; speed skating; tap dancing; foul shooting in basketball; juggling; chipping in golf; sorting in cards; bowling; baseball; swimming; karate; and others. Motor learning included such nonsport tasks as maze tracing and mirrored tracing.

Of the 98 studies located, 60 were suitable for meta-analysis. The basic result of the meta-analysis (Feltz & Landers, 1983) is that mental practice of a motor skill influences performance slightly but consistently better than no practice at all. Another finding is that when effects are examined on cognitive (informational) components of the task, mental practice has more powerful effects on those cognitive components than on motor components.

Learning many motor tasks, perhaps all to varying degrees, involves cognitive components such as the sequence of movements and spatial arrangements. For example, in fly casting, one must know and have encoded symbolically a particular sequence: feeding a few feet of line through the ferrules past the tip of the rod; lifting the rod, and thus the line, with the connecting leader vertically overhead and slightly behind while keeping the wrist rigid; allowing the rod to flex and power the line to the rear; then bringing the rod forward while again keeping the wrist rigid. This oversimplified and incomplete sequential description of a bit of procedural knowledge can be imaged as knowledge, of course in symbolic form. Imagery provides the help often needed to master such cognitive elements; then that knowledge can be deployed in the motor performance. Mentally imaging the sequence and the arrangement in space augments learning.

To examine the possibility of imagery having more powerful effects on cognitive components of tasks than on motor components, Ryan and Simons (1981) formulated an ingenious experiment. They worked within the idea that tasks can be placed on a continuum from cognitive to motor components. Two tasks were to be performed: standing on a stabilometer platform keeping it as steady as possible as a primarily motor task, and solving a maze as more of a cognitive task. The maze required that one handle be moved for horizontal progress through the maze and a second handle be moved for vertical movement. Coordinating the movement of the hands on the handles moved a stylus in and through the maze.

There were three groups in this experiment. The physical-practice group was given 12 trials on each task; the mental-practice (imagery) group was given one actual practice trial, nine mental, and then two more actual practice trials; and the no-practice group was assigned one actual trial, ten minutes' rest and two actual trials. On the primarily motor task, the platform balance, there were no effects for mental practice, with the actual-practice group superior to the other two groups. On the motor task with more cognitive elements, the maze, the imagery group did as well as the actual-practice group, with both the imagery group and the actual-practice group significantly better than the no-practice group. Remember that the imagery group had only three actual practice trials as compared to the 12 trials of the actual-practice group! Also, the imagery group had the same number of actual practice trials (three) as the no-practice group! Very similar findings are reported by Ryan and Simons (1983) in a later experiment.

One of the major reasons that actual practice of motor skills is believed to be critical for mastery is that *practice entails knowledge of results*. One performs and observes accuracy or inaccuracy. Observing actual results is lacking in mental practice, yet mental practice works. Zecker (1982) examined this belief about knowledge of results with four conditions: mental practice, physical practice with knowledge of results, physical practice without knowledge of results and a control. The task was tossing beanbags at a target. As a pretest, each subject tossed the beanbag at a target 20 times.

Subjects in the physical practice had 40 practice trials in which they could observe results. Those in the mental practice condition were instructed to image the entire toss from the beginning of the toss until it was released from the hand. Then they were asked to mentally practice without physical movement for 40 trials and to inform the experimenter when they had completed those 40 trials. Those subjects in the physical-practice-but-no-knowledge-of-results group tossed the bag; but, for each trial as the bag left the hand, the lights were extinguished and white noise was provided which masked auditory feedback. Controls played frisbee. Following the experimental manipulation all subjects tossed the bag 20 times, a posttest measure of performance. The mental practice group showed the greatest pretest-to-posttest improvement. The practice-without-knowledge-of-results group improved more than the practice-with-knowledge-of-results group. The physical-practice-with-knowledge-of-results group actually performed worse on the posttest than on the pretest, in contrast to all other groups whose performance improved! It may be that the extensive and repetitive practice with knowledge of results was excessive, so excessive that this "massed" practice became harmful to performance. The main finding, however, that mental practice induces such performance gains despite the absence of knowledge of results, is very exciting.

Some possibility exists that a part of imagery or mental practice is the inclusion of an *imaged outcome*, perhaps the imaginal equivalent of knowledge of results. Woolfolk, Murphy, Gottesfeld and Aitken (1985) investigated this possibility for golf putting by having several conditions for college undergraduates. Experimental conditions included imagery of the putting stroke with the ball rolling into the cup (the outcome), imagery of the putting stroke with the ball missing the cup, imagery of the stroke only, imagery of the successful outcome only (the ball rolls into the cup) and imagery of the unsuccessful outcome only (the ball misses the cup). The subjects who imaged the unsuccessful outcome suffered a decline in putting accuracy, but those who imaged success did not increase accuracy. The main point, however, is that imaging outcomes can have effects. Other studies—Gould, Weinberg and Jackson

(1980), for example—have demonstrated effects for imaging successful outcomes.

There is also some research combining imagery and observational learning (Housner, 1984). Learning by observing a model performing has been a major strategy within social learning theory (Bandura, 1969; Bandura & Jeffrey, 1973). Imagery may be the complementary, perhaps necessary, mechanism for observational learning and for no-trial (no-practice) learning. That is to say that the learner observes a model performing motor activities and forms a mental picture in the mind of the performance. Forming such images can lead to substantial improvement (Housner, 1984).

In the Housner (1984) investigation a variety of leg, trunk, arm and head movements were modeled and then observed by subjects. The motor movements varied systematically in complexity, with some having four parts, some seven parts and some ten. Subjects with high imaging ability performed more accurately than those with low imaging ability across the three levels of complexity. High imagers reported using imagery more than low imagers.

By way of summarization of the research on imagery in motor learning, there is enough evidence to support the use of imagery. No advocate of imagery would recommend the replacement of physical practice with mental practice, with or without models and with or without imaging successful outcomes. Many advocates do, however, recommend imagery or mental practice as a *complement* to physical practice. That recommendation can be made with more confidence and enthusiasm for the learning of the symbolic or cognitive components of motor learning.

Pictures, Maps, Illustrations

Imagery has also been examined as an aid to recalling pictures, drawings and illustrations. Kosslyn, Ball and Reiser (1978) had subjects learn to draw a map of an island containing seven objects such as a hut, tree, well and rock and then asked subjects to form an image of the map. The drawing showed that the subjects had learned the map. Subjects could place objects in relation to others on the map seemingly by scanning the image.

An interesting focus of this study was to determine whether scanning time was a function of distance between objects on the map. Subjects were, for instance, asked to locate the tree on the map and then asked to view the rock. The further apart the objects were, the longer it took to locate the next object. This constitutes evidence of imagery as a real mental representation that retains some of the properties of that which is being represented.

In another investigation of instructional effects of imagery on complex arrays of information, Larson et al. (1985) combined instructions for imagery, verbal mnemonics (such as rhyming) and production of drawings and graphs for one condition. They also combined instructions for correcting inaccurate information, detecting omissions and detecting key ideas (selecting) for another condition. The materials to be learned were two 2,500-word passages, one on geography (plate tectonics) and another on ecosystems, taken from college introductory texts. Pairs of students cooperatively studied the material. Subjects were tested for recall and transfer. The group receiving the set of instructions including imagery performed significantly better on transfer but worse on recall.

Procedural Knowledge

While many of the skills discussed are procedural, they are also motor. Now we look at studies which include procedural knowledge that is at least partially verbal.

Trollip (1979) examined the possibility of supplementing computer-based flight training with imaging. Specifically, the subject of training was flight holding patterns. The skills involved are complex, and, furthermore, some are procedural rather than declarative. Part of the innovativeness of this study is the use of computer-aided instruction instead of the more standard on-the-job training supplemented by simulators.

Controls were given ground school instruction by a lecturer in a class-room setting, but experimentals were given their ground training with computer-aided instruction supplemented with encouragement to visualize. After the training the students were required to fly a series of holding patterns (accompanied by an instructor and an experienced observer!) under varying conditions of no wind, crosswind and tailwind and to make a procedure turn. Performing to these requirements involves attending and responding to a substantial amount of information including speed, altitude and location. Instrument panels provide some of this information, while control tower personnel provide some. The information must be integrated rapidly and proper responses made. The experimental group made significantly fewer critical errors than controls and were superior to the controls on all measures including time to perform correctly, number of trials to criterion, altitude errors and total errors. On the very difficult crosswind patterns, the experimentals were even more efficient than the controls.

In another study which included complex and procedural skills, Lindberg and Lawliss (1988) combined imagery with a progressive relaxation technique. Subjects were being prepared for childbirth. The women who received the imagery-aided treatment were more relaxed during labor and delivery when compared to controls.

In this section we have seen that the formation of images can aid learning and recall for many kinds of tasks, for a wide variety of knowledge domains and for both declarative and procedural knowledge. The representative studies discussed include recall for words, sentences, long passages, pictures, psychomotor tasks and complex forms of procedural knowledge. The knowledge domains include many of those taught in formal education. The media include computers, text and pictures.

ISSUES

In this section we discuss the research on several important issues, including developmental considerations, imposed versus self-generated imagery, training, concreteness, interaction, vividness and bizarreness. These latter four issues are formulated as ways to add force to the image.

Developmental Considerations

While the very young are able to visualize and can, as young as kindergarten age, benefit from instructions to image (Levin, Ghatala, DeRose, & Makoid, 1977), ability to use visualization systematically and efficiently improves with age, probably into adulthood. Just because young children can, under propitious situations, benefit from imagery instructions (Ryan, Ledger, & Weed, 1987) does not mean that they necessarily will. For example, Goldston and Richman (1985) found that their subjects, children age six, did not benefit from instructions to image. There is mixed evidence about the age in which children's learning and recall may be expected to improve under imagery instructions, particularly with self-generated imagery. Some have suggested that by age eight to ten, generally, benefits of instructions to image for learning and recall may accrue (Pressley, 1976, 1977; Pressley, Gariglia-Bull, Deane, & Schneider, 1987). While individuals differ greatly within age, imagery skills should be sufficiently developed around the ages of eight–ten to the extent that benefits can be expected. Furthermore, visualization skills will improve into adulthood and become more efficient (Kosslyn, 1980, pp. 407–437).

The mixed evidence for age-related restrictions may be due to sampling difficulties of two types. With any human skill or trait there may be substantial individual differences, differences so great that it is difficult to sample confidently. Mixed results may be a function of nonrepresentative sampling of persons within age groups. Another type of sampling problem contributing may be task sampling. That which is or is not imaged can vary greatly. To this date little exists by way of the development of standardizing sets of tasks and stimuli, although several tests have been developed and progress is being made (Ahsen, 1986).

Supplied Compared with Self-Generated Imagery

Should students generate their own images or should images be supplied? Any answer to this question must contain qualification. If visualization skills are poorly developed, it is better to supply images (Carrier, Karbo, Kindem, Legisa, & Newstrom, 1983). If, however, visualization skills are developed or if they have been learned, it is best to have students construct their own images (Jamieson & Schimpf, 1980). This question is further complicated by the expectation that a picture or visual supplied will necessarily be imaged by the student. It should not be expected that students will visualize a supplied illustration or picture in the absence of prompting or in the absence of personal experiences of the students which have validated the worth of imaging as a cognitive strategy. This is yet another proof that the best instructional design is based on knowledge of the target students.

There are several complicating factors, one of which is the comparative quality of the supplied or self-generated image with respect to its fidelity to the task being learned. By *fidelity*, we mean the accuracy of the image, the extent to which the image contains reasonable representations of the relevant components of the task or stimuli. Suppose, for example, the task is to learn and remember the structure of the human heart. A student-generated image might be very incomplete, whereas a text or teacher-supplied illustration should be more complete. Age (Reese, 1977; Pressley, 1977) and mental ability (Campione & Brown, 1977) are other complicating factors.

From the discussion on developmental considerations, one may conclude that an important watershed for self-generated imagery is middle childhood, around ages eight to ten (Pressley, 1977). Prior to that age encoding, learning and recall effects are more likely to occur when images are supplied. After that age the better technique is to encourage students to form their own images.

Training

Pressley (1976), with third-grade students, found that a combination of training to image and instructions to image improved recall of contents of story passages. This training consisted of students making up images between story segments while they read and being shown examples of good pictures, those pictures which represent the material accurately.

In a study with first-year mechanical engineering students, Parrott (1986) attempted to train for the visualization of movement and the generation of images and imaginal associations. The training program consisted of eight one-hour sessions, scheduled weekly. During these sessions subjects practiced these forms of visualization. Parrott found that this training led to increased use of imaginal processes in performance and at times altered the subjective nature of the visualization experience.

In another study using undergraduate students, Yates (1986) trained by having subjects practice visualizing cubes and dice and manipulating images of those objects. The training period varied from 60 to 90 minutes. The training improved performance on a paper-folding exercise.

Ohlsen, Hortin and Newhouse (1984) gave graduate students a 30-minute slide and lecture presentation designed to teach them about imagery. Included in the presentation were a definition of imagery, ways to use imagery in teaching and learning, examples of learning using imagery and exercises. The training had positive significant effects on a transfer task consisting of solving visual puzzles.

The studies presented in this section are illustrative studies of training for imagery. Other studies are discussed in Pressley (1977) and Pressley and Levin (1983). As a general rule, imagery training has positive effects on learning. Also, in general, training effects increase into adulthood. We now turn to research issues about increasing the power of images.

Concreteness

Concrete is a deceptively simple word in the context of cognition. It means "existing in reality, perceptible by the senses." This meaning poses some problems, particularly for learning words, since all words are abstract (Bugelski, 1971, 1977). Furthermore, all knowledge is abstract. Thus the phrases "concrete words" and "concrete knowledge" are oxymorons. Nonetheless, there is some psychological utility to the phrase "concrete words" in that some words represent persons, places or things—objects or events which are accessible to the senses. The utility reflects itself in mental imagery.

How necessary is concreteness in the formation of images? There is some agreement that concrete words and concepts are more readily and easily

FIGURE 9-1
Powerful additives for images with definitions and examples.

Additive	Definition	Examples
Concreteness	Entries in the image include persons, places or things; that which exists in reality or is perceptible by the senses, tangible.	Image of tree or cube or motor activity vs. truth, hypothesis or beauty.
Interaction among Items	Entries in the image are affiliated or connected.	Topic: Sources of energy. Visualize blob of oil flowing around a lump of coal.
Interaction with Context	Entries in the image are connected to topic.	Include in above image a sun as a symbol for energy. A ray of sunshine is black and liquid, spilling over a lump of coal.
Vividness	Items in the image are clear, distinct and forceful.	Change above image to a coalminer tossing the sun into a bubbling pool of oil.
Bizarreness	Images that are weird, unusual or incongruous.	Topic: Petroleum products. Giant hot tub is filled with bubbling petroleum. Bubbles burst with great force, casting products from the tub.

imaged than those which are abstract. What is important is what happens in the mind of the person on seeing or hearing the word or the concept name (Bugelski, 1977; Richardson, 1980a). The word *tree* may call to mind an image of an oak tree, but the more abstract word *democracy* may or may not. There may be imaginal associations brought to mind by *democracy*, such as a polling booth, but the image may be more remote from the concept than an image of an oak tree is to the concept of "tree." Such remoteness may reduce any effects imagery might have.

There is some evidence that concreteness has positive effects on learning which are experimentally separable from imagery effects (Richardson, 1980b). Thus, the student who images concrete material may reap the benefits of both concreteness and imaging.

One caveat should be mentioned. Some individuals are such skilled imagers that they appear to be able to visualize even abstract material. Some are able to visualize very abstract symbols—printed words, for example—to the point that it is helpful in spelling (Sears & Johnson, 1986). Still others have the capability of *eidetic imagery*. This is a very vivid type of imagery, as though the person is actually seeing the object or event (Ahsen, 1977; Haber, 1979; Jordan, Davis, Kahn, & Sinnott, 1980; Kunzendorf, 1984; Marks & McKellar, 1982; Pavio & Cohen, 1979). It was once thought that eidetic imagery was a capability limited to childhood and that it disappeared by adolescence. More recent research has demonstrated that this is not true.

Interaction

By interaction is meant that when the task is composed of two or more items or components, it is best if these items are visualized as acting on each other. Suppose, for example, the task is to recall pairs of words such as *piano-cigar* (from Wollen, Weber, & Lowry, 1972). The pairs are better recalled if they are shown interacting, if the piano is smoking the cigar.

Beggs and Sikich (1984) add to the possibilities of richness of interaction in images by experimentally demonstrating that the image should include the context of association of the pairs of words. For example, if *cake-ring* were to be paired in the image, *wedding* would be the context. Combining the pair of words and the context in the image is a better aid for recall than merely pairing the words in an image.

As a result of his analysis of related research, Higbee (1979) concludes that interaction does aid recall. Furthermore, other research has demonstrated the importance of including context in the interactive image. Thus, part of imagery training and the use of imagery in teaching and design would be to highlight the potential of interaction.

Vividness

According to Higbee (1979) a vivid image is one that has clarity, distinctness and strength. Descriptors of vividness also include emotionality, colorfulness and forcefulness. Within the imagery research vividness has been investigated as a trait of the image and as a trait of the object or material imaged. Either has positive effects on recall and heightens the effect of imagery. Thus vividness is similar to concreteness in that both vividness and imagery aid learning.

In one representative study of vividness as a property of material studied, Montague and Carter (1973) investigated the power of vividness in paragraphs of passages. Two versions of these paragraphs were written. In one version vivid words (italicized in this text) such as "The cobra *whipped* . . . ," "Its *smooth brown* body *grew taut* . . . ," and "The mongoose *seized the leathery throat* . . . ," were included. In the other version less vivid words were used, such as "The cobra *lifted* its head . . . ," "Its *dark-colored* body *assumed* a posture . . . ," and "The mongoose *gained hold* of the throat. . . ." Subjects read these passages, with half of them given instructions to image. Words were categorized into function words (articles, conjunctions and prepositions) and substance words (nouns, pronouns, verbs, adjectives and adverbs). The vivid, image-evoking substance words in the passages were recalled better than the nonvivid words in the passages. Vividness had no effect on recall of function words. Instructions to image interacted with vividness on recall of synonyms for words used in the passage. These authors think that the vivid words evoked the use of imagery by all subjects, whether or not they were given instructions to image.

In a similar vein Wharton (1980) revised passages from college-level history texts for more vividness. Not only did students rate the passages as more interesting, but also comprehension was enhanced by the revised version of the text.

Bizarreness

The idea that images should be *bizarre*—that is, weird, unusual, incongruous—extends through the history of imagery as an aid to learning and memory. Higbee (1979) notes that the findings are mixed for this variable. He emphasizes that one reason bizarreness may not always promote recall is that some persons may have problems making up bizarre images. For those who have problems, Higbee suggests creating images that are vivid, interactive and interesting. Those who are comfortable with and who can formulate bizarre images will probably benefit.

In this section we presented an overview of several issues which are important in the research and use of imagery. We discussed the issues of development (age), supplied versus self-generated imagery, training, concreteness, interaction, vividness and bizarreness. We cast concreteness, interaction, vividness and bizarreness as powerful additives to imagery. These are summarized in Figure 9-1 with definitions and examples. We now examine some of the characteristics of images other than vividness and bizarreness.

CHARACTERISTICS OF IMAGES

Mental images are pictorial analogues of something physical, somewhat like pictures in the mind. Most people are capable of forming these visual representations and then "scanning" them for detail. Images are thought to have two primary sources: some can be formed from experiencing external events and objects and others can be formed from contents of mind (Piaget & Inhelder, 1969, 1971). Most people can observe an event or object and immediately form a mental, seemingly visual, representation. So also can most people form an image of something recalled, such as the house in which they lived many decades before. There is considerable variation both within individuals and among individuals as to how long images are recalled.

The simile that images are "like pictures in the mind" is helpful to a degree. Yet images are more like videotapes or movies than still photographs, for they are plastic, dynamic and modifiable (Anderson, 1985, pp. 89–95). As one, for example, recalls the hotel suite on the ridge in Lugano from last summer, one can "walk" through and scan the entryway, the bedroom to the right, the bath, the bedroom to the left and some of the furnishings, the glass doors and the balcony. From the balcony one can mentally scan the lake, the boats with slack sails tacking at their leisure, the speeding power boats whose spreading wakes tear the natural painting in the quiet water, the town center to the left and well below the hotel, the surrounding mountains and the changing light as the day passed. In the evening fireboats sprayed sparkling fountains of bright colors.

The richness of images allows the representation and storage of substantial amounts of information. It has been said that a picture is worth a thousand words. That may or may not be true. For recall, however, it is more likely that an image can be worth a thousand words. One can mentally "walk" through or scan the image for reconstruction of large numbers of bits of information. One can focus deliberately on parts of the image and generate substantial amounts of detail.

For example, one might try to reconstruct a mental picture of one's home at age 12. It is very likely that one can move through the image of the home from room to room. Furniture can probably be visualized as well as paintings, contents of cabinets, views from windows and even some guests.

FIGURE 9-2
Characteristics of images.

Images Are:
1. Pictorial analogues in mind
2. Modifiable
3. More like videotape than a still photograph
4. Divisible into parts which can be inspected
5. A result of learning
6. Teachable

The idea that an image might contain substantial amounts of information should not be taken to mean that an image is unlimited in the number of "bytes" of information represented and recalled. Normal limits of images may be similar to those described by Miller (1956) and Meehl (1954) for verbal representation. This limit should be the subject of future research. Whatever the limit is, it would be subject to individual differences.

Following Figure 9-2, other characteristics of images are that they can be learned and that the skill can be taught. Some people seem to have modest imaging skills but seem to improve those skills with instruction and maturation. There is some agreement that by age eight to ten years imagery can be self-generated.

GENERAL RULES FOR USING IMAGERY IN INSTRUCTIONAL DESIGN

In this section we present the specifications summary (Figure 9-3) and discuss important implications of the research on imagery for teaching and instructional design. Consistent with our emphasis on strategy learning are the objectives of not only learning imagery as a cognitive strategy but also using imagery to learn content.

We have emphasized that imagery is a multipurpose strategy, and that should be obvious as you inspect Figure 9-3. There are a few restraints which you should understand: those of concreteness and medium or low data tonnage. Also you should note that imagery is another strategy to aid the outcome of motor learning.

Student learning to use imagery should most often be seen as a gradual process. For some its use is alien, so that the task is to encourage its use gradually by prompting—by giving instructions to "form a mental picture." Ideally, students who are strangers to the strategic use of imagery become convinced of its utility in learning through use during instruction and study and, as they learn, they become comfortable with it. The conviction and increasing comfort should lead to use in their study and mastery of more tasks and content as well as different types of tasks and content.

Particularly in the early stages of imagery use, instruction should contain *prompting* (please note Figure 9-4). Students should be told to form a mental picture of the content to be learned. Prompts should be specific to the content and task. It is important to provide objects, pictures, charts, spatial arrays or illustrations for children up to ages eight to ten as aid for visualization. This could be a good rule also for those adolescents and adults who report difficulty or discomfort with the use of imagery. Such provisions should not be as necessary for sophisticated visualizers. For very difficult content or tasks, supplied stimuli may be necessary even for more sophisticated students.

It is probable that *modeling* can be a very effective aid for imagery use (Figure 9-4). Teachers and designers may describe their images and share how that image helps their recall and performance. An additional modeling

FIGURE 9-3

Specifications for imagery.

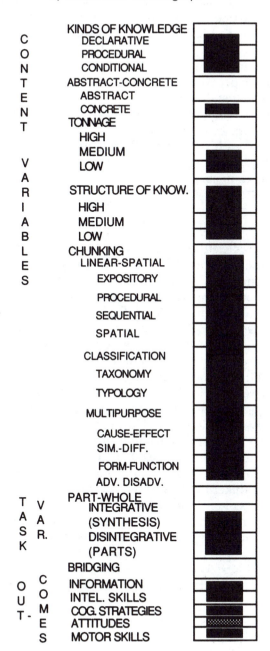

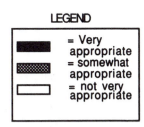

LEGEND

■	= Very appropriate
▨	= somewhat appropriate
□	= not very appropriate

FIGURE 9-4

Rules for the use of imagery in design.

1. Prompt—Give instructions to visualize (often absolutely necessary). Say: "Form a picture of _____ in your mind."
2. Model the use of imagery.
3. Reinforce their formation and use.
4. Images should be vivid.
5. Items to be recalled should interact.
6. Include context in the interactive image.
7. Suggest and encourage concreteness.
8. Provide instructions for bizarreness with caution.
9. Fidelity is necessary.
10. Avoid overloading an image.

effect which could be predicted in motor learning is that of the model performing the task for the student while the student observes and visualizes (Housner, 1984). The student may then mentally, visually practice.

Reinforcement is another important component in instructional uses of imagery. Students can talk about the image formed, and then designers or teachers and perhaps peers could comment on the desirability of any attempt and the attributes of the image shared. Attributes include vividness, interaction, concreteness, bizarreness and fidelity. Review of Figure 9-1 should help in the use of these additives as one uses imagery in design.

Finally, it is important to avoid overload. Good images are complete representations of major items to be remembered; that is, effective images have fidelity. It is, however, possible to pack the image with too many items or bytes of information. We suggest that, without further research, the optimal number of bytes to include is about nine. Designers may wish to determine this limit for their knowledge domain and for their target students through trial and error, through tinkering. It is better to formulate a new and associated image than to overload any one image.

In Chapter 1 we introduced the idea that the technology of instructional design is partially tinkering, toying with ideas and experimenting—essentially trial and error. The strategy of imagery, turned to design techniques, should provide many ideas for this trial and error. Each of the ten rules for the use of imagery is a guide, each of which may require tinkering for the most effective use of imagery in instruction.

HYBRIDIZATION

In the last chapter we presented the idea that visual images may be rehearsed. Here it is important to emphasize that while students are engaged in any of the rehearsal strategies, some visualization may occur. Given the legion of uses of imagery in both verbal and motor learning and in most knowledge domains, imagery is likely to be combined with most of the other strategies.

SUMMARY

In this chapter we presented the strategy of imagery, discussed some representative studies of its instructional uses, discussed research on major issues about the characteristics of effective images and provided guidelines for effective uses of imagery as a technique in instructional design and classroom learning. We have shown that the formation of mental images aids recall in a variety of learning tasks such as word associations, vocabulary learning, extended prose learning, visual arrays, motor learning and complex learning of procedures. We have seen that imagery effects extend beyond mere recall to transfer.

We have avoided direct mentioning of imagery in mnemonics in this chapter. Several mnemonic systems depend on mental visualization. These we discuss in the next chapter.

EXERCISES

1. Rate yourself from one to ten (ten = high) on imagery skills. Why do you think you rate at this level? Before this course has anyone encouraged you to use imagery? Has reading this chapter encouraged you to develop your imagery skills?

2. Choose several items of knowledge with which you feel familiar, or even expert in. Rate each on their imageability on the same scale, from one to ten. Provide a rationale for this rating.

REFERENCES

Ahsen, A. (1977). Eidetics: An overview. *Journal of Mental Imagery, 1*, 5–38.

Ahsen, A. (1986). Prologue to unvividness paradox. *Journal of Mental Imagery, 10*, 1–8.

Anderson, J. R. (1985). *Cognitive psychology and its implications.* New York: Freeman.

Anderson, R. C., & Hidde, J. L. (1971). Imagery and sentence learning. *Journal of Educational Psychology, 62*, 526–530.

Anderson, R. C., & Kulhavy, R. W. (1972). Imagery and prose learning. *Journal of Educational Psychology, 63*, 242–243.

Bandura, A. (1969). *Principles of behavior modification.* New York: Holt, Rinehart and Winston.

Bandura, A., & Jeffrey, R. W. (1973). Role of symbolic coding and rehearsal processes in observational learning. *Journal of Personality and Social Psychology, 26*, 122–130.

Beggs, I., & Sikich, D. (1984). Imagery and contextual organization. *Memory and Cognition, 12*, 52–59.

Bower, G. H., & Winenz, D. (1970). Comparison of associative learning strategies. *Psychonomic Science, 20*, 119–120.

Bugelski, B. R. (1971). The definition of the image. In S. Segal (Ed.), *Imagery: Current cognitive approaches*. New York: Academic Press.

Bugelski, B. R. (1977). Imagery and verbal behavior. *Journal of Mental Imagery, 1*, 39–52.

Campione, J. C., & Brown, A. L. (1977). Memory and metamemory development in educable retarded children. In R. V. Kail, Jr., & J. W. Hagen (Eds.), *Perspectives on the development of memory and cognition*. Hillsdale, NJ: Lawrence Erlbaum Associates.

Carrier, C., Karbo, K., Kindem, H., Legisa, G., & Newstrom, L. (1983). Use of self-generated and supplied visuals as mnemonics in gifted children's learning. *Perceptual and Motor Skills, 57*, 235–240.

Feltz, D. L., & Landers, D. M. (1983). The effects of mental practice on motor skill learning and performance: A meta-analysis. *Journal of Sport Psychology, 5*, 25–57.

Giesen, C., & Peeck, J. (1984). Effects of imagery instruction on reading and retaining a literary text. *Journal of Mental Imagery, 8*, 79–90.

Goldston, D. B., & Richman, C. L. (1985). Imagery, encoding specificity, and prose recall in 6-year-old children. *Journal of Experimental Child Psychology, 40*, 395–405.

Gould, D., Weinberg, R., & Jackson, A. (1980). Mental preparation strategies: Cognitions and strength performance. *Journal of Sport Psychology, 2*, 329–339.

Haber, R. N. (1979). Twenty years of haunting eidetic imagery: Where's the ghost? *Behavioral and Brains Science, 2*, 583–629.

Higbee, K. L. (1979). Recent research on visual mnemonics: Historical roots and educational fruits. *Review of Educational Research, 49*, 611–629.

Housner, L. D. (1984). The role of visual imagery in recall of modeled motoric stimuli. *Journal of Sport Psychology, 6*, 148–158.

Jamieson, D. G., & Schimpf, M. G. (1980). Self-generated images are more effective mnemonics. *Journal of Mental Imagery, 4*, 25–33.

Jordan, C. S., Davis, M., Kahn, P., & Sinnott, R. H. (1980). Eidetic-imagery group methods of assertion training. *Journal of Mental Imagery, 4*, 41–48.

Koslow, R. E. (1987). Sex-related differences and visual-spatial mental imagery as factors affecting symbolic motor skill acquisition. *Sex Roles, 17*, 521–527.

Kosslyn, S. M. (1980). *Image and mind*. Cambridge, MA: Harvard University Press.

Kosslyn, S. M., Ball, T. M., & Reiser, B. J. (1978). Visual images preserve metric spatial information: Evidence from studies of image scanning. *Journal of Experimental Psychology: Human Perception and Performance, 4*, 47–60.

Kunzendorf, R. G. (1984). Centrifugal effects of eidetic imaging on flash electroretinograms and autonomic responses. *Journal of Mental Imagery, 4*, 67–76.

Larson, C. O., Dansereau, D. F., O'Donnell, A. M., Hythecker, V. I., Lambiotte, J. G., & Rocklin, T. R. (1985). Effects of metacognitive and elaborative activity on cooperative learning and transfer. *Contemporary Educational Psychology, 10*, 342–348.

Levin, J. R., Ghatala, E. S., DeRose, T. M., & Makoid, L. A. (1977). Image tracing: An analysis of its effectiveness in children's pictorial discrimination learning. *Journal of Experimental Child Psychology, 23*, 78–83.

Lindberg, C., & Lawliss, G. F. (1988). The effectiveness of imagery as a childbirth preparatory technique. *Journal of Mental Imagery, 12*, 103–114.

Marks, D., & McKellar, P. (1982). The nature and function of eidetic imagery. *Journal of Mental Imagery, 6*, 1–124.

Meehl, P. E. (1954). *Clinical versus statistical prediction. A theoretical analysis and a review of evidence*. University of Minnesota Press.

Miller, G. A. (1956). The magical number seven plus or minus two: Some limits on our capacity for processing information. *Psychological Review, 63,* 81–96.

Montague, W. E., & Carter, J. F. (1973). Vividness of imagery in recalling connected discourse. *Journal of Educational Psychology, 64,* 72–75.

Ohlsen, R. L., Hortin, J. A., & Newhouse, B. (1984). Training students for imagery and solving visual puzzles. *Reading Improvement, 21,* 324–328.

Parrott, C. A. (1986). Visual imagery training: Stimulating utilization of imaginal processes. *Journal of Mental Imagery, 10,* 47–64.

Pavio, A. (1971). *Imagery and verbal processes.* New York: Holt Rinehart and Winston.

Pavio, A., & Cohen, M. (1979). Eidetic imagery and cognitive abilities. *Journal of Mental Imagery, 3,* 53–64.

Piaget, J., & Inhelder, B. (1969). *The psychology of the child.* New York: Basic Books.

Piaget, J., & Inhelder, B. (1971). *Mental imagery and the child.* New York: Basic Books.

Pressley, M. (1976). Mental imagery helps eight-year-olds remember what they read. *Journal of Educational Psychology, 68,* 355–359.

Pressley, M. (1977). Imagery and children's learning: Putting the picture in developmental perspective. *Review of Educational Research, 47,* 585–622.

Pressley, M., & Levin, J. R. (Eds.). (1983). *Cognitive strategy research.* New York: Springer-Verlag.

Pressley, M., Cariglia-Bull, T., Deane, S., & Schneider, W. (1987). Short-term memory, verbal competence, and age as predictors of imagery instructional effectiveness. *Journal of Experimental Child Psychology, 43,* 194–211.

Reese, H. W. (1977). Imagery and associative memory. In R. V. Kail, Jr., & J. W. Hagen (Eds.), *Perspectives on the development of memory and cognition.* Hillsdale, NJ: Lawrence Erlbaum Associates.

Richardson, J. T. E. (1980a). Concreteness, imagery, and semantic categorization. *Journal of Mental Imagery, 4,* 51–58.

Richardson, J. T. E. (1980b). Mental imagery and stimulus concreteness. *Journal of Mental Imagery, 4,* 87–97.

Ryan, E. D., & Simons, J. (1981). Cognitive demand, imagery, and frequency of mental rehearsal as factors influencing acquisition of motor skills. *Journal of Sport Psychology, 3,* 35–45.

Ryan, E. D., & Simons, J. (1983). What is learned in mental practice of motor skills: A test of the cognitive-motor hypothesis. *Journal of Sport Psychology, 5,* 419–426.

Ryan, E. D., Ledger, G. W., & Weed, K. A. (1987). Acquisition and transfer of an integrative imagery strategy by young children. *Child Development, 58,* 443–452.

Sears, N. C., & Johnson, D. M. (1986). The effects of visual imagery on spelling performance and retention among elementary students. *Journal of Educational Research, 79,* 230–233.

Sheehan, P. W. (1972). *The function and nature of imagery.* New York: Academic Press.

Trollip, S. R. (1979). The evaluation of a complex computer-based flight procedures trainer. *Human Factors, 21,* 47–54.

Ward, F. (1989). Images for the computer age. *National Geographic, 175,* 718–751.

Wharton, W. P. (1980). Higher-imagery words and the readability of college history texts. *Journal of Mental Imagery, 4,* 129–147.

Wollen, K. A., Weber, A., & Lowry, D. H. (1972). Bizarreness versus interaction of mental images as determinants of learning. *Cognitive Psychology, 3,* 518–523.

Woolfolk, R. L., Murphy, S. M., Gottesfeld, D., & Aitken, D. (1985). Effects of mental rehearsal of task motor activity and mental depiction of task outcome on motor skill performance. *Journal of Sport Psychology, 7*, 191–197.

Yates, F. (1966). *The art of memory.* London: Routledge & Kegan Paul.

Yates, L. G. (1986). Effect of visualization training on spatial ability test scores. *Journal of Mental Imagery, 10*, 81–92.

Zecker, S. G. (1982). Mental practice and knowledge of results in the learning of a perceptual motor skill. *Journal of Sport Psychology, 4*, 52–63.

CHAPTER 10

Mnemonics

In this chapter we discuss strategies which are "high-tech" for low-structure knowledge. Mnemonics have been called "artificial aids for memory." As learners we all have had to memorize relatively logically disconnected items. Sometimes the number of items seems overwhelming, sometimes there are only a few. Some of us have developed or have been taught "tricks" which help. Two notorious examples of these tricks are "HOMES" to aid remembering the names of the North American Great Lakes and "ROY G. BIV" to aid recall of the colors of the rainbow. These tricks are labeled *mnemonics*. The two examples given are just one type of mnemonic called "single use" or "first letter."

Mnemonics were particularly critical to predominantly preliterate societies or nonliterates in societies in which only a few were literate, for books serve as repositories of knowledge. Books are in part artificial memory aids. The advent of writing somewhat reduced the need for commitment to memory. One could always check the written material. It is not surprising then that the innovation of writing had its critics. For example, consider Julius Caesar's claim: ". . . . through reliance upon written records students relax their diligence in learning by heart and impair their memory" (Joseph Pearl's translation of *Caesar's Gallic War*, 1962, p. 194). Many nonliterates needed to remember considerable detail and relied on mnemonics for that recall, so it should not be surprising that systematic mnemonics and imagery have a very extended history (Yates, 1966).

In this chapter we continue the presentation of the fourth family of cognitive strategies, those of general purpose. We now turn to the strategies called mnemonics. Mnemonics are devices which aid recall. Some of these strategies capitalize on imagery and some do not.

Mnemonics have been called "artificial memory" because they have little to no relationship with the content to be recalled (Bellezza, 1981). That is, the material is so ill-structured that, without the artifice, about the only other strategy appropriate would be rote learning (or repetition). This is not to say that one could not use mnemonics to learn well-structured knowledge; but when knowledge has even modest structure it is best to use other learning strategies.

In the following sections of this chapter we first provide an overview of four common types of mnemonics, then discuss some of the research on each type. This is followed by a designers' guide, a section on hybridization and finally a chapter summary.

FOUR TYPES OF MNEMONICS

In this section we present an overview of four types of the most widely used and researched mnemonics. (Please see Figure 10-1 for a concept map of these four types.) The first type of mnemonic is keyword. *Keyword* is a technique for remembering word pairs. Suppose, for example, the task is to remember the capital city of a state: Annapolis, Maryland. First, a keyword is obtained for the name of the state: Maryland = marry. Then get a keyword for the name of the city: Annapolis = apple. The final step is to connect the two keywords: Two apples getting married. Note that there is an element of bizarreness in the connective, and, furthermore, sometimes the connectives lend themselves to imagery because of the concreteness contained. When the connectives do not particularly lend themselves to imagery they are called verbal keywords.

Students are often required to learn numerous word pairings such as states and capitals. Other pairings, the learning of which is often required in formal education, are countries with major product, inventors with major invention, words with synonyms, words with antonyms and authors with titles. The verbal keyword can help recall of this kind of material in substantial ways.

Other keywords, named imagery keywords, rely even more on imagery and have been used particularly in research and development on learning second language vocabulary equivalents. For example, the Spanish word "carta" (postal letter) looks like the English word "cart," so a letter is imaged in a cart. For another example, the Spanish word "perro" (dog) is pronounced as "pear oh" so a dog can be imaged eating a pear.

A second major type of mnemonic is *chain*. As the name implies, these can be deployed to help one remember strings or chains of items in order, in contrast to the keyword method which was designed for word pairs. There are three subtypes of chain mnemonics. The first subtype is links. In links, imagery is used to connect the first two items; another image is used to connect items two and three; then another image is used to connect items three and four. These pairings are continued through the list.

A second subtype of chain mnemonics is story in which a rhyme or story is created as an aid. A well-known example of a rhyme is "Thirty days hath

FIGURE 10-1
Types of mnemonics.

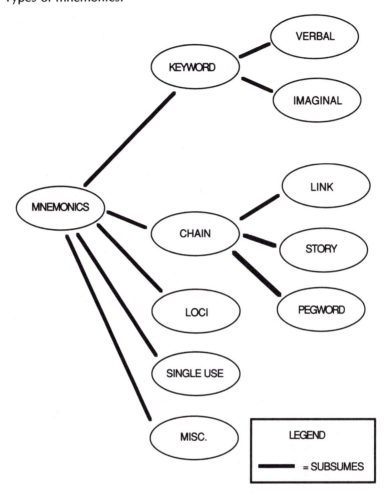

September . . ." which is used to recall the number of days in each month of the year. The other option is to create a story in which the items to be recalled are parts of the story.

A third subtype of chains is the pegword. First, it is necessary to memorize ten or more pairs each consisting of a number (one through ten or more) and a high-imagery word which rhymes with the number. The rhyming seems to aid recall. This is a well-known sequence: one is a bun, two is a shoe, three is a tree, four is a door, five is a hive, six is fix, seven is heaven, eight is a gate, nine is wine and ten is a hen. Notice that each word is the name of a concrete object which is easily imaged for most people. After this is memorized, new items to be recalled are imaged with the keyword. The image provides the item to be recalled while the number provides the order. Figure 10-2 is a pegword example to help you remember the four types of mnemonics.

FIGURE 10-2
A pegword mnemonic for the four types of mnemonics.

One is a bun [image a *key* (keyword) in a hamburger bun].

Two is a shoe (visualize a *chain* in the shoe).

Three is a tree [picture *locusts* (loci) in a tree].

Four is a door [image a door with a *pizza for a doorknob and a home* attached (pizza and home are examples or partial examples of single-use codes)].

The third type of mnemonic is called the *method of loci*. This method consists of visualizing a familiar place such as a street or a room. The items to be recalled are imaginally placed in the larger image of the familiar place. This is the method said to have been used by ancients such as the Roman senators as an aid for recall of long speeches (Yates, 1966).

The method of loci can be so well developed that phenomenal amounts of information can be committed to memory quickly, sometimes with one presentation (Ross & Lawrence, 1968; Briggs, Hawkins, & Crovitz, 1970). In one development early in the nineteenth century (von Feinaigle, 1813), a room as a place to store imaged items was divided into 50 squares using the floor, walls and the ceiling. Each square was numbered and a familiar object was to be imaged in each of the 50 squares. That image would be used as a way of imaginally connecting and locating the item to be recalled. In each room the 50th square on the ceiling was a code to transition to the next room. Thus the system was infinitely expandable. One had to memorize the systematic layout, the images to fit into the squares and then, as new information was committed to memory, each item could be visualized with the image in the square. Obviously this is a very elaborate system and strains our modern perspective about just how much of logically disconnected items we ought to be required to commit to memory.

The fourth type is *single-use coding*. Many examples of these involve using the first letters of each word to be remembered to create another word or a sentence. A well-known example of the word variation of single use mnemonic is "HOMES" for the names of the five Great Lakes in North America (unfortunately this does not help to remember the location from west to east or east to west). Another is "ROY G. BIV," used to code and recall the primary colors. A frequently used sentence code for names of the planets from the sun outward is "My very educated mother just served us nine pizzas." Obviously each first letter in the sentence is the first letter of the name of a planet.

There are numerous miscellaneous mnemonics in the literature which we do not discuss in this book, primarily because we have located little research and development on them. We merely mention several of these here. One is semantic encoding, in which the original stimulus is encoded into something meaningfully related to it. Suppose, for example, in vocabulary learning one is to learn the meaning for the word *origin*. *Origin* can be turned into *egg* and *egg* can be imaged. A similar mnemonic is *phonetic encoding*, in which the sound of the original stimulus is used for encoding. There are also mnemonic systems for the recall of number strings by converting numbers to letters in a systematic way, then using the letters to generate familiar words. These miscellaneous mnemonics are discussed in Pavio (1971) and/or Bellezza (1981).

Notice that most of the types of mnemonics briefly presented in the foregoing entail the use of imagery. In the following section we present samples of research on these four types.

RESEARCH

In this section we discuss some of the research on the four types of mnemonics. The amount of research available on these types varies greatly. The keyword method has been researched more extensively than the others. This research has been conducted with subjects of varying ages including children and young adults.

Keyword

The keyword method of forming an image is based on part or all of a word to be learned and including in that image cues to aid recall of another word or some item of information has been researched extensively in recent years. It has generally been demonstrated as an effective way to learn: vocabulary in one's first language (Pressley, Levin, & Miller, 1982; McDaniel & Tillman, 1987; McDaniel, Pressley, & Dunay, 1987); names of famous persons (Shriberg, Levin, McCormick, & Pressley, 1982) and their accomplishments (Peters & Levin, 1986); famous artists and paintings (Carney, Levin, & Morrison, 1988); second language vocabulary, including verbs (Miller, Levin, & Pressley, 1980) and nouns (Atkinson, 1975; Pressley, 1977; Pressley & Levin, 1978); and states of the United States and their capitals (Levin, Shriberg, Miller, McCormick, & Levin, 1980).

It is interesting that these studies have extended the use of the keyword method to so many topics and that this method usually results in significant effects on learning. It is equally interesting to show how this method compares with other more traditional methods of vocabulary learning. Three such studies are discussed next.

Pressley, Levin and Miller (1982) examined effects for six different conditions on recall of 32 very-low-frequency English words. In the first condition subjects were instructed to use the imagery keyword method for each word and its definition. That is, for the word *carlin* subjects were asked to form an image of an old woman driving a car. In the second condition subjects were instructed to construct meaningful sentences in which the keywords were related to their definitions. For *carlin*, for example, the sentence might be "The old woman was driving a car." In the third condition students were provided with sentences which were related to the meaning of the word. For the fourth condition students were asked to construct a sentence from which the meaning of the word could be inferred. For the fifth condition a sentence was presented and subjects were asked to judge whether the word was used correctly in the sentence. For the final, control condition subjects were asked to try to remember the meaning of the words. It is assumed that subjects in this condition used their usual strategies for learning vocabulary. The recall of subjects in the imagery keyword condition was superior to that in all other conditions.

In another contrast study, McDaniel, Pressley and Dunay (1987) compared the keyword method with one other condition. Definitions of 30 low-frequency English words were learned in the other condition by placing each of them in the context of paragraphs showing how the word was used and meaning could be inferred from the paragraphs. Subjects in the keyword condition recalled more meanings for immediate recall and did as well as the other group in a one-week delay test.

In a third contrast study McDaniel and Tillman (1987) compared the recall of subjects who were asked to use the keyword method with subjects who were instructed in how to infer meaning from a passage of three sentences and then asked to use that inference in learning 60 vocabulary words. Subjects in the keyword condition recalled more meanings when they were cued with the word and asked to provide the meaning, but there was no significant difference between the recall in the two conditions when learning was measured with free recall. When, however, the data were reanalyzed according to who claimed on a questionnaire to have actually used the keyword method, the advantage of keyword use was even more apparent.

One possible criticism of some of this research is that the research might be biased against methods other than keyword because of slow presentation rates across conditions (Hall & Fuson, 1986). Hall and Fuson argue that the slow presentation rate is necessary for the keyword method and that subjects could learn much faster under conditions researched and similar to those conditions. Pressley (1987) responded to this criticism by varying presentation rates. The advantage of the keyword method remained despite the time of presentation.

Chain

Bellezza (1983) found a significant effect on immediate recall for the link method. You may recall that the link method is the formation of an image which includes the first two items to be recalled, then the formation of an image which includes the second and third, and so on. In this study, for example, *window* and *child* were imaged together and then *child* and *ship*. In the first image the child was visualized breaking a window, and in the second image a child was visualized sailing a ship.

Delin (1969a) compared the link method with one control group. Subjects using linking mastered the list of words more rapidly and made fewer errors during the period leading to mastery. It is interesting that these young adult subjects were simply asked to form vivid and active images of the pairs, but were given no practice or demonstrations on the use of linking. In a similar study (Delin, 1969b), the superiority of link formation was found for longer-term recall.

Another chain method is the story mnemonic. Ghatala, Levin, Pressley and Lodico (1985) demonstrated that children could be trained to remember words by making up a story which included the words. Those trained to use this method retained more than did the controls. Their data appear to support the idea that the children continued to use this strategy even when they were not instructed to do so.

In an older study (Bower & Clark, 1969), the story technique was compared with one control treatment. The learning task was formidable, consisting of 12 lists of ten words each. Controls were simply told to study and learn each list. The narrative or story treatment consisted of brief instructions to ". . . make up a story relating the items to one another. Specifically, start with the first item and put it in a setting which will allow other items to be added to it. Then, add the other items to the story in the same order as the items appear. Make each story meaningful to yourself. Then, when you are asked to recall the items, you can simply go through your story and pull out the proper items in their correct order" (p. 181).

After the twelve lists had been presented, subjects were tested on recall of each list from the first list to the twelfth. Subjects in the story condition remembered almost seven times as many words from the lists. It was also noticed that for the control subjects recall was influenced greatly by study time (more time equals better recall), whereas the story subjects' recall was not. These findings are dramatic, and the instructions for the story treatment seem to be models for this technique.

In a later study with more comparison groups, Bower and Winzenz (1970) looked at effects on both reproduction and recognition memory. There were four learning-strategy treatments: repetition, reading word pairs to be recalled in a meaningful sentence, subjects' creation of a meaningful sentence and the creation of an image including the word pairs. Significant differences in both reproduction and recognition recall were found among the groups, with recall best in the imagery group, second best in the story (sentence-creation) group, third in the sentence reading and last in the rote repetition group.

How well do the positive effects of the story technique on recall hold up over time? Boltwood and Blick (1970) compared single-use codes, story and a control which they called "clustering" (the words learned were unrelated to each other, so that meaningful grouping or clustering was not possible). One week later and again eight weeks later the story technique was superior as an aid to recall.

Bellezza, Cheesman and Reddy (1977) ran a series of experiments on the story method. Their basic strategy was to examine the number of words recalled as a function of the creation of a meaningful sentence using the words. In one of the experiments recall effects of this sentence creation were compared with making sentences into stories. For these first two experiments the sentence creation was superior to being told that the words were to be remembered, and the story creation was somewhat superior in aiding recall to sentence creation, but the difference was not significant.

Stories as linking mechanisms can often be supplemented with imagery. That is to say that subjects form mental images of items in a story they are creating. Lesgold and Goldman (1973) found this to help recall, particularly when the images were unique. Santa, Ruskin and Yio (1973) also found that imagery supplementation of stories aided recall when compared to rote repetition, stories only and pegword, among others.

The third chain method is pegword. Foth (1973) found that the use of the pegword resulted in superior recall when compared to controls for words rated as concrete, but not for abstract words. Since the pegword mnemonic relies on imagery, this is understandable.

Is it possible that the use of the pegword technique again and again with very little time between uses would produce interference? In one study located this was not the case (Morris & Reid, 1970). Subjects were instructed to learn six lists of ten words each. The experimental group was asked to use pegword while the controls were asked to memorize the lists. Lists were presented only once on audio tape. The use of pegword had a significant effect on recall, and, in addition, the superiority of pegword use did not decline over the recall of the successive lists. Apparently there was no interference. No other research has been located which tests the possibility of interference beyond the extent in this study.

All of the pegword studies presented up to this point involve imagery. One study located used a variation of pegword without instructions to image (Wood & Bolt, 1970). In this study, the standard inclusion of imagery in pegword resulted in no significant differences. To our knowledge, this finding has not been replicated. Furthermore, it is very difficult to explain how pegword could be effective without the inclusion of imagery, particularly when there is so much research supporting the power of imagery.

Method of Loci

Lee and Edwards (1981) compared the method of loci with two other treatments. The learning task consisted of a list of 20 words to be remembered. The loci, or place of the central image, was a house, and the items to be remembered were familiar objects typically associated within a house, garage and lawn. The loci subjects were taught to image themselves moving from one location to another and were asked to associate imaginally the items with the specific location. On a handout they were given a string of sentences depicting the location and including the item to be remembered. Here are the first three sentences: The *bed* in the bedroom. The *rug* beside the bed. The *mirror* on the wall. The subjects imaginally moved through the house and grounds forming the images. Subjects in the second condition were to elaborate the items verbally by creating a sentence containing the first and second word, then the second and third and so on. Subjects in the third condition were given 20 abstract words which were different from the words in the other two conditions and were asked to use any technique for recall that they felt would be helpful. *Subjects in the loci treatment recalled twice as many items as each of the other treatments.*

In the Lee and Edwards (1981) study the items to be recalled and embedded in the larger image (the loci) are items normally found in the familiar place imaged. That is, the bed was located in the bedroom and the table was in the kitchen. In a study in which items were not necessarily found in the place of the loci (Ross & Lawrence, 1968), subjects used the method to recall 40 items each day for four successive days. Each list was presented only once. There were no control or comparison groups in this study. Both immediate and delay recall were exceptionally good, particularly when it is considered that the lists were presented only one time. Furthermore, the recall of the different lists did not interfere with each other. This is interesting in that subjects used the same familiar loci (a walk around the grounds of the University of Western Australia) for the different lists.

These studies and most others employ the standard instruction to place and image items in a familiar place. One research effort (Briggs, Hawkins, & Crovitz, 1970), however, resulted in outstanding recall when subjects were provided with a place in which to embed the items. In this study a fictitious map of Gorky Street was drawn on a classroom chalkboard. On this "map" were placed 20 locations on which items were to be imaged. Thus it seems that the use of a place already familiar to subjects is not essential to the method.

Single-Use Codes

Manning and Bruning (1975) compared effects on recall for several techniques including single-use codes and stories. They were also interested in the effects of abstractness and concreteness. They found that single-use codes combined with high imagery was superior for abstract word recall while concrete word recall was aided best by the descriptive story technique. It could be that subjects used imagery on the concrete items without instructions, but that the instructions induced more imagery for the more abstract material.

Pash and Blick (1970) used a first-letter code as an aid to recall. Two different lists of nine "words" each were presented. One list was called unmeaningful because the words were merely strings of letters which look like words but are not. The other list, called meaningful, consisted of real English words. For both lists the first letter of the words, when arranged appropriately, spelled the word *education*. Recall of the subjects actually using the first-letter coding was significantly better than those not using the code for both lists.

As with other strategies, a question often asked is whether it is best for the designer or teacher to supply a single-use code or have subjects or students originate the code themselves. This was investigated by Kibler and Blick (1972), who found no difference between the two on immediate recall but that with delay intervals of one and four weeks the experimenter-supplied mnemonics were superior. Given the usual position that it is better typically for students to personalize the use of strategies presented in this book, perhaps the experimenter codes were better designed and more appropriate for the material learned in this experiment.

In this section we discussed the research on the four types of mnemonics. This research clearly demonstrates the usefulness of mnemonics as an aid to memory. In the following section we discuss a few limitations, reservations and caveats.

RESERVATIONS AND CAVEATS

The most important restriction on the use of mnemonics is that they should be used for low-structure or nonmeaningful material (Anderson, 1985, p. 173). It is obvious from the research that these mnemonics provide "high-tech" strategies for this kind of knowledge. It is equally obvious that substantial amounts of material taught in formal education are low in structure or in inherent meaningfulness.

Often we hear the criticism that the use of mnemonics is undesirable because it is preferable for students to "learn meaningfully." This is true, but this criticism follows from ignoring the facts that mnemonics are recommended specifically for nonmeaningful material and that it is futile to go about trying to learn something in a meaningful way if it lacks structure or meaning.

Another criticism is that material learned with the aid of mnemonics tends to be forgotten within a few hours or, at best, within a few months. While this criticism may be valid, it should be remembered that mnemonics aid recall for a period and are superior to no strategies or to strategies often used by untrained students. Also material learned with mnemonics sometimes is retained for long periods. It is likely that in such cases that knowledge is rehearsed occasionally or used frequently to the point that the device used disappears, but the knowledge remains. Perhaps the knowledge ultimately is embedded in assorted schemata or structures after continued use. Medical students, for example, often use a single-use code beginning with "On old Olympus' tiny top a Finn and German viewed some hops," to remember the names of major cranial nerves. While none of us would particularly want our brain surgeon to recite this mnemonic over a diagnosis or the operating table, it is preferable to not recalling at all. By the time the medical training is complete that knowledge is probably embedded in a variety of deep-knowledge structures. The mnemonic has served as a stop-gap measure until related structures are developed.

Another criticism is that the amount of time needed to learn something with a mnemonic may be greater than with rote learning or with some other individually developed method. This may be true, but since mnemonics often result in more effective recall (more information retained longer) than rote learning, that disadvantage is outweighed.

This caveat is related to that of the need for training. It is true that these strategies must be learned, as must other strategies. The benefits, however, can be impressive.

Another criticism is that the use of mnemonics can interfere with comprehension when they are used with material which has structure or meaningfulness; that is, the student may fail to see the inherent organization or structure. This is a familiar problem even in rote learning. This criticism can be avoided by encouraging the use of mnemonics only on those materials which lack structure.

This leads to the caveat that students could use mnemonics when better strategies could be used. Throughout this text we have discussed the goal of metacognitive sophistication, that of students knowing strategies and knowing which strategies work best for which materials. If the designer or teacher models this sophistication and if this sophistication is included as a continuing instructional objective, students are unlikely to fall into this trap.

In this section we discussed some of the common criticisms or reservations about the use of mnemonics. If the designer honors the rule that *mnemonics are "high-tech" strategies for low-structure knowledge*, these criticisms can be avoided. In this section we have been guided by the thorough review and analysis of Bellezza (1981), along with a host of other references.

DESIGNERS' GUIDE

The designer who follows the high-tech for low-structure rule is well on the way to proper deployment of mnemonics in design. You will notice that the specifications communicated in Figure 10-3 include structure, and that mnemonics are recommended primarily for low-structure knowledge. Also, please notice that somewhat different specifications exist for each of the types of mnemonics listed in the columns.

Following the rule of high-tech for low structure, the first step in the use of mnemonics in design is to determine whether the material has its own structure, meaningfulness or organization. If the material is well structured it is much better to use some other strategy which is more suited to the material.

The one possible exception to this is the use of the mnemonic as a "stopgap" measure. That is to say, the material has considerable meaningfulness or structure, but knowledge of that structure is not considered achievable in the lesson, course or unit being planned. In such a case the designer initiates or encourages the use of mnemonics for temporary learning and defers learning of the structure (or deeper comprehension) for targeting in later instruction.

Following the frame in Figure 10-4, the material should be examined to determine which types of mnemonics to encourage students to use or to develop for their use. Material or content which is essentially pairs of words or items, as in the earlier discussions of the keyword technique, should be seen as candidates for keyword use. Longer series of content lend themselves to the three types of chain mnemonics, to the method of loci or single use codes.

FIGURE 10-3

Specifications for mnemonics.

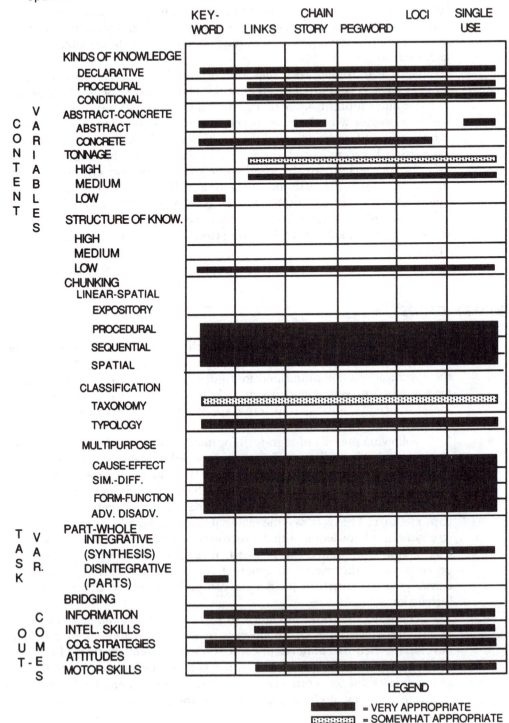

FIGURE 10-4

Designers' guide to the use of mnemonics.

Step	Explanation	Condition	Decision
1.	Is there structure in the content?	yes	Use other strategies.
		no	Go to step 2.
2.	Decide about information clusters.	word pairs	keyword
		more than 2 ("integrative")	chains, loci, single-use codes
3.	Is the material abstract?		chain: link or story, single-use code
	Concrete?		pegword, key-word, loci
4.	Create mnemonic.	Consider prior learning and general knowledge background of students.	

Another attribute of the content other than structure or number of items is the relative concreteness. If the material is abstract, the chain link, chain story or single-use code could be used. Pegword, keyword and the method of loci require that the material be imageable. This is not to say that in some cases links, stories or single-use codes could not be supplemented with imagery. Image supplementation, of course, depends on concreteness and the learner's ability to image.

The next step is to create the mnemonic based on the conditions and decisions as outlined in Figure 10-4. In the fourth step it is essential to consider the prior learning and general background of the target students. In Figure 10-5 we provide some help in designer use by providing standardized instructions for initiating and encouraging use of the major types of mnemonics. In summary there are four basic steps in the use of mnemonics: deciding about the inherent structure of the content, the amount of information in the clusters, the relative abstractness and the creation of the mnemonic itself.

For those who might use mnemonics extensively we recommend *A Dictionary of Mnemonics* (London: Eyre Methun, 1972). This may be difficult to obtain, but could be very helpful for it is a large collection of widely used mnemonics for specific materials.

We also recommend that you review the chapter on imagery since so many of the mnemonics involve imagery. Particularly, it is helpful to be aware of the important "additives" to imagery which are contained in Figure 9-1 on page 180.

FIGURE 10-5
Recommended instructions for the major types of mnemonics.

Type	Task	Instruction (say or write)
Keyword		
	Words associated with meanings or other words	Look at the first word. Think of a word that looks or sounds like it. Now look at the second word (or meaning) and think of a word that
Verbal		looks or sounds like it or part of it. Now think of a phrase or short sentence that connects the two. It may help to form an image of the phrase or sentence.
Imagery		Think of a word that can be imaged which is like all or part of the first word. Now image the second word (or meaning) interacting with that first image.
Chain		
	Words or items in a series. This could include steps in procedural knowledge.	
Link		Form a mental picture of the first two words acting together (interacting). Now form an image of the second and third together. Now the third and fourth together (and continue if necessary).
Story		Make up a story which connects these items to one another. Start with the first item and put it in the story setting. Then, add the other items to the story in the same order as the items appear. Make the story meaningful to you. When you recall the items, you can go through your story and pull out the proper items in their correct order (Bower & Clark, 1969, p. 181). It may help to visualize as you create the story.

FIGURE 10-5 (continued)

Type	Task	Instruction (say or write)
Pegword		Memorize: One is a bun. Two is a shoe. Three is a tree. Four is a door. Five is a hive. Six is fix. Seven is heaven. Eight is a gate. Nine is wine. Ten is a hen. (May be continued for longer lists.) Now, image the first item in the bun, the second in a shoe, the third in a tree and so on.
Loci	Series of items	Think of a place very familiar to you. It should be a place with lots of detail. It could be your room or your street. Now form a mental picture of the first item to be remembered somewhere in the image. Move to another part of the image and put the next item in the image. Continue until you have located all the items in the image. When you need to remember the items, just "walk" through your image and "see" the items you placed there.
Single-use Codes	Series of items	Look at each of the items you want to re-remember. Take the first letter of each word and use them to create a word which is familiar to you or which you can memorize. OR Use the first letter of each word to create new words. Then use the new words to make a sentence. Now be sure to memorize the new sentence. (It may help to give examples.)

HYBRIDIZATION

As we emphasized in both this and the previous chapter, most of the mnemonics involve imagery as an intrinsic part of the strategy. For those mnemonics which do not, most could be supplemented with imagery. Thus the most important strategy combined with mnemonics is imagery.

We have also seen how rehearsal has been combined with other strategies discussed in other chapters. Rehearsal, particularly repetition and cumulative rehearsal, will often be necessary in learning and practicing the mnemonic after it has been developed or presented.

In addition, there may be parts of concept maps and frames which are difficult to learn or which may be supplemented with mnemonics. These include concepts and words with attributes and meaning and lists of items. It is also appropriate to use mnemonics in the first phases of procedural and conditional learning as a supplement to appropriate types of concept maps and frames.

SUMMARY

In this chapter we discussed the artificial strategies known as mnemonics. We have seen that there are several types, each of which was developed for specific purposes to fit requirements of content. We have also found that considerable research has been conducted which exists as testimony to their utility.

With the completion of this chapter we conclude the discussion of the nine cognitive strategies. In the next and final two chapters we present a discussion of phases of instructional design which are critical in designing instruction. For this we present a procedural explanation called the Instructional Design Template.

EXERCISES

1. Select at least one important set of information from this text which you think you would have trouble remembering for a test. Create a single-use code to help you remember this. Make a note to test yourself on this two days from now.

2. Select another set of information from this text which you might have a problem remembering. Select a mnemonic other than the one you used for question one and use it to help you remember this. Make a note to test yourself on this two days from now.

3. After the two-day delay, how effective were the mnemonics in helping you remember?

REFERENCES

A Dictionary of Mnemonics. (1972). London: Eyre Methuen.

Anderson, J. R. (1985). *Cognitive psychology and its implications.* New York: Freeman.

Atkinson, R. C. (1975). Mnemotechnics in second-language learning. *American Psychologist, 30,* 821–828.

Bellezza, F. S. (1981). Mnemonic devices: Classification, characteristics, and criteria. *Review of Educational Research, 51,* 247–275.

Bellezza, F. S. (1983). The spatial-arrangement mnemonic. *Journal of Educational Psychology, 75,* 830–837.

Bellezza, F. S., Cheesman, F. L., II, & Reddy, B. G. (1977). Organization and semantic elaboration in free recall. *Journal of Experimental Psychology: Human Learning and Memory, 3,* 539–550.

Boltwood, C. E., & Blick, K. A. (1970). The delineation and application of three mnemonic techniques. *Psychonomic Science, 20,* 339–341.

Bower, G. H., & Winzenz, D. (1970). Comparison of associative learning strategies. *Psychonomic Science, 20,* 119–120.

Bower, G. H., & Clark, M. C. (1969). Narrative stories as mediators for serial learning. *Psychonomic Science, 14,* 181–182.

Briggs, G. C., Hawkins, S., & Crovitz, H. F. (1970). Bizarre images in artificial memory. *Psychonomic Science, 19,* 353–354.

Caesar, J. (1962). *Caesar's Gallic War* (Joseph Pearl, Trans.). Great Neck, NY: Barron's Educational Series.

Carney, R. N., Levin, J. R., & Morrison, C. R. (1988). Mnemonic learning of artists and their paintings. *American Educational Research Journal, 25,* 107–125.

Delin, P. S. (1969a). The learning to criterion of a serial list with and without mnemonic instructions. *Psychonomic Science, 16,* 169–170.

Delin, P. S. (1969b). Learning and retention of English words with successive approximations to a complex mnemonic instruction. *Psychonomic Science, 17,* 87–89.

Foth, D. L. (1973). Mnemonic technique effectiveness as a function of word abstraction and mediation instructions. *Journal of Verbal Learning and Verbal Behavior, 12,* 239–245.

Ghatala, E. S., Levin, J. R., Pressley, M., & Lodico, M. G. (1985). Training cognitive strategy-monitoring in children. *American Educational Research Journal, 22,* 199–215.

Hall, J. W., & Fuson, K. C. (1986). Presentation rates in experiments on mnemonics: A methodological note. *Journal of Educational Psychology, 78,* 233–234.

Kibler, J. L., & Blick, K. A. (1972). Evaluation of experimenter-supplied and subject-originated first-letter mnemonics in a free-recall task. *Psychological Reports, 30,* 307–313.

Lee, S., & Edwards, P. (1981). Retrieval of abstract nouns as a function of mnemonic instructions and reading ability. *Journal of Mental Imagery, 5,* 117–126.

Lesgold, A. M., & Goldman, S. R. (1973). Encoding uniqueness and the imagery mnemonic in associative learning. *Journal of Verbal Learning and Verbal Behavior, 12,* 193–202.

Levin, J. R., Shriberg, L. K., Miller, G. E., McCormick, C. B. & Levin, B. B. (1980). The keyword method in the classroom: How to remember the states and their capitals. *The Elementary School Journal, 80,* 185–191.

Manning, B. A., & Bruning, R. H. (1975). Interactive effects of mnemonic techniques and word-list characteristics. *Psychological Reports, 36,* 727–736.

McDaniel, M. A., Pressley, M., & Dunay, P. K. (1987). Long-term retention of vocabulary after keyword and context learning. *Journal of Educational Psychology, 79,* 87–89.

McDaniel, M. A., & Tillman, V. P. (1987). Discovering a meaning versus applying the keyword method: Effects on recall. *Contemporary Educational Psychology, 12,* 156–175.

Miller, G. E., Levin, J. R., & Pressley, M. (1980). An adaptation of the keyword method to children's learning of foreign verbs. *Journal of Mental Imagery, 4,* 57–61.

Morris, P. E., & Reid, R. L. (1970). The repeated use of mnemonic imagery. *Psychonomic Science, 20,* 337–338.

Pash, J. R., & Blick, K. A. (1970). The effect of a mnemonic device on retention of verbal material. *Psychonomic Science, 19,* 203–204.

Pavio, A. (1971). *Imagery and verbal processes.* New York: Holt Rinehart and Winston.

Peters, E. E., & Levin, J. R. (1986). Effects of a mnemonic imagery strategy on good and poor readers' prose recall. *Reading Research Quarterly, 21,* 179–192.

Pressley, M. (1977). Children's use of the keyword method to learn simple Spanish vocabulary words. *Journal of Educational Psychology, 69,* 465–472.

Pressley, M. (1987). Are keyword method effects limited to slow presentation rates? An empirically based reply to Hall and Fuson (1986). *Journal of Educational Psychology, 79,* 333–335.

Pressley, M., & Levin, J. R. (1978). Developmental constraints associated with children's use of the keyword method of foreign language vocabulary learning. *Journal of Experimental Child Psychology, 26,* 359–372.

Pressley, M., Levin, J. R., & Miller, G. E. (1982). The keyword method compared to alternative vocabulary-learning strategies. *Contemporary Educational Psychology, 7,* 50–60.

Ross, J., & Lawrence, K. A. (1968). Some observations on memory artifice. *Psychonomic Science, 13,* 107–108.

Santa, J. L., Ruskin, A. B., & Yio, A. J. H. (1973). Mnemonic systems in recall. *Psychological Reports, 32,* 1163–1170.

Shriberg, L. K., Levin, J. R., McCormick, C. B., & Pressley, M. (1982). Learning about "famous" people via the keyword method. *Journal of Educational Psychology, 74,* 238–247.

von Feinaigle, G. (1813). *The new art of memory.* (3rd ed.). London: Sherwood, Neely and Jones.

Wood, G., & Bolt, M. (1970). Type of instruction, abstractness, and mnemonic system. *Psychonomic Science, 21,* 91–92.

Yates, F. (1966). *The art of memory.* London: Routledge & Kegan Paul.

CHAPTER 11

Instructional Design Template: Part I

The previous chapters in this book are discussions of cognitive strategies which we consider to be particularly relevant for use in instruction. In this chapter and the next, we present the Instructional Design Template (IDT), which is a procedural explanation (see Chapter 2) of instructional design. Specified in the IDT are the decisions we recommend be made before deciding which of one or more of the cognitive strategies should be used in the instruction being designed, as well as subsequent decisions in the instructional design process.

In this chapter, the IDT is presented and described generally, along with suggestions for its use. Also included in this chapter is a detailed description of the first of six phases in the IDT. The first phase is entitled "The Situational Audit." Its purpose is to help the instructional designer focus first on the context in which the instruction is to occur and from which the significance of the instruction can be derived and communicated to the students and others. A detailed description of the other five phases of the IDT are presented in the next chapter. These five phases present ways that the instructional designer can zoom [an analogy suggested by Reigeluth and Stein (1983)] his or her focus from the context to specific decisions to be made in designing the instruction.

In the title of this and the next chapters, *template* is being used metaphorically. Much as a physical template guides the hand or the machine, the IDT can guide the instructional designer. It can help the designer "see the forest from the trees" in the designing process and, at the same time, facilitate giving attention to details throughout the process.

Understanding each of the terms in the title of this chapter can contribute to one's comprehension of instructional design. *Instruct* means to impart knowledge in a systematic manner. *Instruction* refers to an outline or manual of technical procedures. It also pertains to the action, practice or profession of a teacher. A *design* is a plan or layout. *Design* can also refer to the structural form of something, regardless of the medium employed. *Template* means a gauge, pattern or mold (as a thin plate or board) used as a guide to form a piece being made.

In Chapter 1, we stated that, in our view, recent contributions of cognitive science have numerous implications for instructional design. Those implications include the following:

1. In our complex society, people need to learn how to learn. This necessitates dramatically broadening the goals of instruction to include that the learners will be able to know and appropriately use cognitive strategies.

2. Instructional design should use cognitive strategies as a means of instruction.

3. Teachers are to be role models and reward the use of cognitive strategies in the teaching-learning transaction.

4. Knowledge of, the appropriate use of, and attitudes toward cognitive strategies are to be included in what is focused on in instructional testing and evaluation.

It is important to view the significance of what is to be learned from the perspective of both the learner and society. This necessitates developing and maintaining situational awareness on the part of the instructional designer and others involved in the design process and permits establishing significance broadly and explicitly.

The IDT can be used by beginning as well as more advanced instructional designers much as airplane pilots with all levels of expertise use preflight checklists. On important and potentially complex matters, thinking that one can outgrow or become too experienced to use a checklist can be perilous at best. The use of an appropriate checklist can help the instructional designer remember each of the key decisions to be made and make explicit the recommended sequence for considering those decisions.

Prompts are included in the IDT, much as a user-friendly computer program assists the user with instructions or suggestions at critical points. The IDT provides the instructional designer help about how to process each decision and provides alternatives to consider, when applicable, for each decision.

The IDT can be used in evaluating instructional designs as well as instruction itself. Finally, the IDT can be used in troubleshooting instruction, much as an airplane pilot uses a checklist in an emergency. The instructional designer and/or instructor can use the IDT in troubleshooting instruction, assisting the instructor in determining whether or not the design itself and all aspects of it have been implemented as intended. If the instruction has actually been implemented as intended but is not working well, the instructional designer and/or the instructor can use the IDT to select other alternatives for some or all of the key decisions in order to revise instruction.

DESCRIPTION OF THE IDT

As depicted in Figure 11-1, the IDT consists of six phases. Also as depicted in that figure, each phase contains between one and seven sequential decision points, labeled 1.1 through 6.4, which function as subroutines for the phases in which they appear.

A complete version of the IDT is presented in Figure 11-2. For 25 of the 28 sequential decision points which appear in that figure, alternatives to be considered are presented along with instructions for documenting each decision. For the remaining three decision points, instructions alone are presented. The instructional design which results from the use of the IDT is similar to the design that an architect develops for a house. It contains the shape and style of the house along with many general features to be built into it. The general contractor and the subcontractors work with that architectural design, sometimes in consultation with the architect, to build the house, making modifications as necessary to meet the wants, needs and expectations of the owner. Similarly, the instructor implements the instructional design, revising it and providing details to a greater or lesser extent (Merrill, 1983; Reigeluth, 1983) as the situation requires. It is important to consider strategic planning and implementation together. Likewise, we recommend dealing with instructional design and its implementation in instruction as integrally related activities. For example, the instructional designer needs to consider the nature and extent of involvement of the potential learners and/or learners both in developing the instructional design and during the implementation of the instruction itself.

We suggest that the designer accompany the completed IDT with a narrative, explaining each decision point in the same sequence that appears in the IDT. That narrative should communicate the nature of the intended instruction much as a story teller describes a trip or adventure. In doing so, the instructional designer should seek to make explicit the ways that the various decisions interrelate and build upon each other.

Users of the IDT have indicated that there are typically two or more *stages* in the courses or programs that they have designed. Sometimes such stages were preplanned. At other times they resulted from significant changes in the situation and/or perceptions of the situation in which the instruction occurs. In using the IDT, a Roman numeral one (i.e., "I") can be placed next to the alternative(s) in each decision point most appropriate for the first stage; a Roman numeral two (i.e., "II") next to the alternative(s) most appropriate for the second stage; and so forth.

A brief description of each of the six phases in the IDT and of the sequential decision points in it are presented next. These descriptions are accompanied by a concept map, depicting the phase and the decisions to be made in it.

FIGURE 11-1
Concept map of template.

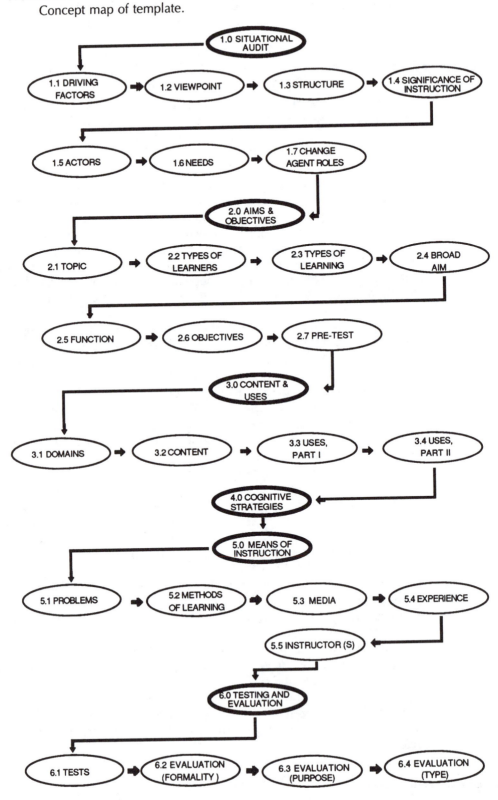

FIGURE 11-2
Instructional design template (IDT).

Phases and Sequential Decision Points	Short Explanation
1.0 SITUATIONAL AUDIT	
1.1 Driving Factors: (Check all that pertain.) ____ economic ____ social needs ____ legal considerations ____ physical ____ need for cognitive strategies ____ other (Please specify _____ _____.)	Each alternative represents a factor from the societal context that may make it important for persons to learn what is to be taught because of the likely benefits from doing so and/or negative consequences from failing to do so.
1.2 Viewpoint Taken: (Check only one.) ____ functionalist ____ conflict ____ critical	Each alternative refers to quite a different viewpoint that can be taken in designing and implementing instruction.
1.3 Structure of the Situation: (Check only one.) ____ well defined ____ moderately well defined ____ ill defined	Available, applicable designs can be used with relatively well-defined situations; hand-tailored ones must be used with less well-defined situations.
1.4 Significance of the Instruction: (Indicate percentage for each of the following.) It is assumed that the instruction will: ____ contribute to cultural awareness or knowing and understanding of a culture ____ contribute to practical and/or problem-solving ability contribute to meaningfulness of life through: ____ helping person(s) realize their full potential ____ helping person(s) understand and cope with negative circumstances that are not likely ever to improve	Each alternative is a different type of assumed benefit of the instruction to the learner(s) and/or society. In other words, each alternative represents a different statement about why instruction may be of value or worth to individuals and/or society.

FIGURE 11-2 (continued)
Instructional design template (IDT).

Phases and Sequential Decision Points	Short Explanation
_____ helping persons learn to learn (become meta-cognitively sophisticated) 100% Total	
1.5 Actors to Be Involved: (Check only one or indicate sequence.) _____ educator(s) alone _____ learner(s) alone _____ educator(s) with major involvement; learner(s) with minor involvement _____ learner(s) with major involvement; educator(s) with minor involvement _____ expert in knowledge domain _____ transactive	Each alternative indicates a different actor or combination of actors who can be involved in designing and implementing the instruction as well as the nature of the power relationship between them.
1.6 Needs: (Check all that are to be used, and indicate sequence, if applicable.) _____ normative _____ expressed _____ felt _____ comparative _____ anticipated or future	Each alternative indicates a different type of need on the part of the learners or potential learners.
1.7 Change Agent Roles: (Check all that are to be used, and indicate sequence, if applicable.) _____ solution giver _____ resource linker _____ process helper _____ catalyst	Each alternative indicates a different way that the instructor(s) and/or learners can aid the learning process in instructional activities.

2.0 BROAD AIM AND SPECIFIC OBJECTIVES

2.1 Topic: (Define the topic; describe the boundaries of the topic; and provide examples of what the topic is and is not.)	The topic refers to the kind of knowledge, attitudes, or skills to be learned.

FIGURE 11-2 (continued)
Instructional design template (IDT).

Phases and Sequential Decision Points	Short Explanation
2.2 Types of Learners: (Indicate percentage of each.) _____ scientists or disciplinarians _____ students of the sciences or disciplines _____ practitioners in applied field(s) _____ students of applied field(s) _____ other (Please specify_____.) 100% Total	Each alternative indicates the main occupational orientation of the learner(s) and the role of the learner(s) relative to that occupation.
2.3 Types of Learning: (Indicate percentage of each.) _____ accretion _____ tuning _____ restructuring 100% Total	Each alternative indicates how the learner(s) are expected to process what is being learned.
2.4 Broad-Aim: (Describe.)	The broad aim is the main, intended effect of the instruction on individuals and/or society.
2.5 Function: (Check all that pertain.) _____ pass exams or tests _____ become licensed or credentialed _____ acquire required knowledge, attitudes or skills _____ update their knowledge _____ experience something _____ practice something _____ develop cognitive strategies (learn to learn) _____ other (Please specify _____.)	The function of the instruction refers to why the learner(s) need to know or be able to do what is to be learned.
2.6 Objectives: (Provide meaningful examples.)	Each objective should indicate: the significance of what is to be learned; what the learner will be able to do after the learning experience; under what conditions; at what level to be satisfactory; and according to whom and/or what.

FIGURE 11-2 (continued)
Instructional design template (IDT).

Phases and Sequential Decision Points	Short Explanation
2.7 Use of Pretest or Preassessment: (If none, please specify. Otherwise, check all that pertain.) _____ written _____ oral _____ situational _____ problem solving _____ self-reporting _____ preassessing ability to use cognitive strategies _____ none _____ other (Please specify: _____.)	Pretests and preassessments can be used to provide evidence of the level of the learner's(s') attainment of what is to be taught.
3.0 CONTENT AND USES	
3.1 Instructional Domains: (Indicate percentage for each of the following.) _____ cognitive _____ affective _____ psychomotor 100% Total	These alternatives refer to whether the instruction is intended to bring about changes in thinking, attitudes and/or skilled performance.
3.2 Instructional Content: (Indicate percentage for each of the following.) _____ theories or concepts from the disciplines or sciences _____ ways of thinking and acting like a disciplinarian or scientists _____ generalizations from applied field(s) _____ ways of thinking and acting like persons in applied field(s) _____ other (Please specify: _____.) 100% Total	Each alternative indicates a different main orientation of what is to be learned. The first two alternatives refer to knowledge that is more abstract than the third and fourth alternatives. The first and third alternatives refer to knowing what; the second and fourth to knowing what and knowing how.
3.3 Uses of Knowledge, Part I: (Indicate percentages for each of the following.) _____ explicit _____ tacit 100% Total	Explicit knowledge can be expressed and used. Tacit knowledge cannot be actually expressed but may provide a useful perspective.

FIGURE 11-2 (continued)
Instructional design template (IDT).

Phases and Sequential Decision Points	Short Explanation
3.4 Uses of Knowledge, Part II: (Indicate percentages for each of the following.) _____ replicative _____ associative _____ applicative _____ interpretive 100% Total	Each alternative indicates a way that the learner(s) is expected to be able to use what is learned in the instruction.

4.0 COGNITIVE STRATEGIES

(Mark each by placing an *a* by the name of the strategy if strategy is to be taught, *b* if it is to be activated in the learner, *c* if it is to be used to convey the content and *d* if there is no planned use of the strategy in the design.)

_____ frames, type one _____ frames, type two _____ concept mapping _____ advance organizer _____ metaphor _____ chunking _____ rehearsal _____ imagery _____ mnemonics	Each of the cognitive strategies has been described and illustrated earlier in this book. The nature of what is to be learned and the learners should be taken into consideration in selecting and sequencing cognitive strategies to be used in the instruction.

5.0 MEANS OF INSTRUCTION

5.1 Problems: (Indicate percentage of each type.) _____ well defined _____ moderately well defined _____ ill defined 100% Total	These alternatives refer to how well defined, from the perspective of the learners, are the problems to be used in the instruction or to which the instruction is to be related.
5.2 Methods of Learning: (Indicate percentage of each type.) _____ autonomous _____ guided inquiry _____ reception _____ cognitive apprenticeship 100% Total	The designer needs to take into consideration the nature of what is to be learned, the learner(s), and the instructor(s) in selecting and sequencing the methods of learning to be used.

FIGURE 11-2 (continued)
Instructional design template (IDT).

Phases and Sequential Decision Points	Short Explanation

5.3 Media:
(Check all that are to be used.)
_____ film
_____ lecture
_____ discussion
_____ demonstration
_____ panel
_____ seminar
_____ symposium
_____ field trip
_____ computer
_____ other (Please specify:

_____

_____.)

It is recommended that media be selected and sequenced, not only to facilitate the learning of knowledge, attitudes and/or skills but also to facilitate the cognitive processing of what is learned.

5.4 Experience:
(If none, please specify. Otherwise, indicate percentage of each.)
_____ concrete
_____ reflective observation
_____ abstract conceptualization
_____ experimentation
_____ none
100% Total

These alternatives refer to the types of experiences to be used in the instruction or to which the instruction is to be related. Consideration should be given to how experiences are to be cognitively processed.

5.5 Instructor(s):
(Indicate percentage of each.)
_____ person(s) selected for knowledge, attitudes and/or skills relative to sciences or disciplines
_____ person(s) selected for knowledge, attitudes or skills relative to ways that disciplinarians or scientists think and act
_____ persons selected for their knowledge, attitudes or skills relative to generalizations in applied field(s)
_____ persons selected for knowledge, attitudes or skills regarding ways that persons think and act (including how

These alternatives are oriented similarly to the alternatives in 2.2 (Types of Learners) and 3.2 (Instructional Content) above.

FIGURE 11-2 (continued)
     Instructional design template (IDT).

Phases and Sequential Decision Points	Short Explanation

they solve problems) in applied field(s)
_____ other (Please specify:

_____
_____.)

100% Total

6.0 TESTING AND EVALUATION

6.1 Tests:
     (If none, please specify. Otherwise, indicate percentage of each.)
_____ problem solving
_____ demonstration or performance
_____ recall with written or oral test
_____ testing for cognitive strategy learning
_____ other (Please specify:

_____
_____

_____ none
100% Total

These alternatives refer to different ways to determine ability, achievement, interest, etc. on the part of the learners. The test(s) should be relevant to the nature of what has been learned (including cognitive strategies) and situationally appropriate.

6.2 Evaluation (Extent of Formality):
     (If none, please specify. Otherwise, indicate percentage of each.)
_____ informal
_____ formal
_____ none
100% Total

Efforts to determine the value or worth of the instruction can range from relatively informal to relatively formal (systematic and/or using standard instruments).

6.3 Evaluation (Purpose):
     (If none, please specify. Otherwise, indicate percentage of each.)
_____ formative
_____ summative
_____ none
100% Total

Formative evaluation is used to suggest ways to improve instruction; summative evaluation, to facilitate decision making about whether or not to continue what is evaluated, and, if so, in what ways and/or at what level.

FIGURE 11-2 (continued)
Instructional design template (IDT).

Phases and Sequential Decision Points	Short Explanation
6.4 Evaluation (Type): (If none, please specify. Otherwise, indicate percentage of each.) ____ internal ____ external ____ none 100% Total	Internal evaluation is done by a person(s) involved in designing and/or implementing the instruction; external evaluation, by a person(s) without such involvement.

1.0 SITUATIONAL AUDIT

The first phase in instructional design, as we view it, is the situational audit composed of seven subroutines, which are numbered 1.1 through 1.7. Much as it is essential for an airplane pilot to establish and maintain situational awareness throughout a flight, it is crucial for the instructional designer to focus first and foremost on the situation for which the instruction is to be designed and the potential meaning of that situation for the students and others who are or will be involved in or affected by the instruction. Starting the design process with a situational audit can facilitate doing so.

Flight safety tends to be affected by situational awareness (Schwartz, 1987). Costly errors are likely to occur when there is low situational awareness. Such errors can result from fixation or preoccupation. For example, the pilot's attention may be focused on the instrument panel, and he or she may not be aware that the wings of the plane are icing up or that the plane is on a collision course with another plane.

Similarly, early and ongoing situational awareness is essential in instructional design and the resulting instruction. In instructional design and instruction, situational awareness is the accurate perception of the factors and conditions that affect the instruction and those involved in these processes.

Establishing the significance and meaningfulness of instruction is not something that is merely done after the instructional design occurs. This should be done first in instructional design and then be attended to as a continuous function throughout the rest of the designing of the instruction as well as its implementation and evaluation. Decisions made in designing and implementing instruction should be governed by what establishes and retains the significance and meaningfulness of the instruction for the students, teachers and others who have a stake in the instruction. Significance and meaningfulness seldom come spontaneously or cheaply. They are usually the result of hard work on the part of instructional designers, teachers and students.

In some circumstances, curricular specialists play a role in establishing the significance and meaningfulness of instruction. If so, instructional designers should become thoroughly knowledgeable about whatever the curricular specialists have developed that is relevant to the instruction being designed. If not, establishing the significance and meaningfulness of the instruction has to be accomplished by instructional designers and/or teacher with or without the assistance of students.

A central way of establishing the significance and meaningfulness of instruction is to situate it sociologically and psychologically. This is similar to what an architect does to enhance the value of a house to the client by situating it well ecologically and in relationship to the client's lifestyle. The first few tasks in instructional design involve considering factors in the broad, societal context (Gagne, Briggs, & Wager, 1988, p. 39) and the specific situation (Farmer, Buckmaster, & LeGrand, 1988) in which the instruction is to take place. Those factors may include economic conditions, social needs, legal considerations or physical conditions. Of particular importance are factors that are likely to necessitate or help the instruction and those that may limit it.

The designer may already be somewhat familiar with those factors and the specific situation from prior experience. He or she may need to learn more about the broad and/or specific aspects of the situation from written descriptions and/or from interacting with persons who are knowledgeable about them.

The initial response to the first as well as other decision points in the IDT can be revised subsequently if and when additional information or reflection indicate that doing so is necessary or would be beneficial.

Each of the key decisions is discussed in the following in the order in which it appears in the IDT. The components of the first phase, the situational audit and the relationships among them are depicted in Figure 11-3.

1.1 Driving Factors

Much as the effective executive (Drucker, 1967) focuses primarily outside the organization in making key decisions, the instructional designer is

FIGURE 11-3
1.0 Situational audit.

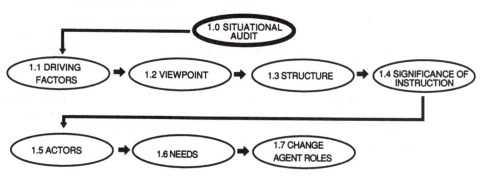

advised to consider the nature of the broad, societal context in which the instruction is to exist. According to Katz and Kahn (1978, pp. 122–125), that environment may be more or less turbulent. Resources in it may be more or less uniformly distributed and/or more or less scarce. A variety of external factors can facilitate or limit the development and implementation of a particular instructional design effort and the resulting instruction. Those external factors may include political, legal, economic and/or physical considerations. They may present themselves in the form of laws, norms or social needs. In any case, in dealing with the first key decision, the instructional designer identifies all of the important external factors which are thought to impact the instruction.

The significance of the instruction being designed is rooted in those external, driving factors. Making those driving factors explicit can help the instructional designer with subsequent decision points. They can also be used in getting others to assist in the design process and in marketing the resulting instruction. Accurate knowledge of the driving factors can be invaluable in communicating the potential value or worth of the instruction to learners and those others who have a stake in the instruction such as instructors, funders, evaluators and administrators.

For example, a change in a law may have extensive implications for how a certain drug can and cannot be used medically. Employers may be willing to hire or increase the remuneration of individuals who have taken an approved course and, as a result of having done so, been certified under a new law to administer the drug. Awareness of the change in the law permitted an instructional designer to make timely revisions in an existing course in order to get it approved for certification.

1.2 Viewpoint Taken

There is an old adage that states: "Assumption is the mother of foul-up." Instructional designs are, of course, based on assumptions. Unexamined assumptions tend to compromise instructional design and the instruction that results from it. Sometimes examination of one's assumptions results in concluding that they can be built upon with little or no revision. At other times such an examination leads to replacing one or more assumptions. Changes in the assumptions upon which an instructional design is based can change the resulting design considerably.

According to Good (1959, p. 44), the term assumption refers to any one of the propositions from which a train of reasoning starts or which is necessary to the solution of a problem. Good notes that assumptions are usually taken as self-evident but may be true only hypothetically. He adds that assumptions are not explicitly stated but left implicit.

Particularly problematic for instructional design are unexamined assumptions about the goals of the instruction. If the instructional designer(s), the instructor(s), the learners, the administrator(s), the funder(s) and/or the sponsor(s) of the instruction are on a fundamentally different wave length or are basically in disagreement concerning the goal and/or the value of the instruction, difficulties are likely to be encountered and, unless rectified, can seriously compromise the learning experience.

There are three quite different viewpoints regarding the proper goal of education today (Cervero, 1988). Assumptions about learners, educators, content and process can be examined in the light of these differing viewpoints. Decisions at each point in the IDT are likely to be at least partly determined by the viewpoint taken about the goal of education. Moreover, the nature of the instructional design as a whole is likely to reflect the viewpoint taken. As with cognitive strategies, it would seem desirable to make the viewpoint of the education explicit for all concerned so that individuals can choose freely and on an informed basis whether or not to participate in the instruction that has been designed. In some situations, it may be desirable to let the learners or potential learners as well as others who have a stake in it have a say as to which viewpoint is to underlie the instruction, and to have the matter settled consensually.

The three viewpoints are: the functionalist viewpoint, the conflict viewpoint and the critical viewpoint. Each of these viewpoints is described briefly in the following, and implications for instructional design are noted.

The Functionalist Viewpoint. This viewpoint has been dominant in the social sciences for the past few decades (Cervero, 1988). Many individuals' understandings tend to be based on assumptions and tenets from the functionalist viewpoint. From this perspective, problem solving can be made rigorous by scientific theory and technique. It is assumed that most practical problems are well formulated, unambiguous and can be solved by the application of scientific knowledge. From this viewpoint, consensus, order and equilibrium are valued, and there tends to be considerable agreement about the proper ends of society.

From this perspective, education is viewed as mainly a technical process with the main purpose of helping individuals learn to contribute to society. Education is to reinforce the status quo and further the power and responsibility of those with technical expertise.

The Conflict Viewpoint. Persons who hold a conflict viewpoint are likely to challenge functionalist understandings (Cervero, 1988). They tend to be particularly concerned about power relationships and the extent of agreement in society about value issues. From their perspective, there is considerable conflict between groups in society for power, status and money. Knowledge, skills and orientations can be used by such groups in their quest for social rewards. Within this perspective, the misuse of expertise is seen as capable of disabling people.

Persons who take a conflict viewpoint are likely to provide educational interventions at the social-structural level and not just at the individual level. Such interventions can include community activities, community organization and liberating education. For example, a union organizer may choose to design a course for workers from a conflict viewpoint. That decision may well affect some or all of the subsequent decisions to be made in designing the course.

The Critical Viewpoint. People holding this viewpoint, according to Cervero (1988), stress the need for individuals to be critically aware of the choices they make and their implications. They challenge the validity of the problems that experts tend to address and the special characteristics of the knowledge that they use to do so. This perspective shares with the functionalist perspective the importance of experts working on well-defined problems with research-based knowledge. Persons who take a critical viewpoint consider the key to practice is deciding which problems to address. They see the important problems as being ambiguous and characterized by uniqueness, uncertainty and value conflicts. Moreover, they tend to think that the main source of professional knowledge is not only textbooks but also, and even more important, repertoires of examples, images and understandings that are acquired through practice.

Persons with a critical viewpoint tend to seek to help individuals face the ethical implications of societal inequities. Within this perspective, the need for experts is recognized, but, because expertise is seen as value-laden, it should be constrained. Moreover, the need for it and how it is to be used should be open to critical, public discussion.

From this viewpoint, it is important to abandon the idea that there is consensus about professional quality. Expert knowledge is viewed as being embedded in values which reflect a particular view of society. Every educational program is a statement of the need for a particular form of technical knowledge and a statement about the proper educational ends. The key questions are: "Why should the learners have this knowledge and to what ends will it be put?" as well as "Who will decide on the content of the instruction and on the basis of what criteria?" The main features of these viewpoints are presented in Figure 11-4.

Students of instructional design may come to the study of it with any one of these three viewpoints or without a well-articulated viewpoint. They may have acquired that viewpoint from their parents, friends and/or teachers. In any case, it is very much to their advantage and important for them to become critically aware of which viewpoint they are espousing and the implications for instructional design.

Some students of instructional design may implicitly find themselves asking questions from a functionalist viewpoint. They may feel pressure to attain technical expertise that will work with relatively well-defined educational problems and in common instructional situations. Such a student may say: "Don't bog me down with a lot of theory and confuse me with ambiguity and complexity. Make instructional design simple and technically sound. I may eventually learn how to handle the ambiguous and the more complex." It is tempting simply to respond to such requests and describe instructional design mainly from a functionalist perspective.

FIGURE 11-4

The main features of the functionalist, conflict and critical viewpoints.

Viewpoint

	Functionalist	*Conflict*	*Critical*
Key Concepts:	expertise	power	dialectic
Key Assumptions:	one-way application of knowledge to solve problems	one-way application of knowledge to solve problems	individuals need to interact with situations and be critically aware of choices and implications of them.

Many books and articles about instructional design have, of course, been written from the functionalist perspective and are widely available. They present much technical expertise which can be used in its existing form for designing instruction from a functionalist viewpoint. Much of that expertise can be used without adaptation in designing instruction from a critical viewpoint; some of it must be adapted for such use. Such technical knowledge is necessary for the instructional designer to know, but may not be sufficient.

In today's world, instructional design does not merely involve the application of cut-and-dried theories and techniques to well-formulated problems. To be sure, there may well be times when the use of such an approach will work satisfactorily. At other times, however, the instructional designer has to interact with situations which are ambiguous and fraught with uniqueness, uncertainty and value conflict.

Under such circumstances, instructional designs must be constructed for the particular situation. Merely designing by formula or applying prototypic designs would be inappropriate. The instructional designer will not only need to know and apply appropriate theories and techniques but also be critically aware of the choices made and the implications of those choices. How driving factors from the societal context are interpreted and cognitive strategies are used in the instruction may well affect the meaningfulness and effectiveness of the instruction.

The IDT was developed to aid instructional design in both relatively well-defined and relatively ill-defined situations. Moreover, the template provides a basis for the instructional designer to examine the situation in which the design is to be used and interact with it. The template helps to determine whether the situation is conducive to the use of a functionalist, conflict or critical viewpoint.

Instructional design from a functionalist viewpoint and from a critical viewpoint are contrasted in Figure 11-5. It should be noted that the viewpoint taken considerably affects the nature of each of the key concepts listed in the column at the left of that figure.

The authors of this book think that it is important for instructional designers to know not only specific techniques for use in instructional design but also how to use those techniques with critical awareness. Such critical awareness includes adequately taking into consideration contextual factors, alternative forms of those techniques and the consequences of choices made among alternatives. It involves, when situationally appropriate, designing instruction in which not only content but also the use of cognitive strategies for processing content, critical awareness and the use of knowledge can be learned.

1.3 Structure of the Situation

The specific situation for which the instruction is being designed can be well defined, moderately well defined or ill defined (Lippert & Farmer, 1984, p. 40).

A well-defined situation is one which the designer can understand and deal with by using a standard model. Moreover, there is reason to think that under similar circumstances most instructional designers elsewhere, who are knowledgeable about what is to be taught, would use that model for understanding the situation and developing an instructional design for use in it. In other words, the model taken would be widely considered to be applicable for understanding the situation and designing the instruction under such circumstances. The model selected may be one of those described in Reigeluth (1983) or elsewhere such as Gagne and Briggs's prescriptive model of instruction (Aronson & Briggs, 1983), Gropper's behavioral approach (Gropper, 1983), Landa's algo-heuristic approach (Landa, 1983), Collins' cognitive approach (Collins & Stevens, 1983), Merrill's component display approach (Merrill, 1983), Reigeluth's elaboration theory approach (Reigeluth & Stein, 1983) or Keller's motivational design approach (Keller, 1983). Or the selected approach may be a domain-specific one which has been developed for a special purpose such as teaching students to pass the Certified Public Accountant (CPA) examination.

A moderately well-defined situation is one in which there is no one standard way to understand the situation and design the instruction for it. Rather, there are two or more alternative ways of understanding the situation and/or of designing the instruction in it. When alternatives exist, a satisfactory way of selecting among such alternatives should be available.

Triangulation (Lippert & Farmer, 1984, p. 45) may be used in selecting among alternatives. Triangulation is a graphic technique designed to help the problem solver visualize decision making. The approach is to weigh each alternative against relevant practical and theoretical criteria. The alternative which best fits all of the criteria should be the best selection for the situation.

FIGURE 11-5

Instructional design from a functionalist viewpoint and a critical viewpoint.

Viewpoint

	Functionalist	Critical
Key Concept:	expertise	dialectic
Main Application to:	well-formulated problems/situations	well- or ill-formulated problems/situations
Instructional Design Tools: Outcomes of Instruction	mainly intended and anticipated	intended and unintended; anticipated and unanticipated
Varieties of Learning:	lower order to higher order	emphasis on application, valuing and performance
Task Analysis	bottom up (parts to whole)	top down (whole to parts) and/or bottom up (parts to whole)
Objectives	specific, behavioral; often many and fixed; clear-cut and agreed-upon criteria	specific, behavioral with significance explicit; usually fewer and more global; more flexible; sometimes uses clear-cut and agreed-upon criteria; otherwise, uses being above a gray area and avoiding specific errors; may require value clarification when faced with important differences about values or standards
Methods and Media	largely used to convey content	used to facilitate conveying content and cognitively processing content or experience
Testing, Evaluation, and Accountability	usually uses types of objectives described above from the functionalist viewpoint	goal related and/or goal free; uses types of objectives described above from critical viewpoint

A situation is ill defined if it cannot be dealt with by the designer either as a well-defined or moderately well-defined situation. In some instances, other designers might be able to deal with a particular situation as well or moderately well defined. The person who is actually doing the instructional design, however, may not have the necessary knowledge or skills that permit doing so. Therefore, he or she may have to deal with the situation as ill defined. Doing so may be aided by the use of heuristic strategies such as those presented by Davis (1973).

Heuristic strategies provide aid for working with ill-defined problems or situations. They go beyond mere trial and error. Typically used heuristic strategies include:

The Use of Analogy. This involves taking into consideration resemblances between objects, situations or ideas which are similar. (See Chapter 7 for use of analogy in *learning*.) Should similarity be extensive, reasoning from analogy may be helpful. If resemblance is merely partial or superficial, marking significant differences, reasoning from analogy may be misleading. (You may wish to review material in Chapter 7 on seduction.) Two situations may appear somewhat similar, suggesting that the instructional design that worked well in the other situation may be applicable to the current situation.

The Use of Bionics. Bionics is the use of biological prototypes for the design of human-made systems. It has also been defined as the study of the structure, function and mechanisms of plants and animals to gain design information for analogous man-made systems. For example, the design of a spider's web may suggest a pattern to use in networking with a variety of organizations to identify needs and recruit students for a particular course or program being designed.

The Use of Synectics. This is done through joining together apparently unrelated elements. For example, the designer might consider using both nurses and electricians in understanding the need for a course or program on safety in the hospital.

The Use of Idea Checklists. The checklist strategy is the use of a list that could suggest solutions suitable for a given problem or for understanding a specific situation. An idea checklist essentially stimulates nonobvious and nonhabitual idea combinations. The IDT itself is a checklist for instructional design.

The Use of Attribute Listing. This consists of step-by-step isolation and modification of individual attributes of the situation being addressed. The first key decision point, 1.1 (Driving Factors), is an attribute list, designed to help the designer isolate the most significant external factors affecting the instruction.

The Use of Morphological Synthesis. This is a logical extension of attribute listing. It involves identifying two or more major dimensions or attributes of the situation. One then lists ideas from each of these dimensions. Finally, one evaluates the different combinations and permutations of these. For example, a designer may select only legal and economic aspects of the situation, list major considerations from each and evaluate different combinations and permeations of them to identify a promising focal point for a lesson, course or program.

The Use of Brainstorming. This strategy stems from the principle of deferred judgment. Harsh criticism and evaluation interfere with flexible idea production. In brainstorming, criticism is delayed; imaginative ways of understanding the situation and dealing with it are welcomed; quantity is wanted; and combination and improvement are sought. After many ideas are generated, they can be evaluated. A representative group of individuals who are familiar with different aspects of the broad, societal context and the specific situation may be brought together to brainstorm ways of understanding the situation and implications for the instruction. Brainstorming can be done either by a group or an individual.

1.4 Significance of the Instruction

Education, and learning more generally, can benefit individuals and society in several ways (Farmer, Buckmaster, & LeGrand, 1988; Apps, 1973). They can contribute to cultural awareness or knowing and understanding of a culture. That culture may be the majority culture in a geographic region, a minority culture or the "culture" of an organization or occupational society. Basic education and liberal arts are both assumed to make such contributions. So also is preparatory education for entering a profession and international travel.

Education can also contribute to practical and/or problem-solving ability. Sometimes individuals learn, by engaging in a variety of activities, to perform practical tasks or to solve real-life problems. Such know-how can enhance daily living. Having individuals who can do practical tasks and solve real-life problems is essential for a technological society.

Education can also contribute to meaningfulness of life in two different ways. It can help persons realize their full potential. For example, a re-entry program in a community college may help persons "be all that they can be" personally, vocationally and avocationally.

Moreover, education can contribute to the meaningfulness of life through helping persons understand and cope with negative circumstances that are not likely to ever improve. What is learned about one's medical condition and prognosis in a hospice for the terminally ill may help one be realistic about one's expectations regarding the likely progression of the disease and one's physical condition in the future.

Instruction can be designed to benefit individuals and society in any one of these ways or in any combination of them. Care must be taken to avoid concluding that attaining what was intended is necessarily beneficial to individuals *and* society.

1.5 Actors to Be Involved

It is important to select the actors for design and instruction (Farmer, Buckmaster, & LeGrand, 1988). The actors include those who are to determine the nature of the context and specific situation; who are to design the instruction; who are to teach; and/or who are the learners. The designer should specify whether educator(s), the learner(s) or both are to be involved in designing and implementing the instruction. Also at issue is the power relationship between the educator(s) and the learner(s). The educator(s) or the learner(s) can design and implement the instruction alone; either one can have a major role and the other a minor role in doing so; or they can function transactively (i.e., mutually) with both taking a substantive but not predominant role.

1.6 Needs

Instructional needs can be identified in five quite different ways (Bradshaw, 1974; Briggs & Wager, 1981; Burton & Merrill, 1977):

Normative Needs. Normative needs are determined by comparing the current situation and a relevant norm. Such norms can include what experts have described as "normal" or "desirable" (Farmer, Buckmaster, & LeGrand, l988).

Expressed Needs. Expressed needs are based on statements of individuals that indicate that they need something and are willing to expend time and/or money to attain it.

Felt Needs. Felt needs consist of lacks, hurts or gaps that are experienced by individuals who have not stated them in the form of expressed needs and/or who are unable or unwilling to put time or money into addressing such needs.

Comparative Needs. Comparative needs are identified by contrasting what has benefited persons elsewhere with what has been provided locally. It is assumed that persons locally are in need of whatever it was that benefited similar individuals elsewhere.

Anticipated or Future Needs. Anticipated or future needs are ones which are likely to occur or be identified at some time in the future.

The following is an illustration of how all of these five ways of identifying instructional needs can be used to identify the needs for instruction. The designer is likely to learn something quite different about the situation and the needs for the instruction from each way of identifying instructional needs.

Social workers and other professionals in a community may know that the average reading level of the adults in the community is considerably below the national norm. From this information, an instructional designer concludes that there is evidence of a normative need for adult literacy training in the community.

A spokesperson for a large church in the community informs the instructional designer that a group of 75 functionally illiterate adult members of the church have indicated their willingness to spend an evening a week strengthening their ability to read. This is viewed by the instructional designer as expressed need.

The instructional designer learns from a social worker in the community that there is a large concentration of adults in a nearby housing development who have considerable trouble reading and writing. No requests for instructional assistance have been received from them. They can be assumed to have a felt need.

Adults in similar communities have benefited from a certain type of functional literacy program which has not been available locally. The instructional designer concludes that adults locally are in comparative need of such instruction.

When the functionally illiterate adults in the community have learned to read and write, they are likely to be in need of courses to prepare them to get the equivalent of a high school diploma. Based on this projection, the instructional designer concludes that there is an anticipated or future need for such a course and decides to design into the functional literacy courses knowledge, attitudes and skills which are thought to be prerequisite to GED courses.

Sometimes the instructional designer will be able to identify needs having implications for instruction in all of the five ways specified above. At other times, it may be impossible or unfeasible to determine need for instruction in one or more of these ways. If possible, determining needs in two or more of these ways is desirable, since each way tends to cross-validate the other ways.

1.7 Change Agent Roles

If the instructional designer is revising existing courses or programs, he or she is likely to act as a change agent. In any case, the instructional designer will need to decide what change agent role(s) the instructor(s) is intended to play in the instruction being designed. As we view it, instruction is always supposed to bring about desirable change. By definition, instruction is intended to bring about desirable changes in knowledge, attitudes or skills. Change agents can play one or more of four possible roles: solution giver, resource linker, process helper or catalyst (Havelock, 1973).

Solution Giver. In designing and implementing instruction, educators can give solutions to problems or provide content. For example, an instructional designer may be a specialist in biology and use that expertise in designing a biology course for use in a community college to replace an outdated course. In so doing, the instructional designer is being a solution giver.

Resource Linker. Educators can help identify and establish links with resources in the form of experts, written material or media. For example, the designer provides an updated list of references for a course and makes them available in the college library. Thereby the designer is being a resource linker.

Process Helper. Educators can assist in the learning and/or problem-solving processes. For example, the designer decides to teach the course and provides guidance (i.e., acts as a process helper) to the students in the course during their experiments in the laboratory.

Catalyst. Educators can act as catalysts, seeking to stimulate reluctant individuals to assist in instructional design, participate in learning activities, engage in solving problems or become involved in other actions. Educator(s), learner(s) or both can play a catalytic role. Under some circumstances, it may be necessary and appropriate for them to do so. Neither educators nor learners have the inherent right or obligation to act catalytically. They should not, however, avoid the catalytic role merely because of inhibition or ideology (Farmer, Buckmaster, & LeGrand, 1988). For example, in the laboratory, one student aids another student (i.e., plays a catalytic role) by helping that student grasp the real-life relevance of what is being learned in a particular experiment.

As with the five ways of establishing the need for instruction, any one or a combination of the change agent roles can be used both in instructional design and instruction. What is accomplished by playing one of these roles may be complemented and/or reinforced by playing one or more of the other roles.

SUMMARY

In this chapter we presented the Instructional Design Template (IDT) and suggested ways to use it in making decisions in designing instruction. We have also started our more detailed description and explanation of specific aspects of the instructional design process by focusing on the first phases of the IDT which is entitled the "Situational Audit." Such an audit is done first to establish significance and meaningfulness in the instructional design. The next phase in the IDT is determining the broad aim and specific objectives of the instruction, both of which are viewed as being derived, at least in part, from the instructional designer's understanding of the situation in which the instruction is to be implemented both socially and psychologically.

EXERCISES

1. What are the main advantages of starting instructional design with the type of situational audit described in this chapter?
2. Think of a specific type of instruction which you have designed or might

design. Then conduct an imaginary situational audit relative to it, explicitly using the first phase and its seven sequential decisions as a checklist in doing so. This exercise is very important as an aid to understanding the value of the IDT.

3. When, if ever, would a functionalist or conflict viewpoint be appropriate for use in instructional design rather than a critical viewpoint?

REFERENCES

Apps, J. (1973). *Toward a working philosophy of adult education.* Syracuse, NY: Publications in Continuing Education.

Aronson, D. T., & Briggs, L. J. (1983). Contributions of Gagne and Briggs to a prescriptive model of instruction. In C. M. Reigeluth (Ed.), *Instructional-design theories and models: An overview of their current status.* Hillsdale, NJ: Lawrence Erlbaum Associates.

Bradshaw, J. (1974). The concept of social need. *Ekistics, 220,* 184–187.

Briggs, L. J., & Wager, W. W. (1981). *Handbook of procedures for the designing of instruction* (2nd ed.). Englewood Cliffs, NJ: Educational Technology Publications.

Burton, J. K., & Merrill, P. F. (1977). Needs assessment: Goals, needs, and priorities. In L. J. Briggs (Ed.), *Instructional design: Principles and applications.* Englewood Cliffs, NJ: Educational Technology Publications.

Cervero, R. M. (1988). *Effective continuing education for professionals.* San Francisco: Jossey-Bass.

Collins, A., & Stevens, A. L. (1983). A cognitive theory of inquiry teaching. In C. M. Reigeluth (Ed.), *Instructional-design theories and models: An overview of their current status.* Hillsdale, NJ: Lawrence Erlbaum Associates.

Davis, G. A. (1973). *Psychology of problem solving—Theory and practice.* New York: Basic Books.

Drucker, P. F. (1967). *The effective executive.* New York: Harper & Row.

Farmer, J. A., Buckmaster, A., & LeGrand, B. (1988). Situational-specific approaches. *Lifelong Learning: An Omnibus of Practice and Research, 12,* 8–13.

Gagne, R. M., Briggs, L. J., & Wager, W. W. (1988). *Principles of instructional design* (3rd ed.) New York: Holt, Rinehart and Winston.

Good, C. V. (Ed.). (1959). *Dictionary of education.* New York: McGraw-Hill.

Gropper, G. L. (1983). A behavioral approach to instructional prescription. In C. M. Reigeluth (Ed.), *Instructional-design theories and models: An overview of their current status.* Hillsdale, NJ: Lawrence Erlbaum Associates.

Havelock, R. (1973). *The change agent's guide to innovation in education.* Englewood Cliffs, NJ: Educational Technology Publications.

Katz, D., & Kahn, R. L. (1978). *The social psychology of organizations* (2nd ed.). New York: Wiley.

Keller, J. M. (1983). Motivational design of instruction. In C. M. Reigeluth, (Ed.), *Instructional-design theories and models: An overview of their current status.* Hillsdale, NJ: Lawrence Erlbaum Associates.

Landa, L. N. (1983). The algo-heuristic theory of instruction. In C. M. Reigeluth (Ed.), *Instructional-design theories and models: An overview of their current status.* Hillsdale, NJ: Lawrence Erlbaum Associates.

Lippert, F., & Farmer, J. (1984). *Psychomotor skills in orthopedic surgery.* Baltimore: Williams & Wilkins.

Merrill, M. D. (1983). Component display theory. In C. M. Reigeluth (Ed.), *Instructional-design theories and models: An overview of their current status*. Hillsdale, NJ: Lawrence Erlbaum Associates.

Reigeluth, C. M. (Ed.). (1983). *Instructional-design theories and models: An overview of their current status*. Hillsdale, NJ: Lawrence Erlbaum Associates.

Reigeluth, C. M., & Stein, F. S. (1983). The elaboration theory of instruction. In C. M. Riegeluth (Ed.), *Instructional-design theories and models: An overview of their current status*. Hillsdale, NJ: Lawrence Erlbaum Associates.

Schwartz, D. (1987). Training for situational awareness. Paper presented to The Flight Safety Foundation, Fortieth International Air Safety Seminar, Tokyo, Japan, October 28, 1987.

CHAPTER 12

Instructional Design Template: Part II

The Instructional Design Template (IDT) was presented and described in general in Chapter 11 along with suggestions for its use. A detailed description of the first phase (1.0 Situational Audit) was also presented in that chapter. The other five phases of the IDT, beginning with the second phase (2.0 Broad Aim and Specific Objectives), are described in greater detail in this chapter.

2.0 BROAD AIM AND SPECIFIC OBJECTIVES

The second phase of instructional design is focused on the broad aim and specific objectives of the instruction and consists of subroutines 2.1 through 2.7. Decisions about the topic, types of learners to be instructed, types of learning, the function of the instruction and type(s) of pretest or preassessment to be used are also included in this phase. A concept map of the second phase, including each of the subroutines in it, is presented in Figure 12-1.

2.1 Topic

At this point, the question is: "What is the instruction to be about?" In other words, what is to be taught and learned? It is absolutely essential for the instructional designer to define the topic. A standard educational reference such as *Good's Dictionary of Education* (1959) and an unabridged dictionary can be useful in this regard. Next, the instructional designer should specify the boundaries of the topic. Finally, the designer should provide:

FIGURE 12-1
Aims and objectives.

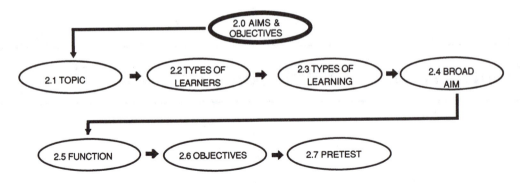

1. clear example(s) of what is in the topic;
2. clear example(s) of what is not in the topic;
3. ambiguous example(s) of what appears not to be in the topic but actually is; and
4. ambiguous example(s) of what appears to be in the topic but actually is not.

2.2 Types of Learners

We recommend that the types of learners be considered before the types of instructors. This is consistent with Gagne, Briggs and Wager's (1988, p. 3) distinction between designing instruction rather than teaching. According to those authors, it is important to take into consideration all of the events that may have a direct effect on the student, not just those set in motion by an individual who is a teacher.

In specifying the type(s) of learners, one states the characteristics of the learners, including the nature and extent of their knowledge, attitudes, values and skills relative to specific professions or other occupations, when they enter the instruction. Doing so permits situating the instruction relative to the learners rather than classifying the learners in terms of (1) what is to be taught; (2) what is thought they need, want or like; or (3) what is taken to be the nature of their interests or motivations.

The type(s) of learners for which the instruction is being designed can include scientists or disciplinarians, students of the sciences or disciplines, practitioners in applied fields, students of the applied fields or others. Persons in these categories differ greatly. Scientists and disciplinarians have been trained to think very abstractly. In other words, their knowledge is intentionally apart from any particular or concrete object. What they know, how they think, their values and attitudes and their skills are likely to be influenced strongly by their respective sciences or disciplines. When persons are in the role of students of the sciences or disciplines, it can be assumed that they seek to learn to think and act, at least in part, in ways that are valued by the science(s) or discipline(s) which they wish to enter. Moreover, they are likely to want to conform to the values and attitudes that are generally espoused in those sciences or disciplines.

Practitioners of the applied fields intentionally think at a different level of abstraction than scientists and disciplinarians. In other words, their knowledge is less far from concrete objects. Professionals and others in the applied fields are characterized by their ability to use "knowledge in action" (Ruesch, 1975) in beneficial ways. In this use, they are able to do practical tasks and solve real-life problems which others cannot. On the other hand, it can be assumed that persons who are in the role of students of applied fields seek to learn to think and act similarly to those who are in the applied fields. They also want to attain values and attitudes that are typically espoused by those in the applied fields.

The learners may include persons who are in none of the foregoing categories. Such individuals may not yet have chosen a particular career or may not wish to become scientists or disciplinarians. Moreover, they may not have entered nor wish to enter a profession or any of the other applied fields.

For example, an individual may wish to learn to play music "by ear" rather than to learn to play in a more formal manner. To design instruction about musical theories and how to read music for such individuals would seem to be inappropriate and contrary to the students' explicit wishes.

2.3 Types of Learning

According to Rumelhart and Norman (1978), learning can occur through accretion, tuning or restructuring. Each of these types of learning has been described in Chapter 1 on pp. 14–15. They are summarized and implications for instructional design are suggested as follows:

Learning Through Accretion. In learning through accretion, new facts are added incrementally to what one already knows. The addition does not, however, alter one's information-processing system itself.

Learning Through Tuning. Learning through tuning involves changing the categories one uses for interpreting new information to bring them more in line with functional demands placed on them.

Learning Through Restructuring. Learning through restructuring tends to be more significant and difficult. Such learning occurs when new structures are developed for interpreting new information and for putting a new organization on information that is already stored. Learning through restructuring typically occurs after considerable time and effort and is likely to require a critical mass of unwieldy and ill-formed information to have built up first, necessitating restructuring.

The type of learning that is intended in the instruction can affect the choice of cognitive strategies to be used in that instruction. For example, rehearsal (particularly through paraphrasing) may be the cognitive strategy of choice in an instructional design which mainly seeks to promote learning through tuning, but a metaphor could be used in a design for restructuring. Moreover, the sequencing of cognitive strategies to be used can be affected by the type of learning intended in the instruction.

2.4 Broad Aim

According to Good (1959), the terms *aim*, *goal*, and *purpose* have similar meanings. All are references to a foreseen end that gives direction to an activity. *Goal* can be used broadly to mean an aim or purpose. It can also be used more narrowly to refer to the objective or end to be attained in any behavior situation.

In 2.4 (Broad Aim), the instructional designer is expected to describe the foreseen end of the instruction broadly. The relationship between the broad aim and specific objectives is depicted in Figure 12-2 (see next page).

Figure 12-2 can perhaps be explained best by the use of the "moose hunt story" presented in Box 12-1. It was synthesized from numerous reports of somewhat similar experiences that appear from time to time in sporting magazines. The moose hunt story can be explained by relating each aspect of the story to Figure 12-2.

BOX 12-1: THE MOOSE HUNT STORY

A man who lived near Chicago wanted to go moose hunting in Minnesota during his vacation. He phoned ahead and made a reservation with a moose hunting guide.

On the first day of his vacation, he put his hunting equipment into his recreational vehicle (RV) and was about to leave for Minnesota. But, being a conservative sportsman, he went back into the house, got his fishing equipment, and put it in the RV.

When he got to the sports store in Minnesota where he was supposed to meet the moose hunting guide, he was informed, contrary to expectations, there were no moose in the area, and none could be expected.

Disappointed, he canceled his reservation with the moose hunting guide and headed for a nearby liquor store to buy a case of gin to drown his sorrows during the rest of his vacation.

Before he got there, he decided that excessive drinking was a bad idea and went back to the sports store where he heard that muskies, exciting game fish, were biting well. He hired a muskie fishing guide and caught several near-record muskies during his vacation. When he returned home, he wrote about his experience, sold the article to a sporting magazine and was paid well for it.

FIGURE 12-2

Broad aim and specific objectives.

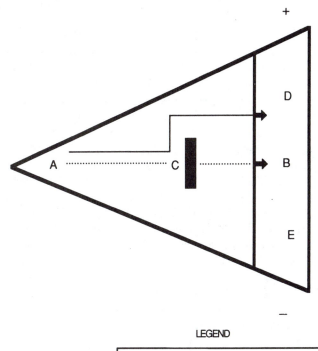

LEGEND

A= Starting point
B= The intitial, specific objective
C= Unforseen barrier to achieving B
D= Alternative, specific, achieved objective
E= An alternative, not-selected objective
-= Undersirable consequences
+= Serendipitous (valuable* but not sought) outcomes

_____

*To be valued, an outcome is not required to be intended. Likewise, some intended outcomes may not be valued.

"A" in Figure 12-2 is the starting point when the decision was made to go on vacation. "B" is the specific objective of going moose hunting in Minnesota. "C" is the unforeseen problem or barrier incurred when it was learned that there were no moose in the vicinity, blocking access to "B" (moose hunting). "−" is a symbol for the undesirable consequences that were avoided by deciding not to remain inebriated throughout his vacation. "D" is an alternative, specific, achieved objective (muskie fishing) that was articulated when the vacationer heard that such fishing was possible and likely to be successful. "E" is one of several other alternative, not-selected objectives, such as hiking or bird watching, which a sportsman might have considered and enjoyed during his vacation. "+" is the serendipitous (valuable but unsought) outcome of having his story appear in print and having received money for it.

Clearly, moose hunting and obtaining moose meat were not the broad aim of the conservative sportsman. His taking along his fishing equipment on vacation was evidence that he realized that he could have a good outdoor vacation in other ways than moose hunting. The broad aim, then, was having a good outdoor vacation, which could have been achieved in a variety of ways. Not all types of activities and outcomes can be considered part of the broad aim. That broad aim had a lower limit and an upper limit. Spending an inebriated vacation ("−") turned out to be below the *lower limit*. Selling the story and seeing it in print were above the *upper limit*, since these were not intended or anticipated before the end of the vacation.

In instructional design, it is advisable to work backwards (Gagne, Briggs, & Wager, 1988, p. 39) from the broad aim. Information learned in order to handle the first ten decision points in the IDT may provide clues about the broad aim of the instruction being designed. What is learned or realized in dealing with subsequent decision point in the IDT, such as 2.6 (Objectives), may help to revise the description of the broad aim, including what can be considered to be its upper and lower limits. It is advantageous, however, to focus on and describe the broad aim itself and its upper and lower limits before dealing with the specific objectives. Otherwise the designer is likely to be overly influenced by those specific objectives and may well erroneously consider the sum of them as constituting the broad aim.

We recommend using the term *broad aim* rather than *educational goals* (Gagne, Briggs, & Wager, 1988, p. 39). As indicated, one usage of the term *goal* has it as interchangeable with *objective*. The broad aim of education and the broad aim of a particular instructional design effort are both more than the sum of the specific objectives.

Educational broad aims can include those human activities that contribute to the functioning of a society (including the functioning of an individual in the society) and that can be acquired through learning. Included in educational broad aims can also be those human activities that help individuals realize their full potential, however they may define the activities and whether or not associated learning contributes to the functioning of society. Also included can be human activities that help persons endure negative circumstances that are not likely ever to improve.

If one or more specific objectives are blocked during instruction, having the broad aim and its upper and lower limits identified can help in efforts to retain the meaningfulness of the instructional experience. Having alternative objectives available and realizing that others may be derivable within the broad aim can be equally advantageous in such circumstances.

In short, the meaningfulness of the instruction may be enhanced if a well-conceived and consensually validated statement of the broad aim and its upper and lower limits has been developed by the instructional designer and is available to the teachers and students. Moreover, if the initial objective(s) cannot be attained or no longer seem desirable, such a statement can be used in identifying worthwhile, alternative objectives within the broad aim. Further, such knowledge can make the learner aware of learning outcomes to be avoided as well as beneficial outcomes that may be realized unintentionally.

2.5 Function

Learners may need to know particular subject matter or skills to: pass exams or tests; become licensed or credentialed; or acquire prerequisite knowledge, attitudes or skills for particular courses, programs or types of employment. They may need to know or be able to do what is to be learned to: update their knowledge or be able and/or permitted to experience or practice something. All of the foregoing are functions of instruction. The instructional designer may find that there are other reasons for learning and instruction. This functional information can affect not only what it is desirable to teach but also the motivation of the learners.

It is advisable for the instructional designer to differentiate between: the "need to know," the "ought to know," the "nice to know" and the "interesting to know." Prioritizing what might be taught is an essential function of the instructional designer. If the "need to know" is missing, potential benefits of the instruction are likely not to be realized. If all that the instruction provides is the "need to know" and if those things that the learners think that they ought to know, that would be nice to know or that they would be interested in knowing are rigidly curtailed from the instructional experience, its meaningfulness can be compromised.

Concerning the "experience something" alternative, the learners may have experienced, be experiencing, plan to experience or have to experience something which necessitates or can be enhanced by particular outcomes. For example, an individual may have done poorly in one course and may wish to attain better cognitive strategies before taking the next course. An individual may be in the midst of a developmental crisis and may wish to learn to understand the experience more adequately and learn ways to cope with it more effectively. An individual may plan to take an international trip and may want to learn about the culture in the countries to be visited. A child may require an operation and may need to learn about hospitals, operating rooms and what to expect and do before, during and after the operation.

Concerning the "pass exams or tests" alternative, an issue is to what extent is it appropriate to key the instruction to specific examinations or tests. For example, special courses are taught to help prepare for the Certified Public Accountant (CPA) examination and the examinations administered by medical specialty boards. Speciality courses are taken by persons who wish to be admitted to law, medical or business schools. In such courses, there may be a deliberate attempt to "teach to the test." The reputation of such a course is likely to depend heavily on the validity of what is taught relative to what is actually tested in the examination and the passing rate of graduates of the course.

In some instances, actual items from previous tests or exams are used in teaching a course or program. In other instances, similar items are substituted for the actual items, which may or may not be available. In some situations and fields, "teaching to a test or exam" is appropriate and encouraged; in others, it is discouraged or forbidden. In any case, it is essential for instructional designers, instructors and learners to know what is appropriate, legal and being done about this in instruction elsewhere.

2.6 Specific Objectives

Instructional objectives can be stated orally or in writing. They can be formally or informally developed and/or stated. According to Good (1959, p. 371), specific objectives are more narrowly focused than broad aims and serve as a guide for a teaching unit. Specific objectives are directed toward the eventual achievement of more general goals, purposes or broad aims. They are statements of results that are desired from that particular instruction.

Educational broad aims and objectives may be the outputs of processes such as curriculum development, program development or needs assessment. They function, however, as inputs in instructional design. Katz and Kahn (1978) have noted that broad aims, purposes, goals and objectives of all kinds are inputs rather than outputs. They may be the outputs of other processes including instruction itself, but, in any case, they are not part of the results or outputs of instruction, although experiences in and the results of prior instruction may be used to modify the objectives for similar instruction in the future.

Objectives are intended outcomes which may or may not be realized. To think of objectives as outcomes in instructional design is to engage in conceptual confusion. Because a traveler plans and wants to get to New York City from Los Angeles next Wednesday (an input in the form of an objective) does not mean that he or she is there (an output). If the traveler is, in fact, in New York City on that Wednesday, then he or she will have achieved the initial objective. If he or she ends up in Chicago on that day and being there has more desirable personal consequences than being in New York City, not having achieved the initial objective is unlikely to be viewed negatively by the traveler. Others who may have had a stake in having the traveler in New York City on that day may, however, view negatively his or her not having achieved the initial objective.

Much has been written (Mager, 1975; Gagne, Briggs, & Wager, 1988; Bloom, 1956; Krathwohl, Bloom, & Masia, 1964) about how to write instructional objectives and their potential benefits. Much has also been written (Atkin, 1969) about their limitations and misuses. Behaviorists tend to stress the importance of stating objectives clearly, precisely and unambiguously. Critics of the behaviorist stance point to potential rigidity and formalism in the way behavioral objectives often are developed and worded. Moreover, critics have noted that many behavioral objectives that were developed in the past were somewhat trivial and too numerous to be used practically in instruction. Reviewers (Melton, 1978; Kibler & Bassett, 1977) of conflicting claims concerning the effects of behavioral objectives have concluded that claims regarding the benefits of their use, particularly under certain circumstances, are inconclusive at best. Those reviewers noted that there may even be limiting effects of their use under other circumstances.

In some situations, ranging from special education for the severely handicapped to continuing professional education, the development of specific objectives is required if the proposed instructional design is to be approved for funding or credit. Under such circumstances, or if the designer wishes to develop specific objectives for other reasons, doing so typically entails: (1) describing what the learner is expected to be able to do after the learning experience rather than conceptualizing the objective in terms of what the learner will be exposed to during the instruction; (2) describing at what level (how well) the learner is expected to perform to be satisfactory; (3) specifying under what conditions or constraints the learners will be expected to perform; and (4) specifying who will judge the performance (Mager, 1975).

We note, however, that if a *critical* rather than a functionalist view of instructional design is taken, the above criteria for instructional objectives should be modified. From the functionalist viewpoint, it is viewed as possible and desirable to specify the exact criteria to be used in describing the satisfactory level, and it may be assumed that there will be considerable external agreement about what that level is. If a critical viewpoint is taken for instructional design, however, the matter of level may be problematic. For certain objectives there may be a single satisfactory level which is extensively agreed upon externally. But the existence of such a criterion should be established by the instructional designer rather than assumed. In other instances, there may be disagreement on the part of reasonable and informed persons about the satisfactory level. Moreover, *satisfactory* may not merely consist of being above a clear-cut point. It may consist of being above a gray area and avoiding certain errors.

According to Lippert, Farmer, and Schafer (1989, p. 38), a relatively weak way of handling who will judge is merely to indicate: "to the satisfaction of the instructor or the learner." Learners may have recourse in the case of capricious grading by a parochial or out-of-date instructor if they can demonstrate that they have met or exceeded standards which appear in relevant references such as textbooks, articles, syllabi and institutional guidelines.

The instructional designer should ensure that these sources reflect the *current, national perspective and associated standards*. Particular instructors may be dated or parochial. Learning the national perspective may be essential for students who have to take nationally developed tests or exams or who have to work subsequently in settings in which persons are expected to perform at a level which is acceptable nationally.

In writing instructional objectives from a critical viewpoint, it is desirable (Lippert, Farmer, & Schafer, 1989, p. 40) to start instructional objectives with a *significance statement*, indicating the main reason(s) why it is important, from the learners' and society's perspectives, for the learners to be able to do what is specified in the objective. Such significance statements can often be derived from and related to the situational audit (the first phase of the IDT) and the broad aim of the instruction.

Developing meaningful and adequate instructional objectives can be challenging. Lippert, Farmer, and Schafer (1989) have noted that development of objectives can be facilitated if developers avoid the following common errors:

1. writing the objectives as directives (i.e., "The learners will type at 60 words per minute.");
2. omitting one or more of the key elements (i.e., what the learner will be able to do, at what level, under what conditions, to whose satisfaction, or the significance statement);
3. writing a trivial (nonsignificant) objective;
4. writing a nonfeasible objective;
5. writing an objective that is too broad in scope;
6. writing an objective which describes the content to be taught (i.e., "By the end of the basic science course, the learners will have been exposed to cellular biology.").

2.7 Use of Pretest

A pretest is typically given in order to determine preexisting skills, aptitudes or knowledge, as a basis for judging the appropriateness and the effectiveness of subsequent treatment. Dick and Carey (1985) have stressed the importance of "identifying entry behaviors and characteristics" of students. The relationships between the pretest, other aspects of instructional design and subsequent instruction are depicted in the following figure adapted from Lippert, Farmer, and Schafer (1989).

A rifle shot cannot correct its direction once it leaves the barrel of the rifle. A heat-seeking missile, by contrast, can seek out its target. The cybernetic cycle works like a heat-seeking missile in that it seeks out and corrects its trajectory toward the target (unlike the rifle bullet). Knowledge, attitudes, skills and performance change frequently. Learners may look the same but may not be. Formal or informal provisions should be built into the instructional design to permit determining the entry level of the learner(s) and adjusting the instructional level as the students and/or the circumstances change.

As indicated in Figure 12-3, the objectives often can be derived from and related to the broad aim. In some instances, those objectives can be validated or refined through the use of a questionnaire administered prior to the instruction. A formal or informal pretest can also be conducted before instruction. Pretests can be written or oral. They can be situational, whereby the learners are observed performing in situations in which they would be expected to use the knowledge, attitudes or skills. Pretests can include contrived or real-life problem-solving activities. Self-reporting by the learners on the extent that they already have the prerequisite knowledge or skills can be

FIGURE 12-3

Cybernetic cycle.

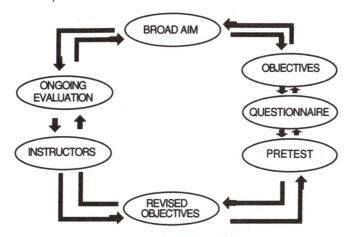

Adapted from *Handbook for Orthopaedic Educators* (11th ed.), 1989, p. 64. Chicago: Committee on Graduate Education, American Academy of Orthopaedic Surgeons. Adapted by permission of American Academy of Orthopaedic Surgeons.

considered a form of pretest in that such feedback from the learners can be used to adjust the instruction.

If the learner(s) knows much or all of what is usually taught or is scheduled to be taught in a course or program and that is determined by pretesting, the learner(s) can be exempted from the course or program or referred to a more appropriate one. Or, it may be possible to revise the course or program to accommodate the proficiency level(s) of the learner(s). One way to do so is a branching approach, whereby all the learners start at the same level but provisions are made for more difficult or advanced learning for those who are able to move readily and rapidly through the easier material or tasks.

At this point, we suggest that the reader review the template in Chapter 11 and use the section on pp. 214–216 dealing with the second phase (2.0 Broad Aims and Specific Objectives) as a checklist in continuing to develop an instructional design for the imaginary situation that was suggested in Exercise #2 at the end of Chapter 11. Included should be the information called for by the prompts for each of the following sequential decision points: topic, types of learners, types of learning, broad aim, function, objectives and pretest.

3.0 CONTENT AND USES

In this section we describe the four subroutines in the third phase of the template. Each pertains to a different aspect of the content of the instruction and anticipated uses of what is learned in it. These subroutines and their relationship to each other are depicted in Figure 12-4.

FIGURE 12-4

3.0 Content and uses.

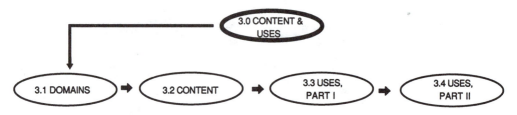

3.1 Instructional Domain(s)

Three domains of instruction have been identified (Bloom, 1956; Krathwohl, Bloom, & Masia, 1964; Simpson, 1966; Gagne, Briggs, & Wager, 1988). The *cognitive domain* pertains to knowledge; the *affective domain*, to attitudes and values; and the *psychomotor domain*, to skills entailing physical action. The cognitive and affective domains are discussed in Chapter 2.

The "head, heart, and hand" analogy (Lippert & Farmer, 1984, pp. 11–13) can be used to understand the relationship between the three domains. For theoretical purposes it may be possible to consider separately how an athlete or surgeon thinks, feels and engages in motor skills. But for instructional design purposes, considering motor skills separately from cognition and affective considerations, or from their appropriate use, would be to inadequately situate them (Brown, Collins, & Duguid, 1988a). It would be like examining a free cutting hand in a surgeon and thinking that in some way that hand was disconnected from and not under the control of the brain and heart of the surgeon. Efforts to develop and maintain psychomotor skills for use in real life should focus not just on the hands of the performers but also on the relationships among their hands, brains and hearts. All are coordinated to do useful tasks. As depicted in Figure 12-5, from the point of view of the professions and other applied fields, central to the three domains are *application (i.e., problem solving), valuing and movement skills.*

The practitioner in the professions and other applied fields uses all three domains. In each domain, the higher levels build on the lower ones hierarchically. For some forms of learning, starting at the bottom of a domain and working up may be advisable. In the professions and other applied fields it may be most appropriate (Lippert, Farmer, & Schafer, 1989, p. 63) to enter at the third level of each domain and "reach down" (i.e., provide remedial instruction) and "reach up" (i.e., provide more advanced forms of instruction) as necessary to further the development of the learner(s).

For example, central to the professions is applying knowledge that is shared with others in one's profession to solve real-life problems. To learn a profession or to keep up to date in it one may need to attain certain knowledge. Such learning is seldom for its own sake but rather to make professional problem solving possible. If the problems to be solved are relatively well defined, problem solving can be done through application of the standard

FIGURE 12-5

Cognitive, affective, and psychomotor domains from the perspective of the professions and other applied fields.

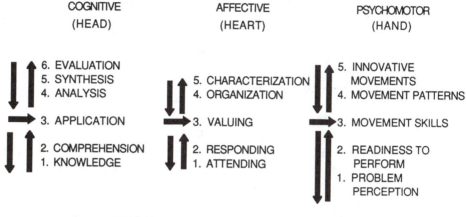

Adapted from *Handbook for Orthopaedic Educators* (11th ed.), 1989, p. 63. Chicago: Committee on Graduate Education. American Academy of Orthopaedic Surgeons. Adapted by permission of American Academy of Orthopaedic Surgeons.

knowledge of the field. Otherwise, it will be necessary to engage in analysis to better understand the problem and/or synthesis to develop a new way of dealing with the problem. The professional must also evaluate what has been done, whether the problem solving, if any, has been appropriately conducted, and/or the effects of that problem solving.

At the core of the affective domain for the professional are the values that are typically held in common. Essential to becoming a professional is accepting the values of one's chosen profession. Initially, one may only be willing to entertain (attend to) a particular value. (The reader may review this domain which was presented in Chapter 2, pp. 48–49.) Then one may be willing to discuss and try out (responding to) that value. Next, he or she may evidence valuing that value. This may include acting voluntarily in accordance with it. At a future time, the individual may generalize (organization) by relating the value to other aspects of work or life. Finally, the individual may have so internalized and accepted that value that actions exemplify it (characterization). Keller (1983) has developed a motivational-design model of instruction in which attention is paid particularly to: arousing the learner's interest or curiosity, establishing relevance from the learner's perspective, capitalizing on the expectancy of the learners and providing learner satisfaction by combining extrinsic rewards and intrinsic motivation.

At the heart of the psychomotor domain for many of the professions are skilled techniques which are used to solve problems or perform physical tasks. In learning such techniques, individuals must perceive the problem and get ready to act on it. To do so, one uses skilled movements and patterns of movements which together constitute the skilled techniques of the profession. Finally, the individual may learn to be innovative about problems in ways that are acceptable to the profession and society.

3.2 Instructional Content

In 3.2 (Instructional Content), the instructional designer indicates the percentage of the content of instruction that is to consist of: (a) theories or concepts from the disciplines or sciences, (b) ways of thinking and acting like a disciplinarian or scientist, (c) generalizations from the applied fields, (d) ways of thinking and acting like person in the applied fields and (e) others as specified.

Which one or more of the foregoing are selected for use in a particular instructional design depends on choices made in the other decision points in the IDT. In turn, the choices made relative to instructional content may well affect how other decision points, such as 5.5 [Instructor(s)], are handled.

The reason that we recommend deciding about the instructional content midway in design and choosing the types of instructor(s) even later is that it encourages fitting the instructional design to the learners with due consideration of the context and situation. This approach is in contrast to designing around instructors and what they know, hoping that what they have to offer and how they typically offer instruction will suffice. In short, we recommend designing instruction to facilitate learning and the needs of learners rather than facilitating teaching and the needs of teachers.

3.3 Uses of Knowledge, Part I

At 3.3 (Uses of Knowledge, Part I), the instructional designer indicates the percentage of intended (1) explicit learning and (2) tacit learning. According to Broudy (1979), when knowledge is used explicitly, the learner remembers what is learned and how to use it and does so consciously and deliberately. By contrast, tacit knowledge is not intended to be applied but rather to be used perspectively. In other words, one becomes aware of tacit knowledge without memorizing it. While one is not intended to recall the specifics of such knowledge exactly, having acquired tacit knowledge permits one to "look at the world" through it.

For example, a person with a tacit knowledge of oriental cultures and religions is likely to view the Orient quite differently on a trip there than one who has never attained such knowledge. Similarly, a physician who has a tacit knowledge of microbiology may view and treat patients' medical problems differently than one who lacks such tacit knowledge.

3.4 Uses of Knowledge, Part II

In 3.4 (Uses of Knowledge, Part II), the instructional designer indicates the percentage of what is to be learned that is to be used: replicatively, associatively, interpretively and applicatively (Broudy, 1988; Eraut, 1985). Each of such uses of knowledge is defined and illustrated briefly below.

Replicative Use of Knowledge. When knowledge is used replicatively, it is put to use in the form in which it was learned. For example, a person may have learned that 25 minus 15 equals 10. He or she may use that knowledge in making a small purchase later the same day.

Associative Use of Knowledge. When one uses what has been learned *associatively*, one sees connections between things that are associated, which he or she otherwise might not have seen. For example, a person may have learned to associate a certain smell in food with the likelihood of spoilage and subsequently use that knowledge in spotting food in the refrigerator that should be discarded rather than eaten.

Interpretive Use of Knowledge. Knowledge used interpretively provides a context in which to understand something or an explanation for something. For example, an adult may experience a "mid-life crisis." He or she may use information, provided by a relative, teacher or friend, that such crises are typical of that age. Such learning may induce greater understanding of human development and also be reassuring.

Applicative Use of Knowledge. Knowledge is used applicatively in understanding and solving relatively well-defined problems or understanding and dealing with relatively well-structured situations. For example, a counselor may learn a standard technique for helping persons understand and cope with being fired from a job. Shortly thereafter, someone who has just been fired seeks help in understanding and coping with the experience. The counselor determines that the standard technique is applicable and uses it to help the client understand what has happened—to put it into perspective.

We again suggest that the reader review the template in Chapter 11 and use the section on pp. 216–217 dealing with the third phase (3.0 Content and Uses) as a checklist in continuing to develop an instructional design for the imaginary situation that was suggested in Exercise #2 at the end of Chapter 11. Included should be the information called for by the prompts for each of the following sequential decision points: domains; content; uses, Part I; and uses, Part II.

4.0 COGNITIVE STRATEGIES

In this section we refer to the cognitive strategies that have been described in greater detail in the first ten chapters of this book and suggests ways of incorporating them in instructional designs. Also included in this section is a presentation of these cognitive strategies in the form of a concept map.

4.0 Cognitive Strategies

In 4.0 (Cognitive Strategies), the instructional designer should examine the list of nine cognitive strategies provided as a checklist and check all that pertain to the instruction being designed. Kirby and Briggs (1980) have suggested that instruction can be viewed as a testing ground for theoretical insights about how persons learn, which includes the use of cognitive strategies. Instructional designers, teachers and students can all use metacognition (Lawson, 1980, p. 145) in making decisions about the cognitive strategies to use in a specific instructional setting. Hopefully, they can all learn from their experience in order to strengthen the fit between what is to be learned and strategies used to do so. Weinert (1987, p. 7) has noted that training in the use of cognitive strategies is particularly successful if additional, special knowledge about the use of these strategies and self-regulatory skills such as monitoring are also taught. Reigeluth and Stein (1983) have noted the difference between *embedded* strategies (which are designed to force the learner to use a specific strategy with or without awareness of doing so) and *detached* strategies (which direct the learner to employ a previously acquired cognitive strategy).

All the cognitive strategies described in this book are presented in Figure 12-6, which is in the form of a concept map. Some are more applicable than others for use with particular content. For example, in some forms of instruction, it may not be possible to use frames, type two, because what is being learned is relatively unstructured. We have discussed in detail the specifications of use of each of these strategies in the appropriate chapter.

As was suggested at the end of the detailed description of each of the previous phases, we again recommend reviewing the template in Chapter 11 with the focus this time on the fourth phase (4.0 Cognitive Strategies). Further, we suggest that the reader use the section on page 217, dealing with the cognitive strategies as a checklist in continuing to develop an instructional design for the imaginary situation that was suggested originally in Exercise #2 at the end of Chapter 11. Remember that any designer can: (1) teach a strategy while teaching content, (2) activate a strategy in the student during the instruction (such as having the student map), or (3) use a strategy to convey content better (present a map). Notice that we have recorded on Figure 12-6 typical uses of each strategy in instruction.

5.0 MEANS OF INSTRUCTION

The fifth phase in the template consists of five subroutines pertaining to means of instruction. These subroutines and their relationship to each other are depicted in Figure 12-7.

FIGURE 12-6
Cognitive strategies with typical design uses.

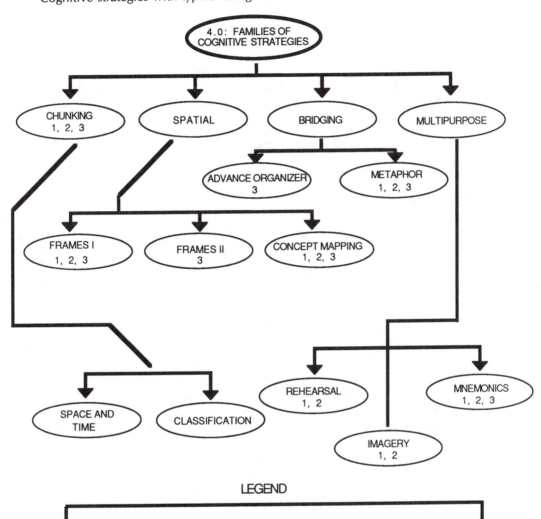

FIGURE 12-7

5.0 Means of instruction.

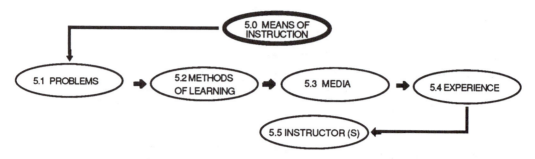

5.1 Problems

In 5.1, the instructional designer is to indicate the percentage of real-life or hypothetical problems to be used in the instruction that are well-defined, moderately well-defined or ill-defined. According to Lippert and Farmer (1984), a *well-defined problem* is one for which there is a single, widely agreed-upon way of understanding and dealing with it, and the problem solver knows that way and how to use it. A *moderately well-defined problem* is (1) one for which there is not a single, widely agreed-upon way but rather two or more acceptable alternatives to select among; and (2) how to select among them is widely agreed upon. Moreover, the problem solver knows those alternatives and this way of choosing among them. An *ill-defined problem* is one that cannot be dealt with either as a well- or moderately well-defined problem. That is, there is no acceptable single way or agreed-upon alternative ways of understanding and dealing with it; or there is no acceptable guide available for choosing among alternatives. Such problems may require the use of heuristic strategies such as the use of analogy, bionics, synectics, idea checklists, attribute listing, morphological synthesis or brainstorming. Each of those techniques is described and illustrated in Davis (1973) and are presented in this book on pp. 228–229.

Algorithms and heuristics are frequently used in solving real-life problems. Landa (1983) has developed an "algo-heuristic" theory of instruction, including empirical propositions and rules for teaching the use of algorithms and heuristics in problem solving. Collins and Stevens (1983) have suggested selecting problems that: illustrate more important factors before less important ones; emphasize concrete rather than abstract factors initially; and are typically incurred frequently or are otherwise more important.

It is often desirable to tailor the type of problems used in instruction to the level of problem-solving expertise of the students and help them learn to solve more difficult problems incrementally. If that level is in doubt, the learner(s) can be asked to solve relatively well-defined problems first. If or when the students can handle them satisfactorily, increasingly less well-defined problems can be used in instructing them and evaluating their ability to understand and solve such problems.

Elshout (1987, p. 267) has noted that benefits from the use of problem solving in instruction are only to be expected if the learner has a good chance of succeeding from the start and if there is as much attention to design and provision of support as is typically provided in direct instruction. Elshout refers to such support as *scaffolding*. Otherwise, undesirable consequences can occur. The use of relatively ill-defined problems is particularly important in teaching higher-order thinking (Resnick, 1987, p. 418) and in teaching real-life problem solving relative to fields in which ill-defined problems are incurred.

5.2 Methods of Learning

In 5.2 (Methods of Learning), the instructional designer is to indicate the percentage of the learning activities that are to entail reception, guided inquiry, autonomous (self-directed) learning (Ausubel, Novak, & Hanesian, 1978) or cognitive apprenticeship. Each of these types of learning is defined and briefly illustrated below.

Reception Learning. In reception learning, the learner reads, hears or observes what is to be learned much in the form in which it is intended to be received. For example, a football player reads a new play that has been diagrammed. He listens to the coach describe what he wants the player to do. Then, on the practice field, he watches the coach demonstrate what he wants the player to do in the new play.

Autonomous Learning. In autonomous learning, the learner is not instructed by another but rather seeks to learn something relatively independently. To continue with the football illustration, the player would be engaging in autonomous learning if, during the next game, he found that a play worked better if he modified his assignment. He learned to do this by watching how the opposing players reacted to the play. During half-time, he told the coach what he had learned. The coach agreed that the player could modify his part in the play in keeping with what he had learned on his own. Such independent behavior may or may not have desirable results. Relatively independent learning and action are encouraged far more in certain positions (such as the linebacker positions) than in others (such as the offensive line positions).

Guided Inquiry Learning. Guided inquiry learning combines some of the characteristics of both reception and autonomous learning. In essence, guided inquiry consists of the following steps (adapted from Lippert, Farmer, & Schafer, 1989, p. 31; Gagne, 1985):

1. The problem is identified.
2. The goal is set.
3. Relevant concepts and materials are arrayed.

4. The learner(s) relates (1) and (3) under guidance . . . until the "Ah ha!" experience.

5. The product and process are evaluated.

6. Discussion.

Each of the above steps in guided inquiry, except the fourth, can be done with or without the assistance of the learner(s). The fourth step is done by the learner(s) under the guidance of the instructor(s).

To continue the football illustration, the player injures his left knee (presenting problem). He wants to return to football as soon as possible (goal). He is examined by an orthopedic surgeon who advises against surgery and goes over with the player alternative treatments of the knee (arraying relevant concepts and materials). When he can return to playing football, the team trainer works (i.e., provides guidance) with him as he tries a variety of movements required of players in his position. The player concludes that he needs more support for the knee and requests a knee brace. The trainer checks out (i.e., evaluates) the basis of that conclusion by examining the player's knee while the player makes the required movements. The trainer also consults with the orthopedic surgeon, who agrees with the decision. When the player first wears the brace, he and the trainer discuss how it should and should not be used.

Landa (1983) has noted that autonomous and guided inquiry methods, in which the learner is expected to discover algorithms and heuristics, tend to be much more difficult and time-consuming than learning and mastering ready-made procedures.

Cognitive Apprenticeship. A recently developed method, cognitive apprenticeship (Collins, Brown, & Newman, in press), combines some of the features of reception learning, guided inquiry and autonomous learning. In that method, coaching (which occurs in the fourth step in guided inquiry) follows modeling by the instructor of the expert behavior that the student wishes to learn. Also included are scaffolding to permit the student to try doing the behavior similarly under supervision of the expert. As warranted, the extent of supervision is lessened (fading) to encourage increasingly autonomous learning and performance. Throughout, articulation of what is being thought is encouraged on the part of both the teacher and the learner. Reflection and exploration are also encouraged, and domain-specific heuristics (derived from general heuristic strategies or unique to the way experts deal with such problems) are explicitly taught in this method.

5.3 Media

In 5.3 (Media), the instructional designer should use the list of media provided in the IDT as a checklist to determine which are applicable for use in the instruction being designed, check all that pertain, and specify the sequence in which they are to be used. These can include the use of film, lecture, discussion, demonstration, panel, seminar, symposium, field trip, computer and many others. While we realize that the computer is more than a medium of instruction, we consider it to be a valuable instructional medium. The literature (Foley & Smilansky, 1980; Gagne, Briggs, & Wager, 1988) contains many descriptions of the various media available in instruction and indicates the advantages and disadvantages of each. Dick and Carey (1985) and Briggs and Wager (1981) provide useful information about media selection.

5.4 Experience

In 5.4 (Experience), the instructional designer should indicate the percentage of each of the following types of experiences (Kolb, Rubin, & McIntyre, 1971) that are to be built into the instruction being designed:

Concrete Experience. In concrete experience, one actually experiences something. For example, the learner(s) may go on a geological field trip and collect fossils. In concrete experiences, it is desirable for the learner(s) to be involved in the experience, making it possible to "feel" the situation and become aware of the problems involved.

Reflective Observation. In reflective observation, one observes something that one wishes to be able to do and reflects on what has been observed. For example, the learners may watch the instructor do an experiment in a chemistry class. If the learning experience is to be meaningful for all of them, it is essential that each learner be able to see what is to be observed. If large numbers of learners want to observe the same performance, it may be necessary to use a remote video or a videotape. The reflective part of reflective observation may involve the use of one or more cognitive strategies to process what has been observed. Schon (1983) has described how professionals can use reflection in practice. The same author (Schon, 1987) has presented ways of teaching professionals and students who wish to enter the professions to be *reflective practitioners.*

Abstract Conceptualization. Experiencing by abstract conceptualization can be done through the use of paper cases, models or computer-based instructional simulation. For example, military engineers can plan defensive strategies and see the effects of their obstacle plans on a "battle," using computer-simulated war games such as MALOS. Developed by Snellen and Murray (1985, 1988), MALOS consists of two versions. One, MALOS-OPS, is a simulation of battlefield obstacle planning and is defensive. A second version, MALOS-QDX, is a simulation of tactical maneuver exercises, both offensive and defensive. The two versions are operational at both Ft. Belvoir and Ft. Leavenworth.

Active Experimentation. Experiencing from experimentation can range from relatively trial-and-error experimentation to formal experiments which use planned procedures under controlled conditions. For example, members of a home economics class can experience different styles of cooking by trying to adapt recipes from other countries to the tastes of their family members.

5.5 Instructor(s)

The instructional designer should next indicate the percentage of each of the types of instructors, classified by type of knowledge or expertise, that are to constitute the teaching faculty. Instructors may be selected for their *knowledge, attitudes* and/or *skills*. For example, the instructional designer may well specify that it would be desirable for a high school class in mathematics to be taught by an instructor who has considerable training and experience in teaching mathematics. Similarly, an instructor with a master's degree in biology may be wanted to teach a course on biology in a community college.

Instructors may also be selected for their knowledge, attitudes and/or skills relative to ways that disciplinarians or scientists think and act. For example, a faculty member who has specialized in historical research may be needed to teach a course designed to help doctoral students in history prepare for their dissertation projects.

Similarly, persons may be selected for their knowledge, attitudes and/or skills relative to generalizations in one or more applied fields. For example, a person with a master's degree in nursing and who has extensive training and experience in trauma nursing may be needed to teach a course on principles of trauma care for nurses. That same nurse could be selected for expertise about thinking and acting as a nurse.

At this point we again suggest reviewing the template in Chapter 11, focusing this time on the fifth section (5.0 Means of Instruction). We suggest using the section on pp. 217–219 on means of instruction as a checklist in continuing to develop an instructional design for the imaginary situation that was suggested in Exercise #2 at the end of Chapter 11. Included should be the information suggested by the prompts for each of the following sequential decision points: problems, methods, media, experience and instructor(s).

6.0 TESTING AND EVALUATION

The final phase of the IDT is 6.0 (Testing and Evaluation). It contains four subroutines, designated as 6.1 through 6.4. Each pertains to an aspect of instructional testing and evaluation. These subroutines and their relationship to each other are depicted in Figure 12-8.

6.1 Tests

In 6.1 (Tests), the instructional designer should indicate the percentage of each of the following to be used in the instruction: testing general and specific problem-solving skills; testing through observing and rating demonstrations or performances; measuring recall with written or oral tests; other

FIGURE 12-8
6.0 Testing and evaluation.

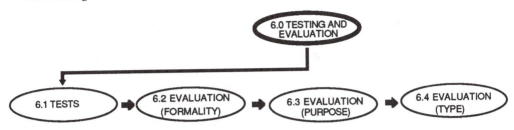

type(s) of testing as specified; or no testing. The selection of the form of testing, if any, to be used is likely to be influenced by the nature of what is taught. Decisions about what is tested and how it is tested will be influenced by the broad aim and specific objectives of the instruction.

If remembering specific information is thought to be important, testing for recall may be appropriate. Ability to recall facts and generalizations, of course, is not sufficient for solving problems, but recall is usually necessary. One cannot apply what one does not know.

On the other hand, if learning to solve a particular type of problem is the focus of the instruction or part of it, then having the learner(s) solve one or more unfamiliar problems of that type would be appropriate. General problem-solving ability may not be sufficient for solving specific problems. Therefore, testing for general problem-solving ability should not be substituted for ability to solve specific types of problems, or vice versa.

If a skill or task has been taught, having the learners demonstrate the skill or perform the task may be an appropriate form of testing. Such an approach may indicate the extent to which the learner is able to do what was intended. It may also reveal errors, weaknesses or omissions and make it possible for the learner to demonstrate proficiency.

In some instances, it may be decided that no form of testing is needed or warranted. Such an approach, however, may result in both the instructor(s) and the learner(s) being deprived of valuable feedback regarding the nature and extent of the learning. Moreover, less will be learned about the effectiveness of the design.

6.2 Evaluation (Extent of Formality)

The instructional designer at 6.2 should indicate the percentage of each of the following to be used in evaluating the instruction: informal evaluation, formal evaluation or no evaluation. Evaluation is determination of the value or worth of something by examining facts, values and judgments and relating them to each other. Remember that if cognitive strategies were taught, they too should be evaluated. If important decisions involving considerable amounts of money, sizable numbers of people or considerable risks are to be made about the value or worth of the instruction, then some type of formal (i.e., systematic) evaluation may be warranted. Otherwise, informal evaluation or even no evaluation may suffice.

6.3 Evaluation (Purpose)

The instructional designer is to indicate what percentage of each of the following is to be used: formative evaluation, summative evaluation, or no evaluation. The purpose of formative evaluation is the suggestion of ways of strengthening a course or program while it is being conducted. The purpose of summative evaluation is to determine whether or not to continue offering the course or program after it has been completed and, if it is to be continued, the details of revision. Useful information about both formative and summative evaluation appear in Gagne, Briggs and Wager (1988); Dick and Carey (1985); and Briggs and Wager (1981).

6.4 Evaluation (Type)

At 6.4, the instructional designer should indicate what percentage of each of the following is to be used: internal evaluation, external evaluation or no evaluation. Internal evaluation is conducted by one or more persons who are on the instructional staff. Such individuals are likely to be very familiar with the course or program but may lack objectivity about it. External evaluation is done by person(s) who are independent of the instructional staff. Such persons may be able to evaluate the instruction with greater objectivity but are likely to be less familiar with it. If resources are available, combining both types of evaluation may be beneficial.

Once again we suggest that the reader review the template in Chapter 11, focusing this time on the section on pp. 219–220 which deals with the sixth phase (6.0 Testing and Evaluation). We recommend using that section as a checklist in further developing an instructional design for the imaginary situation that was suggested in Exercise #2 at the end of Chapter 11. Included should be the information evoked by the prompts for each of the following sequential decision points: tests, formality of the evaluation, purpose of the evaluation and type of evaluation.

FEEDBACK LOOPS IN THE IDT

As indicated earlier in this chapter, we view the IDT as a series of sequential phases, each containing one or more sequential decision points. While we recommend working through the phases and sequential decision points in the order in which they appear in Figure 12-9, we realize that the designer may anticipate certain phases and/or decision points. Briggs and Wager (1981) refer to looking ahead and backtracking. We would caution, however, against focusing first on content, since this may result in designs which are content dominated at the expense of other design considerations.

FIGURE 12-9

Concept map of template.

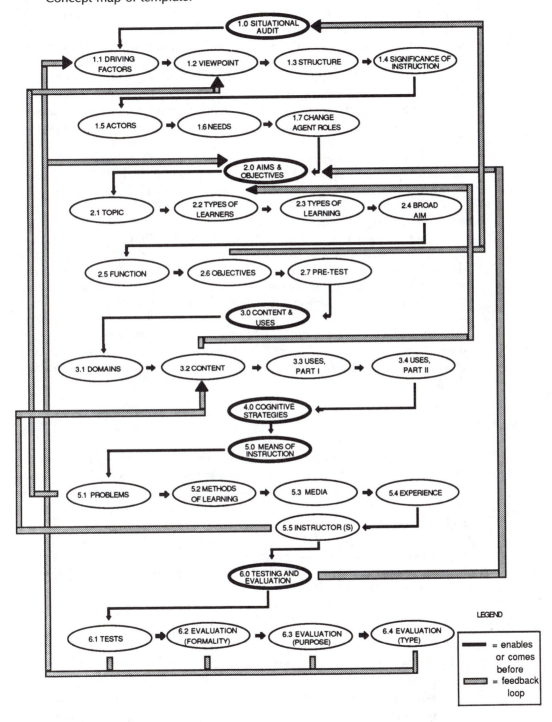

Early design decisions can be made tentatively and changed later if necessary. In other words, they constitute the designer's best initial estimate of how to handle particular decision points. If conditions permit the selection of other choices regarding those decisions, the designer may subsequently loop back to one or more decision points and make revisions which seem advisable in the light of subsequent choices. Frequently used feedback loops are depicted in Figure 12-9. For example, the results of testing (6.1) and evaluation (6.2–6.4) are typically done in light of the aims and objectives (2.0). Or, the results of testing and evaluation can make the designer reconsider the driving factors (1.1) and/or other of the sequential decision points in 1.0 (Situational Audit).

Likewise, the designer may loop back from 5.5 [Instructor(s)] to 3.2 (Content) and 2.2 (Types of Learners) to be sure that the instructional needs of the learners and the content to be provided are well matched. At the same time, the designer can determine whether the types of instructor(s) and learners specified are suitable.

Looping back can be done not only during the design process but also during the instruction. For example, moving from well-defined to less well-defined problems in the 5.1 (Problems) subroutine can be used to help students who start with a functionalist viewpoint at the 1.2 (Viewpoint) subroutine to reconsider that viewpoint and possibly change to a critical viewpoint.

In any case, we encourage the sequential use of the IDT followed by tinkering with it, while always considering the specific situation for which the instructional design is being developed and the content to be taught. Such tinkering can also contribute to increased internal consistency in the resulting design.

SUMMARY

In this chapter we described in detail the second through sixth phases of the IDT. The complete template presented in Chapters 11 and 12 is a detailed and, we hope, complete design system which has been heavily influenced by cognitive science; but it is eclectic in terms of the perspectives which serve as its foundation.

Through the use of a chain map we have represented this complex procedure. We think this can serve not only as another example of concept mapping but also as a model for the representation and presentation of other complex systems which designers face.

EXERCISES

1. Think of the six phases as chunk or sets. What types of chunking is that (from Figure 2-1)?
2. What is the name of the strategy of which Figure 12-9 is an example?
3. Is the material in the IDT declarative, procedural or conditional?

4. To what extent is the following analogy accurate: "The IDT works like a funnel?" What are the limits of that analogy?

5. To what extent does/does not the IDT work like a heat-seeking missile?

6. Be sure that you have followed the instructions after the descriptions of each of the phases (1.0 through 6.0) to use the IDT as a checklist in developing an instructional design for the imaginary situation that was suggested in Exercise #2 at the end of Chapter 11. Now use Figure 12-9 to revise your instructional design, giving due consideration to the design as a whole (the big picture) and feedback loops.

REFERENCES

Atkin, J. M. (1969). Behavioral objectives in curriculum design, a cautionary note. In R. C. Anderson, G. W. Faust, D. J. Cunningham, & T. Andre (Eds.), *Current research on instruction*. Englewood Cliffs, NJ: Prentice-Hall.

Ausubel, D. P., Novak, D. J., & Hanesian, H. (1978). *Educational psychology: A cognitive view* (2nd ed.). New York: Holt, Rinehart and Winston.

Bloom, B. S. (Ed.). (1956). *Taxonomy of educational objectives—The classification of educational goals—Handbook I: Cognitive domain*. New York: McKay.

Briggs, L. J., & Wager, W. W. (1981). *Handbook of procedures for the designing of instruction* (2nd ed.). Englewood Cliffs, NJ: Educational Technology Publications.

Brown, J. S., Collins, A., & Duguid, P. (1989a). Situated cognition and the culture of learning. *Educational Researcher, 18* (1), 32–42.

Brown, J. S., Collins, A., & Duguid, P. (1989b). Debating the situation. *Educational Researcher, 18* (4), 10–12.

Broudy, H. S. (1988). *The uses of schooling*. New York: Routledge.

Broudy, H. S. (1979). Tacit knowing as a rationale for liberal education. *Teachers College Record, 80*, 446–462.

Collins, A., Brown, J. S., & Newman, S. E. (in press). Cognitive apprenticeship: Teaching the craft of reading, writing, and mathematics. In L. B. Resnick (Ed.), *Cognition and instruction: Issues and agendas*. Hillsdale, NJ: Lawrence Erlbaum Associates.

Collins, A., & Stevens, A. (1983). A cognitive theory of inquiry teaching. In C. M. Reigeluth (Ed.), *Instructional-design theories and models: An overview of their current status*. Hillsdale, NJ: Lawrence Erlbaum Associates.

Davis, G. A. (1973) *Psychology of problem solving—Theory and practice*. New York: Basic Books.

Dick, H. S., & Carey, L. M. (1985). *The systematic design of instruction* (2nd ed.). Glenview, IL: Scott, Foresman.

Elshout, J. J. (1987). Problem-solving and education. In E. DeCorte, H. Ludewijks, R. Parmentien, & P. Span (Eds.), *Learning and instruction—European research in an international context* (Vol. 1). Oxford: Leuven University Press and Pergamon Press.

Eraut, M. (1985). Knowledge creation and knowledge use in professional contexts. *Studies in Higher Education, 10*, 117–133.

Foley, R. P., & Smilansky, J. (1980). *Teaching techniques: A handbook for health professionals*. New York: McGraw-Hill.

Gagne, R. M. (1985). *The conditions of learning* (4th ed.). New York: Holt, Rinehart and Winston.

Gagne, R. M., Briggs, L. J., & Wager, W. W. (1988). *Principles of instructional design,* (3rd ed.). New York: Holt, Rinehart and Winston.

Good, C. V. (Ed.). (1959). *Dictionary of education.* New York: McGraw-Hill.

Katz, D., & Kahn, R. L. (1978). *The social psychology of organizations* (2nd ed.). New York: Wiley.

Keller, J. M. (1983). Motivational design of instruction. In C. M. Reigeluth (Ed.), *Instructional-design theories and models: An overview of their current status.* Hillsdale, NJ: Lawrence Erlbaum Associates.

Kibler, R. J., & Bassett, R. E. (1977). Writing performance objectives. In L. J. Briggs (Ed.), *Instructional design: Principles and application.* Englewood Cliffs, NJ: Educational Technology Publications.

Kirby, J. R., & Briggs, J. B. (1980). *Cognition, development, and instruction.* New York: Academic Press.

Kolb, D. A., Rubin, I. M., and McIntyre, J. M. (1971). *Organizational psychology, an experimental approach.* Englewood Cliffs, NJ: Prentice-Hall, Inc.

Krathwohl, D. R., Bloom, B. S., & Masia, B. B. (1964). *Taxonomy of educational objectives—The classification of educational goals: Handbook II: Affective domain.* New York: McKay.

Landa, L. N. (1983). The algo-heuristic theory of instruction. In C. M. Reigeluth (Ed.), *Instructional-design theories and models: An overview of their current status.* Hillsdale, NJ: Lawrence Erlbaum Associates.

Lawson, M. J. (1980). Metamemory: Making decisions about strategies. In J. R. Kirby & J. B. Briggs (Eds.), *Cognition, development, and instruction.* New York: Academic Press.

Lippert, G., & Farmer, J. (1984). *Psychomotor skills in orthopaedic surgery.* Baltimore: Williams and Wilkins.

Lippert, F. G., Farmer, J. A., & Schafer, M. F. (1989). *Handbook for orthopaedic educators,* (11th ed.). Chicago: Committee on Graduate Education, American Academy of Orthopaedic Surgeons.

Mager, R. F. (1975). *Preparing instructional objectives* (2nd ed.). Belmont, CA: Fearon.

Melton, R. F. (1978). Resolution of conflicting claims concerning the effect of behavioral objectives on student learning. *Review of Educational Research, 48,* 291–302.

Reigeluth, C. M., & Stein, F. S. (1983). The elaboration theory of instruction. In C. M. Reigeluth (Ed.), *Instructional-design theories and models: An overview of their current status.* Hillsdale, NJ: Lawrence Erlbaum Associates.

Resnick, L. B. (1987). Instruction and the cultivation of thinking. In E. De Corte, H. Lodewijks, R. Parmentien, & P. Span (Eds.), *Learning and instruction: European research in an international context* (Vol. 1). Oxford: Leuven University Press and Pergamon Press.

Ruesch, J. (1975). *Knowledge in action: Communication, social operations, and management.* New York: Jason Aronson.

Rumelhart, D. E., & Norman, D. A. (1978). Accretion, tuning and restructuring: Three modes of learning. In J. Cotton & R. L. Kalatzky (Eds.), *Semantic factors in cognition.* New York: Wiley.

Schon, D. A. (1983). *The reflective practitioner.* New York: Basic Books.

Schon, D. A. (1987). *Educating the reflective practitioner: Toward a new design for teaching and learning in the professions.* San Francisco: Jossey-Bass.

Simpson, E. J. (1966). The classification of educational objectives, psychomotor domain. *Illinois Teacher of Home Economics, 10,* 110–144.

Snellen, J. E., & Murray, S. L. (1985). *MALOS-OPS: Computer based combat engineer simulation system*. Prepared for the U.S. Army Engineer School.

Snellen, J. E., & Murray, S. L. (1988). *MALOS-QDX: Computer based maneuver simulation system*. Prepared for the U. S. Army Armor School.

Weinert, F. E. (1987). Developmental processes and instruction. In E. De Corte, H. Lodewijks, R. Parmentien, & P. Span (Eds.), *Learning and instruction: European research in an International context* (Vol. 1). Oxford: Leuven University Press and Pergamon Press.

Epilogue

The advances in instructional design resulting from the cognitive revolution are exciting, and we hope that we have channeled some of that excitement to a new generation of designers. That excitement stems largely from the emphasis on internal representation of knowledge as *structure* and *organized processes* (state and process schemata).

For instruction and instructional design an even more exciting and useful revolution could take place as designers struggle with motivation and emotion, the will or affect. The techniques or strategies described in this text are powerful; but without student motivation and stripped of affect they are emasculated. A changeover even newer than the cognitive revolution is the examination of affect as transactive with cognition sometimes called *hot cognition*. A few developments along these lines have an intriguing parallel with the cognitive revolution in that affect is viewed as internal representations (Ortony, Clore, & Collins, 1988) with structural properties including organizations which are both state and process. Should this changeover consolidate in affect as it has in cognition, inordinately powerful implications for design may be in our future. An instructional design technology capitalizing on both *can* and *will* would be formidable.

REFERENCES

Ortony, A., Clore, G. L., & Collins, A. (1988). *The cognitive structure of emotions.* New York: Cambridge University Press.

SUBJECT INDEX

Instructional design template (IDT) (cont'd)
  media, 254–55
  methods of learning, 253–54
  objectives, 235–45
  phases/sequential decision points, 213–20
  pretest, 244–45
  problems, 252–53
  purpose of, 210–11
  situational audit, 220–32
  tests, 256–57
  See also Situational audit
Instructional domains, 46–49, 246–48
Interactive metaphors, 139
Internal evaluation, 258
Interpretive use of knowledge, 249

Keywords, 192, 195–96
Kinds of relationships, in concept maps, 101–2
Knowledge, 15–18, 248–49

Large information sets:
  and concept maps, 105–6
  and frames, type one, 72–73
Learning, 14–15, 17, 87, 253–54
Learning Tool, and concept maps, 100
Links, chain mnemonics, 192
Literal expression, 133
Logical/expository chunking strategies, 44

MALOS (computer-simulated war game), 255
Map-based tests, 106–7
Mapping/outlining, and concept maps, 102–4
Master map, 106
Means of instruction, 250, 252
Media, instructional design template (IDT), 254–55
Metacognition, 18–19
  predecessors of, 26
Metaphor/analogy/simile, 1, 21, 130–50
  differences among, 131–33
Metaphors, 13
  assimilation/accommodation, 138
  attribute metaphors, 139
  comparative metaphors, 139
  compared to advance organizers, 130–31
  and declarative/conditional/procedural knowledge, 139
  designers' guide, 143–47
  development, 134–36
  hybridization, 147
  and imagery, 140–43
  interactive metaphors, 139
  as multipurpose bridging strategy, 140
  and rehearsal, 146–47
  relational metaphors, 139
  research, 134–38
  selecting, 144–45
  similarities/difference, emphasizing, 146
  specifications chart, 142
  as top-down strategy, 140
  topic/vehicle, 133
Method of loci, 194, 198–99
Mind-to-mind contact, and cognitive strategies, 27–30
Mnemonics, 22–23, 74, 91, 127, 191–208
  designers' guide, 201–5
  hybridization, 205–6
  recommended instructions for major types of, 204–5
  research, 195–200
  restrictions on use of, 200–201

Mnemonics (cont'd)
  specifications chart, 202
  types of, 192–95
Modeling, of cognitive strategies, 2–3, 28–29
Moderately well-defined problems, 252
Moderately well-defined situation, 226–28
Moose Hunt Story, 238
Morphological synthesis, use of, 228–29, 252
Motivation, and cognitive strategies, 28
Movement skills, 246
Multipurpose sorting, 50–52
  advantages/disadvantages, 51
  bases for categorization, 52
  causes-effects, 50–51
  forms/functions, 51
  similarities/differences (comparison/contrast), 51

Narration, 41–42
Needs, situational audit, 230–31
Networks, 15–16
Normative needs, 230–31
Note taking rehearsal, 152, 160–62

Objectives:
  instructional design template (IDT), 235–45
    broad aim, 238–41
    functions, 241–42
    learners, types of, 236–37
    learning, types of, 237–38
    specific, 242–44
    topic, 235–36
Obliterative subsumption, 127
Obscure/dated metaphors, 131
Observation frames, 64–65
Order-specific requirement, of procedures, 16
Organizing strategies, *See* Chunking strategies
Origins of prior knowledge, advance organizers versus metaphors, 130
Outlining, compared to concept mapping, 104
Overload, 73–74, 186
Overvaluing, concreteness, 87

Pegwords, 193–94
Perception, and schemata, 8–10
Perceptual sets, 9
PQRST rehearsal strategy, 153–54, 163–64
Preassessment stage, 2, 9
Predicting and clarifying rehearsal, 152, 153, 157–58
Pretests, 244–45
Problem/solution frames, 64
Problem solving, 13, 246
Procedural chunking strategy, 42–44
Procedural knowledge, 16–17, 70–71, 105, 139, 177
Process helper role, 232
Process schemata, 7–8, 13
Programming, analogy between process schema and, 7–8
Propositional knowledge, *See* Declarative knowledge
Psychology of learning, 3–7, 46
Psychomotor domain, 246

Quantitative structure, 39
Question and answering rehearsal, 152, 155–57

Recall:
  and advance organizers, 121, 123
  and chunking, 38

Recall (*cont'd*)
 and framing. 63–64
 and questions, 157
 and schemata, 10
Reception learning, 253
Reciprocal teaching, 18–19, 29
 predecessors of, 26
Reflective observation, experiencing by, 255
Reflective practitioners, 255
Rehearsal strategies, 21–22, 74, 91, 127, 151–69
 activities/definitions, 152–53
 designers' guide, 164–67
 hybridization, 167
 and metaphors, 146–47
 note taking rehearsal, 152, 160–62
 PQRST rehearsal strategy, 153–54, 163–64
 predicting and clarifying rehearsal, 152, 153, 157–58
 question and answering rehearsal, 152, 155–57
 repetition and cumulative rehearsal, 152, 155
 research, 154–64
 restating and paraphrasing rehearsal, 152, 153, 158
 reviewing and summarizing rehearsal, 152, 158–59
 selecting rehearsal strategy, 152, 159–60
 specifications chart, 166
 SQ3R rehearsal strategy, 152–54, 163–64
 training, 164
 underlining rehearsal, 152, 162–63
Reinforcement:
 of cognitive strategies, 29
 and imagery, 186
Relational metaphors, 139
Repetition and cumulative rehearsal, 152, 155
Replicative use of knowledge, 249
Resource linker role, 231–32
Restructuring, 15, 88
 and frames, type one, 70
 learning through, 237
Reviewing and summarizing rehearsal strategy, 152, 158–59

Scaffolding, 253
Scanning/retrieval, and concept maps, 105–6
Schemata:
 functions of, 7–13
 and learning/comprehension, 10
 and perception, 8–10
 quintessential, 13–14
 restructuring of, 15
Schema theory, 5–7, 19
Science texts, frame categories, 64–65
Scripts, 13
Selecting rehearsal strategy, 152, 159–60
Semantic encoding, 194–95
Semantic networks, 15
Sentence variation, single-use coding, 194
Sequencing, 41–42
Similarities/differences (comparison/contrast), as multi-purpose chunking strategy, 51
Simile, 1, 21, 130–50
Single-use coding, 194–95
 research, 199–200
Situational audit, 220–32
 actors involved, 230
 change agent roles, 231–32

Situational audit (*cont'd*)
 driving factors, 221–22
 educational viewpoints, 222–23
 needs, 230–31
 significance of instruction, 229
 structure of situation, 226–29
Skeleton frame, 65
Solution giver role, 231
Sorting, multipurpose, 50–52
 See also Chunking strategies
Spatial learning strategies, 20
Spatial/linear chunking strategies, 38–45
 logical/expository, 44
 procedures, 42–44
 space, 40–41
 time (narrative/sequencing), 41–42
Spider maps, 94–95
 kinds of relationships, 101
SQ3R rehearsal strategy, 152–54, 163–64
State schemata, 7–8
Story, chain mnemonics, 192–93
Story frame, 62
Strategy training, 29–30
Subsumption theory, 118
Summarizing rehearsal strategy, 152
Synectics, use of, 228, 252

Tacit knowledge, 248
Task/content, matching cognitive strategies to, 26–27
Taxonomies, 45–49, 53, 67
Teaching, reciprocal, 18–19, 29
Template, *See* Instructional design template (IDT)
Testing/assessment, and concept maps, 106–7
Tests, 256–57
 pretests, 244–45
Text structure, 40
Three-dimensional frames, type one, 72–73
Time-dependent requirement, of procedures, 16
Topic/vehicle, metaphors, 133
TOTE units, 13
Training:
 in concept mapping, 97–100
 in imagery, 179–81
 rehearsal strategies, 164
 strategy, 29–30
Triangulation, 226
Tuning, 14–15, 88
 and frames, type one, 70
 learning through, 237
Typologies, 49–50, 53

Underlining rehearsal strategy, 152, 162–63

Valuing, 46, 246, 247
Vee diagrams, and concept maps, 99
Verbal keywords, 192

Waldoes, cognitive strategies as, 19
Well-defined problems, 252
Well-defined situation, 226
Well-structured knowledge domains, 16–17
 characterizing, 17
Word variation, single-use coding, 194